TALES OF A
TABLOID
TWITCHER

TALES OF A
TABLOID
TWITCHER

STUART WINTER

NEW
HOLLAND

First published in 2010 by New Holland Publishers
London • Cape Town • Sydney • Auckland
www.newhollandpublishers.com

Garfield House, 86-88 Edgware Road, London W2 2EA, UK
80 McKenzie Street, Cape Town, 8001, South Africa
Unit 1, 66 Gibbes Street, Chatswood, NSW 2067, Australia
218 Lake Road, Northcote, Auckland, New Zealand

10 9 8 7 6 5 4 3 2 1

A CIP catalogue record for this book is available from the British Library.

ISBN 978 1 84773 693 2

Publisher: Simon Papps
Artwork: David Nurney
Editors: Simon Papps and Beth Lucas
Proof-reader: Eloise Wood
Production: Melanie Dowland
Publishing Director: Rosemary Wilkinson
Reproduction by Pica Digital (Pte) Ltd, Singapore
Printed and bound in India by Replika Press

Contents

FOREWORD

I twitched. From about 1979 through until the end of the 1980s. It started nicely but it ended in tears. Well, in fact there were tears throughout, but then snivelling about disastrous dips doesn't really count – it can be heard emanating from the backs of cars in dingy service station car parks with dismal regularity. I like to say that I got better, was cured of the obsessive urge, but that's a lie. In truth I got busy and found not even being able pursue a tick even more painful than actually missing the bird. And then in my aching absence the whole twitching phenomena went big, became a business, got very crowded and became an arena where a thick skin and extreme levels of tolerance are essential attributes to survive. Since neither are amongst my fortes I've not felt brave enough to return to the fold, instead birding by myself. But reading this fabulous book I'm left feeling very envious, clearly I've been missing out on a lot, not only birds but principally lots of amazing adventures and plenty of fun, too.

For a start I might have been able to twitch in tune with Stuart himself. He effuses all the requirements of a good companion: keen, resourceful, armed with a wry sense of humour and a serious side which is marked with a genuine concern for conserving birds and wildlife. He is also wonderfully modest and devoid of an ornithological ego – a blight of so many so-called 'serious birders'. He constantly champions the strengths of others and never seeks to inflate his own. Most of all, though, he has a rich catalogue of anecdotes which he recounts here with great gusto and in enjoyably down-to-earth prose. Extracts from his pieces penned for the papers also chart the evolution of modern birding, not just twitching but so many other aspects of our passion, and his timely and intelligent use of these words have certainly helped to shape and secure the future of some of Britain's birds.

I am confident that you will be hugely entertained by these pages, but also that you'll recognise the author as undoubtedly one of Britain's best birding blokes. Even though he hasn't seen … a Puffin!

Chris Packham

'Hello, Bird Fair...'

The Bat that flits at close of Eve
Has left the Brain that won't believe
The Owl that calls upon the Night
Speaks the Unbeliever's fright.

—William Blake, *Auguries of Innocence.*

The indefatigable smell of Bird Fair was in the air — a distinctive
concoction of wet grass, warm bodies, exotic foods, cold beer and fear.
Mine. Every apology to Mark Cocker, one of my favourite writers, for
plagiarising the opening lines of his seminal *Birders: Tales of the Tribe*,
but I am a Fleet Street hack. It's what we do: lurk in the shadows and
beg, steal and borrow the words of others to inform, entertain and
inspire our readers. We are neither celebrities nor banner holders, merely
messengers. That's unless we get shoved suddenly into the limelight.

Bird Fair, August 1998, and this was to be my Andy Warhol
moment. Centre stage, enthusiastic applause ringing out and a glowing

introduction as bright as the spot lamps beaming down from the light gantry; those 15 minutes of global fame promised to each and every member of humanity by the celebrated Sixties pop art legend had begun ticking on my watch. I sampled the sultry air in the lecture tent: still the essence of wet grass and still the aroma of my uncertainty. Newspapermen are not public speakers, a voice cautioned in my head. I hatched a small, dry cough and began to speak. The microphone projected my voice into the four distant corners of the darkened marquee. Each syllable reverberated in the humid, under-canvas atmosphere, making them sound mature, husky; perhaps even sexy. The front row faces laughed at my opening joke, a hokey one-liner rehearsed countless times in the days running up to my big appearance.

'Hello, Bird Fair,' I had wanted to scream like some rock god on an open-air stage massaging the crowds into a frenzy. I decided to stay with the script, one that I knew all too well and one that I hoped would pave the way to more public appearances. For this Bird Fair was to be my rite of passage, a metamorphosis from hackneyed wordsmith to 'personality' at the biggest, most eclectic, gathering of birders the world ever sees. Thousands of similar-minded souls, hooked on the pleasure derived from looking at creatures that weigh mere grams, had gathered like the wildebeest of the Serengeti to walk the tented meadows bordering Rutland Water – and celebrate birds in all their glory. Many, I had persuaded myself, were there to see and listen to me. Well, the Bird Fair programme had emblazoned my talk as one of the star attractions of the opening day. 'Tales of the Tabloid Twitcher', said the Bird Fair brochure, promising a 'humorous account' of the activities of a national newspaperman turned birder. Soon the joke would be on me.

After four years of writing the weekly 'Strictly for the Birds' column in the *Daily Star*, I had been convinced by others that I had enough material to fulfil a request to give a half-hour talk at the Bird Fair. Keeping tabs on the twitching scene, getting the occasional 'exclusive' from the RSPB and reading the newswires – one of my main duties as a news editor on the newspaper – helped me to produce a welter of stories for the first-ever weekly birding column in a British national tabloid. After the initial approach by the Bird Fair's organisers asking me to give a lecture, I had set to work rifling through my newspaper cuttings for anecdotes that would bring a smile to an audience looking for something of a departure from the 'birdier' fare most speakers deliver.

There was plenty of material but it would be the way, to quote a certain Irish comedian, I told 'em that would make a difference on the day. I set about honing my act, listening to stand-up comics on late night laughter shows and even setting up a video camera on a tripod in the lounge to polish my timing and delivery. The kids heard it so many times they became word perfect themselves, aping my mannerisms and reeling off the punch lines before I reached them. It would cost me a portable television set each to get them back up into their bedrooms so I could perfect my repertoire. As the countdown began, I assembled the slides I needed to illustrate my talk, begging many a national newspaper picture editor to let me borrow profile photographs of Prince Charles, Bill Oddie, Sir David Attenborough and Sir Peter Scott, to name but a few; name-dropping was going to feature heavily in my routine. On the eve of the Bird Fair, I had one final dress rehearsal in front of an audience of one – the cat – soaked up imaginary applause and went to sleep dreaming of showtime.

Anyone who has attended the British Birdwatching Fair, to use its formal title, cannot fail to have been touched by its unique atmosphere, a blend of merry olde England village fete and high-brow sales convention. By the late 1990s the Bird Fair had become one of the key dates on the birdwatching calendar, with only the most committed twitchers, those who feared that being ensconced at Rutland Water would leave them in danger of missing the arrival of an early autumn rarity on some Scottish outcrop or Cornish headland, being noticeable by their absence.

For all other enthusiasts, the Bird Fair is a great place to catch up with old friends, salivate at the latest optical equipment, browse through books for Santa to deliver, pick up holiday brochures to exotic locations from Alaska to Zambia, renew subscriptions to worthwhile charities, sample the specially brewed local bitters and pick out celebrities as they browse at the same things themselves. Television personalities such as Simon King, Nick Baker, Chris Packham and, of course, Bill Oddie, have become regular fixtures but I am sure I have also seen the likes of former Coronation Street and Royle Family actor Geoffrey Hughes and comedian and quiz show panellist Rory McGrath mooching around the marquees over the years. In fact, parodying radio and television game shows has become one of the Bird Fair's stocks in trade, with some genius devising such spoofs as Just a

Linnet and Call My Ruff to bring a smile to the proceedings. Perhaps one day the economy will allow for big money prize shows to be staged using titles such as Teal or No Teal and Smew Wants To Be A Millionaire.

It says something about the unique atmosphere created by the Bird Fair that, in order to attend, many visitors momentarily disengage from the very thing that drives them to be birdwatchers. Rutland Water, particularly now after millions of pounds worth of habitat creation, must rank as one of the best inland birdwatching locations in the country. The reservoir's muddy margins are a great place to watch shorebird migration in late August, when waders such as Ruff, Black-tailed Godwit, Curlew Sandpiper and Spotted Redshank are passing through *en route* to their distant wintering grounds. Somehow there never seems to be enough time to see everything on view at the Bird Fair and then spare a few moments lapping up the ambience of one of the sheltered lagoons with its own bustling community of waders and wildfowl. To date, I have been to all 21 Bird Fairs and the only impressions they have left in my personal logs have been sightings of the introduced Ospreys and also a Great White Egret in 2003. It says something about the expertise and foresight of the organisers that the event is timed so that people can temporarily switch off their birding radar to socialise and grievously abuse their credit cards without worrying too much about their checklists. Not that it has been an easy transition.

One of my favourite memories relates to twitcher supreme Lee Evans at Bird Fair 1995 when news filtered through that a putative Middle Spotted Woodpecker had been discovered on the Kent coast. The bird was a potential 'first' for the British Isles and, although the species has been making a slow but steady spread in range across Continental Europe, only the most optimistic of commentators would ever have predicted that one would make the 26-mile flight across the formidable barrier of the English Channel. As the bush telegraph went into overdrive, Lee, a life-long collector of rarity sightings that has put him in the top echelons of the twitching community with a tally of more than 500 species seen in Britain and Ireland, went into a state of apoplexy. Thoughts of the woodpecker, with its distinctive sealing wax-coloured head markings, black-and-white body plumage and an open-faced, almost friendly, visage, were just too much for his sensibilities and he fell to the floor in a state of shock. Lee's collapse caused more commotion than the story of the bird. When he finally came round, Lee told me of his ordeal. I did not know whether to smile or cry for him as he explained how he had to be at the Bird Fair to make a living.

'I just had to be here,' he said between gasps. 'I make my living selling bird publications and this was the major event of the year. Then this bird turned up. It was a nightmare. There was talk of it looking weak and exhausted and that it would not survive, so getting there was imperative. Yet I was miles away at this event and I could not leave. It was too much and I collapsed.'

'To make matters worse,' he continued, 'when I came round the lady who revived me was wearing special bird earrings and guess what pattern was on them? Yes, Middle Spotted Woodpeckers!'

Ironically, for all the hullabaloo the news of the woodpecker caused on that fateful Saturday, the British Birds Rarities Committee has never officially accepted its occurrence. Perhaps it was thoughts of another rarity of the magnitude of the Middle Spotted Woodpecker turning up that determined the fashion choices of those early years. It always struck me as a little strange to see people parading around the Bird Fair showground dressed in their best, if somewhat incongruous, outdoor cryptic camouflage garb and with their binoculars and telescope-tripod combos draped over their shoulders as if they had been beamed in by Star Trek's Scotty from the North Norfolk coast. These days, most visitors dress as if they were at a county show or dropping in for a pub lunch, with smart windcheaters, linen jackets, pressed chinos and designer jeans replacing the disruptive-patterned parkas and weatherproof trousers of previous years. Indeed, it is only fitting that the event is treated with a degree of decorum. To start with, it is staged in quintessential English countryside on the outskirts of Oakham and under the glare of Burley-on-the-Hill House, a sumptuous 17th century mansion said to have been influenced by Sir Christopher Wren's work, which forms a wonderful backdrop to an event that each year is attended by a VIP list of Government ministers, diplomats, powerbrokers, celebrities and more than 20,000 others who want to celebrate birds and birdwatching. Their efforts since the first event was staged in 1989 have been phenomenal. In all, the 21 Bird Fairs to date have raised more than £2 million pounds for conservation projects and

2009's event, though staged at a time when the economy was in recession, saw both record crowds and proceeds. Bird Fair goes from strength to strength – but it still has moments of foreboding for me dating back to that fateful day in August 1998.

It all began so well. I felt as though I was being treated like royalty. Complimentary tickets and car parking passes had arrived in the post and, on opening the glossy Bird Fair programme, there was yours truly billed as one of the key events of the opening day, with some rather flattering introductory notes about my column. Tales of the Tabloid Twitcher had been given prime time billing and throughout the day I received many a back-slap and handshake from friends, acquaintances and others whose names escaped me, but all promising to be there for my 'big moment.' The butterflies took regular flight in my stomach but I was sure that by adhering to the old army adage of 'perfect-planning-prevents-p***-poor-performance' I would win the day. Oh, how I had planned. My family had never seen me so obsessive in the weeks running up to the lecture. Every story I had ever written about birds had been committed to my memory banks and every funny anecdote regaled so many times that I was supposedly reciting them in my sleep. If I was going to put my head on the line – and there is no more discerning or discriminating group of people as birders *en masse* – then things had to be just so.

The stomach butterflies remained on the wing in the hours leading up to the early afternoon talk, only to be calmed by the reassurance that I could recite any part of my talk off pat. This I was doing under my breath throughout the morning, not only drawing many strange looks, but also meaning that as I was walking around the stands I was absorbing little of the buzzing atmosphere. The last time I had raised my head above the parapet at the Bird Fair had been when I planned to write a story a few years previously about the formation of the Gay Birders' Club – purely from a positive point of how it would enhance the great birdwatching family – but as the message went round that a Fleet Street tabloid journalist was planning some scurrilous exposé, I began to sense a feeling of unease. People were coming up to me in quiet corners and asking how I could be so sleazy as to attempt to ridicule a new and worthwhile organisation? It could not have been further from the truth but left me understanding the evils of prejudice.

With the welcoming applause still ringing in my ears, and squinting to try and make out recognisable faces in the front seats to give me some sense of familiarity with the audience, I began to recount my tabloid tales. There were stories of my foreign assignments with a BBC crew and the most exciting and outrageous birding adventures of those dashing pioneers on the very frontline of the twitching scene. There were silly stories and Scilly stories; there were tales that had filled many column inches in the popular press and some that were too salacious ever to have been laid out in newsprint. The laughs and communal murmurs that punctuated each anecdote felt like a friend guiding me on a journey. As the microphone projected my voice, the slide projector threw up images with perfect precision until ...

Weeks of practice had seen me learning my script off by heart. I knew every story, every slide. With one last click of the carousel, the final image was projected on to the screen. This was it: time for some valedictory words and I could take my bow.

'And those, ladies and gentlemen, are the Tales of the Tabloid Twitcher. Thank you,' I preened, expecting a round of spontaneous applause.

It never came. Instead, from the wings I heard the voice of the master of ceremonies who had introduced me on stage.

'You've still got 15 minutes to go,' he whispered from the sidelines. 'You'll have to find some more material.'

I froze. Adrenalin took over my body functions and my stomach flipped flight-or-fight cartwheels. Those pre-speech butterflies entered my head and prevented any rational thought. Out in the audience the discomfort was tangible. People shuffled on seats. False coughs echoed. Before the lecture, someone had reminded me of the old public speaker's tactic of pretending that the audience was sitting naked as a way of creating an air of superiority when on stage. Now it was me who felt stripped bare: bereft of ideas, exposed to ridicule. In my panic I tried to improvise. Bad idea. My words turned into an incoherent ramble about the beauty of birds and birding. People at the back began to leave. The nervous coughs got louder. I tried a joke but, in my haste, I remembered the punchline was far too risqué for public dissemination and so that got abandoned in mid, hesitant, flow. By now, the compère had seen enough and came to my rescue with a call for 'Any questions?' There was not a single one, except for the wag at the back who shouted: 'Where's the exit?' It was the signal the audience had been waiting for. Like a party of shorebirds taking flight at the sight of a marauding Peregrine Falcon, they vanished. If anyone applauded I never heard it.

I picked up my belongings, collected my slides and began to ask myself where had the talk gone wrong? Only when I looked in my satchel did I see the tell-tale shape of another slide box. Somehow I had managed to blithely rattle off my talk without realising I had missed out a whole chunk of tabloid tales. At last, as they say in the finest traditions of red-top journalism, here is my chance to put the record straight.

Out of the Cold

Youth is, after all, just a moment, but it is the moment, the spark,
that you always carry in your heart.
—Raisa Gorbachev.

The long, harsh winter of 1962–63, the so-called 'Big Freeze', left
the land devoid of birds and many families bereft of hope. Whole
communities were frozen in time. Chamber pots were squeezed under
beds because toilet cisterns had become ice-bound. Meals had to be
cooked on open fires as gas pipes cracked. Roads creaked to a standstill
and cars were left abandoned under towering drifts for weeks on end.
Factories shivered to a halt and schools shut by the thousand. An anti-
cyclone sitting to the north of Britain was to blame; the high pressure
blocking the warming influences of the Atlantic and leaving us in the
grip of an endless stream of Siberian winds and snowstorms. I can still
remember being carried home from a Boxing Day family get-together

in my father's arms when the first saucer-size snowflakes began to fall. Three months later an ugly veneer of dirty brown slush and ice still covered vast tracts of town and country. For many of our common birds, the cold and snows were catastrophic. The Kingfisher population crashed by 85 per cent as streams froze over, leaving them unable to feed. Death by starvation was the fate of millions of other creatures that could not adapt or depart. A nationwide survey was to later reveal that 23 species had suffered appalling losses because of the endless winter, with Grey Wagtail, Goldcrest, Wren, Stonechat, Barn Owl, Snipe, Long-tailed Tit and Green Woodpecker, all largely sedentary species, experiencing massive declines. For the rare and vulnerable Dartford Warbler, the sweeping drifts on its exposed heathland haunts spelt near extinction. In the entire country only 12 pairs made it through to the following spring.

While grown-ups shivered and complained, and conservationists fretted, youngsters thrived in the chaos. School closures meant studies were swapped for sledging. As the Pools Panel decided the results of postponed football matches, snowball fights became the national sport. For me, a somewhat sickly child overcoming a debilitating bout of measles that had kept me away from school for three months the previous autumn, the winter was witnessed largely from behind windows decorated with leaf-like ice patterns. Our terraced council house on a sprawling estate on the outskirts of Luton had no central heating, no double-glazing and, during this modern Ice Age, no means of cooking. Frozen gas pipes meant that my mother had to regularly rustle up sausage, egg and bacon on the living room fire. Power cuts also meant that our black-and-white television sat idle in the corner of the living room, but was I ever bored? No way. Two books, both birthday presents, were to become constant companions as the snows raged. During each day of confinement in our family igloo, I devoured every page, every fact, contained in my little *Observer's Book of Birds*. Archibald Thorburn's exquisite paintings, half published in colour, the other half monotone, created a sense of wonderment. The pinched-mouth Hobby produced by the artist's delicate brush stokes was a particular favourite and I would often stare in the bathroom mirror, sucking in my cheeks to emulate Thorburn's gaunt depiction of this incredible bird that, according to the food section of the book, could catch the fleet-flying Swallow on the wing. Staring with mouth drawn into the mirror was my way of paying homage to an enigmatic bird that seemed so rare and remote that I doubted I would ever encounter one in my lifetime. Thorburn's 'Sparrow Hawk' was another bird that stirred feelings of adventure and awe. Again, I could not wait to see this fierce-looking scourge of garden birds for myself and to celebrate that pending day I would run around the house on outstretched wings uttering its call – '*kee, kee, kee,*' as quoted by my *Observer's* – much to the astonishment of my parents.

My other prized book had the words 'Nature Diary' emblazoned on the front page and carried a chocolate box country scene depicting Red Fox, Red Deer and Badger, as far as I can remember. Sadly, the book was lost long ago, but hopefully it is still languishing in a loft somewhere awaiting rediscovery one day so that it may inspire another child as it once inspired me. Not that my entries, mostly made from inside the confines of our ice-bound house, will carry any great revelations. Yet, more than 45 years on, I can still picture the largely garden observations that had me scribbling in the awful spidery writing that earned more black marks and black looks than anything else I did in an otherwise undistinguished junior school career. The first entry announced the arrival of a flock of Fieldfares in our postage stamp-sized garden. I can still picture these noble thrushes sitting atop the privet hedge, their honey-coloured breasts stippled with inky black flecking and their beady, jet eyes set in faces the colour of the foreboding winter sky. Driven from the farmland wastes that surrounded our island of council houses, the Fieldfares looked forlornly for anything to eat, although in those days old crusts were the only fare thrown out for the birds.

In an early test of my reporting abilities, one entry got headline billing. I can still picture the sight of a dark, shadowy creature dropping from the sky into a neighbour's garden, wings outstretched and, most importantly to this young observer, obviously sporting fingered primary feathers. How I knew that birds of prey had such distinctive wing shapes when all the *Observer's* raptors were painted at rest remains a mystery. Somehow, perhaps through watching too many films at the Saturday morning pictures with them 'damn turkey buzzards' soaring over cowboy-and-indian battlefields, I had become subliminally aware that hawks and eagles ruled the skies on pinions that looked like outstretched hands. The bird that plunged behind the neighbour's fence had just such wings. What could it be? In my first act of 'stringing' – the making up of a spurious sighting of a bird – and also my first, and hopefully last, act of inaccurate reportage, I can still remember the words I wrote: 'Sparrow hawk (sic) in Mr Sharpe's garden.' In hindsight, the bird was most probably a Carrion Crow, but the die had been cast. I had become a 'bird watcher' and reporter in one, excuse the pun, fowl swoop.

A little like it takes some species of gulls or eagles years to mature from their immature plumages into full-blown textbook adulthood, my progression into a binocular-owning member of the bird watching brotherhood was also to take time. The World Cup of 1966, a burgeoning love affair with Tottenham Hotspur and dalliances with both stamp-collecting and astronomy amused and delighted in equal measure during those formative years. Enrolling in the Cub Scouts was character-building and the fields and spinneys on the edge of our urban overspill were great places to build camps, fight imaginary battles and attack wasps' nests. Moving up to secondary school was to reignite my interest in the *Observer's Book of Birds* that had by now lost its dust jacket and been annotated with large ticks to denote my handful of sightings. My snowy 'Sparrow Hawk' was still included although, as I was to find out, the species had ceased to breed in our part of Bedfordshire a few years before the Big Freeze. Mixing with new friends, joining the school's 'Zoo Club' – our school was just five miles from Whipsnade – and having a lesson called rural science on the curriculum, which was supposed to encourage our largely urban school roll to think about careers in agriculture, rekindled my interest in wildlife. Next to our school was a cavernous chalk quarry that had once been used to film an early episode of *Dr Who*, and although strictly out of bounds, it was all too much of a temptation for budding naturalists, with the lure of bird-rich willow scrub that had slowly begun to encroach upon this striking white laceration in the landscape. Small pools also pitted the bottom of the quarry and these were full of newts, most probably threatened Crested Newts, and each specimen was worth a full two shillings on the pocket money black market. For all the warnings about children drowning and falling to their deaths in this most dangerous of playgrounds, the temptation to explore became too much and so one Sunday afternoon a group of us set off on a nature walk to find the quarry's undiscovered secrets. One of the boys brought his father's binoculars – a hefty piece of equipment 'seized from a German U-Boat captain,' so we were reminded – and I took along a set of cricket stumps to use as ice picks to scale the quarry's precipitous slopes, along with a bottle of squash. We saw a Kestrel and Grey Heron but the most exciting sighting was my male 'Hen Harrier' – which soon transpired to be a Common Gull. I had mistaken the pearly grey-and-black wings of the gull for one of England's rarest breeding birds of prey because the binoculars had been grabbed from me before I could focus properly. The squabble over who had 'first dibs' of the field glasses left me vowing never to be caught without binoculars again. So began the long process of saving every penny of pocket money, birthday present postal orders and loose change scavenged from the deep recesses of the family sofa to buy my very own binoculars. By the age of 12 I was proudly cradling my Prinz 10x50s – bought from Dixons for the seemingly astronomical sum of £19 – and letting all and sundry know that I had become not just a watcher of birds but a real, proper bird watcher (notice how bird watcher was still two separate words).

As my voice broke and my juvenile plumage of slicked hair with side parting morphed into a Mod cut, so my horizons for bird finding widened. From trespassing in the quarry, our band began an altogether more dangerous operation: storming the barbed wire bastion that was Dunstable Sewage Farm. The place was bird watching utopia. Vast, glutinous settling beds topped with a foul-smelling crud played host to waders of exotic proportions. Skittish Green Sandpipers, tortoiseshell Turnstones, Bar-tailed Godwits, Ruffs, Dunlins, Little Stints and even the occasional wayward Sanderling, miles from the nearest tidal sweep, would make fleeting visits to the sewage farm during the long school summer holidays, which seemed to have been timed perfectly to coincide with the beginning of the autumn shorebird migration. A Tupperware box full of jam sandwiches and the regulation bottle of squash meant that we could keep a day-long vigil of the comings and goings. At teatime, a mad dash home ensued. To avoid an arduous three-mile hike home along the perimeter road invariably meant taking a short-cut across the grassy bunds that criss-crossed a lake of semi-raw sewage. It was a feat that could only be attempted in dry weather, when the bunds were dry and the crud was at its thickest. On several occasions, the crusty surface failed to support a misplaced footfall and I sank to my waist in the unmentionable. Only after an hour-long hosing down by Dad in the garden was I allowed into the house – grounded, and with warnings of severe punishments if I insisted on going back into the sewage farm. I hated defying my parents but the waders were just too good to miss. Another furtive incursion into the farm resulted in me being brought home supported on friends' shoulders after ripping my shin open to the bone, which required a hospital X-ray and time off school. I still bear the scar to this day. For all the accidents, for all the dousing in raw sewage, I have only one regret about my love affair with 'DSF', as it was affectionately recorded day-after-day in my bird log. A family holiday meant that I was not with Johnny Lynch, my classmate and to this day my close birding friend, when a Marsh Harrier put in an appearance. At the time it was a species which could only be reliably seen in Britain at the Royal Society for the Protection of Birds' most famous reserve, Minsmere. I vowed to see one, and soon.

When a day that you know to be just another Sunday starts off feeling like Christmas Day, something exciting must be in the air. So began a school essay titled 'The best day of my life' which I had submitted as English coursework for secondary school exams. The opening lines follow in the great tradition of plagiarism, being borrowed from the introductory chapter of John Wyndham's classic sci-fi work *The Day of the Triffids*, a chilling novel about flesh-eating plants and the end of the known world. My words, on a far more uplifting note, were used to describe that glorious morning on 17 May 1970, when I awoke knowing that I was about to embark upon an adventure that had been dominating and distracting my attentions for weeks, and resulted in my not doing sufficient revision of Wyndham's disturbing story for my forthcoming exams. The moment that a field trip to the RSPB's flagship reserve on the Suffolk coast had been published by my local natural history club's spring programme I had become totally preoccupied about visiting this bird watching Mecca. By now, I had become a member of the Young Ornithologists' Club or YOC, the junior wing of the RSPB, and hardly an issue of its quarterly magazine *Bird Life* went by without referring to the reserve's incredible bird life. Virtually every bird name mentioned in the journal's articles was only an image in my mind and a picture in my *Observer's Book*, such was my lack of bird watching experience. Without a family car and with Tring Reservoirs the most exotic bird watching venue I had ever visited, it was easy to see how scarce species such as Bearded Tit, Bittern, Avocet and, of course, Marsh Harrier, had remained tantalisingly remote and elusive.

Within minutes of arriving at Dunwich Cliffs car park and looking down on the reserve, with the old Sizewell nuclear power station's ominous outline in the background, I was enjoying an adventure that I can still see to this day in my mind's eye as if it had been recorded on film. Johnny Lynch was also on the trip, which was being run by the Bedfordshire Natural History Society. How they had managed to put up with our infernal questions *en route*, not to mention our travel sickness, I'll never know, but soon they were leading us on to Minsmere's hallowed grounds. My first excitable shouts were aimed at a bird I called out as a Merlin, only to be corrected as a slaty-grey Cuckoo flew overhead, declaring itself with an eponymous burst of song. Moments later, I was getting a first-hand lesson in bird identification as our group entered the public beach hide, opened the shutters and looked out on the reserve's famous Scrape. The moment was as enthralling and breath-taking as anything I have ever witnessed in my life. A carpet of birds, some garrulous and bickering, others sedate and stately, stretched out before my eyes, as if I was in a widescreen 3D surround-sound cinema. Birds that I knew only from paintings in books sprang to life. Avocets tip-toed in the brackish water, their upturned bills sifting for invertebrates; Shelducks patrolled the shallows; Sandwich and Common Terns guarded their small islands, taking flight and screaming at any Black-headed or Herring Gull that came too close for their liking. There was action wherever I looked. Clockwork Dunlins and Ringed Plovers fed on the muddy fringes of the Scrape's islands, which were numbered to make calling out the presence of the birds all the easier. And did we call out bird names? There were Ruff in their flouncy breeding finery, complaining Common Redshanks and Grey Plovers that looked like bewigged judges; striking, sooty-coated Spotted Redshanks and Black-tailed Godwits glorious in their brick-red breeding garb creating beautiful natural contrasts. These longer-legged species were able to enter the Scrape's deeper waters to get their fill of the invertebrate-rich brackish soup. Overhead, a solitary Whimbrel piped its famous seven whistles while the cacophony of tern yelps, Sedge Warbler soliloquies, distant Nightingales and honking Greylag Geese made the aural experience as memorable as the visual one.

All too soon it was time to leave the Scrape's public hide and enter the reserve proper, but before we took the trail inland by the sluice gate the field trip leaders ushered us along the beach path towards Sizewell. I remember thinking that we should be bird watching, not appreciating the architecture of some boring, big lump of concrete. As we made our way through the scrubby bushes that decorate the dunes, our group came to an abrupt halt. Even the experienced leaders began to look excited. Johnny and I were directed to focus our binoculars on what looked like a white plastic bag floating on a small beachside pool. With a shuffle and stretch, the bag took on another shape and revealed itself as a Little Egret. Wow! A 24-carat rarity, a bird that I had seen from a train travelling through the south of France on a family holiday, but never dreamed about seeing in the UK. Back in 1970 Little Egrets were rare vagrants to Britain; their incredible climate change-influenced mass invasion of our shores was still more than two decades away. This close encounter of the bird kind was to remain my bird watching highlight for another 12 years. I lapped up every moment until the egret opened its wings and flapped off towards the wilder reaches of the reserve. Little did I realise then that by the beginning of the 21st century these exotic creatures that conjured up images of Mediterranean salt-pans and marshes would be patrolling the streams and water meadows of my native Bedfordshire.

Our Minsmere adventure continued apace. Bitterns and Bearded Tits made cameo appearances, momentarily emerging from their reedbed haunts to delight our eyes and fill our notebooks. A distant Osprey was called out by one sharp-eyed observer, and although I was able to pick out a distant speck hovering over the Island Mere Hide it was an altogether unsatisfactory encounter with such a charismatic bird. That said, it did not stop me recording Osprey as a 'new bird' with a big asterisk in my notebook – by now I had become a fully-fledged lister.

The adrenalin-fuelled excitement of the morning eased to a more leisurely but equally enjoyable afternoon. We picked our way through the reserve's oak woods, before being ushered back to the Scrape for one final viewing. The kaleidoscope of bird activity continued. Waders, wildfowl and gulls milled about their bird metropolis; I carefully sifted through their countless number looking for anything new. One small gull took my eye. Among the beefy Herring Gulls and sleek Black-headed Gulls, this bird looked minute.

'There's a little gull,' I told one of the group leaders, meaning 'little' strictly in the adjectival sense and hoping he would make the identification.

'Well done,' he responded. 'A first-summer Little Gull. Stuart's found a Little Gull,' the leader broadcast to the rest of the group. I glowed with a mixture of embarrassment and undeserved kudos. The birding elders began to look at me in a new light, no longer the schoolboy nuisance who asked too many questions but a birdwatcher. Note how in an instant the phrase had become one word, with no hyphen – the term that was beginning to carry favour with the more enthusiastic elements of the pastime. It could have been so different – I could so easily have asked: 'What's that small gull?'

Gizza Job...

REPORTER, *n*. A writer who guesses his way to the truth
and dispels it with a tempest of words.
—Ambrose Bierce, *Devil's Dictionary*.

Hormones are funny things. To start with, they are the reason why
males are males and females are difficult to live with (only joking, dear).
They make gawky teenage girls mature into shapely, delectable women
and turn awkward teenage boys with attitudes into awkward men with
attitudes. Chemicals with names such as dehydroepiandrosterone,
androstenedione and dihydrotestosterone also play havoc with your
birdwatching. Football, beer, girls, work, studies, more girls and lots
more beer are all temptations which can disrupt a young birdwatcher's
rites of passage, a journey fuelled by androgen-driven urges that create
terrible distractions and upheavals. More often, hormonally affected
young souls are hurled into a state of suspended animation where
binoculars and notebooks are secreted into lofts or trunks and the

B-word (bird) vanishes from the vocabulary. Perhaps only when a country walk with a girlfriend or an evening of passion in some lovers' lane is interrupted by a churring Nightjar or, if you are particularly lucky, the *ploop....ploop....ploop* of a distant Scops Owl, will those old feelings of birding excitement suddenly replace those charged with testosterone. My birding hiatus between the ages of 16 and 24 was thankfully filled with enough avian excitement – for instance, seeing a Hoopoe on one of the very first dates with my future wife, Annie – to prevent me from hanging up my bins permanently and giving my bird books to a charity shop. School studies also maintained my faith. For instance, Geography A Level provided an opportunity to visit the Hebridean islands of Eigg and Muck, where Black-throated and Red-throated Divers would announce reveille with their eerie morning chorus and nightly beach bonfires were decorated with the ghostly shadows of Manx Shearwaters. College years may have been devoid of birds – studying on the outskirts of London meant I could indulge my other love, Tottenham Hotspur – but the lure of the old sewage farm was always strong on visits home. To this day, the distinct aroma wafting from sewerage systems turns me into Pavlov's dog, salivating at the thought of inland shorebirds.

My first few weeks as a cub reporter on the local newspaper in Hitchin, Hertfordshire, meant doing a tour of duty around the local undertakers to collect obituary notices as well as collecting press notices from the fire station. On one visit, I caught the fleeting glimpse of a small bird as it sallied among the leaves of a beech tree. Its zippy flight was hard to track without my trusty Prinz 10x50s but finally the bird settled on a branch long enough to display its grey-brown plumage and distinctive white wing-bars – a Pied Flycatcher, a species that only makes infrequent stopovers in the Home Counties. The undertakers had never seen someone smiling so much when I called in for the week's death notifications.

Watching birds and working for local newspapers were not always symbiotic activities. I transferred from the *Hitchin Comet* to the *Luton News* yet still found the late-night council meetings, rambling magistrates' court hearings and long days in the office were nurturing my pallid complexion and early stage agoraphobia. Luton is a busy news patch and covering my first fatal light aircraft crash along with all manner of rapes and murders, particularly ones that brought the national boys into town, honed my news sense and began to make me dream about working on Fleet Street one day. My break came when I was offered the chance to work for the regional news agency which supplied the broadsheets, tabloids and television networks with a stream of news from across the northern Home Counties. Day-long magistrates' court hearings became lengthy crown court trials, domestic murders evolved into gangland killings. Stories that were telexed to the outside world would be there in newsprint the next morning, sometimes written word-for-word as they were dispatched. Only my byline was missing, invariably 'bandited' by a staff reporter who hadn't set foot outside London. Still, I loved the job and loved the excitement. One afternoon I resisted the efforts of some particularly tough-looking Regional Crime Squad detectives, who wanted me to leave the court for a hearing that had to be held in public, but which the police would have preferred to be held *in camera*. It turned out that a top supergrass was in the dock, spilling the beans on division-one bank robbers, counterfeiters and long-firm fraudsters. I had my first scoop. The story was on the front page of the *Daily Express* the next morning and senior detectives, respectful of the way I had handled the details that emerged in court, paid the compliment of describing me as a 'crime reporter' the next time our paths crossed. For all the glory of making the front page, it was a much smaller story – a solitary paragraph in the *Daily Telegraph* – that was to prove a more significant achievement.

Detached from the 'grapevine' – the legendary bush telegraph used to pinball the latest vagrant bird information in the epoch before pagers, information lines and mobile phones – I rarely knew what rarities were touching down either nationally or locally. The famous Cheddar Gorge Wallcreeper may have been making headlines in the national press because it attracted thousands of observers, but most rarities came and went without ever coming across my radar. Late October 1977 changed all that. Tring Reservoirs made ornithological history in 1938 when Little Ringed Plovers began their successful colonisation of Britain by breeding in a gravelly corner of one of the three man-made lakes used to balance the Grand Union Canal. Over the years many rarities have made appearances on its tranquil waters or muddy margins: White-winged Black Tern, Least Sandpiper and Alpine Swift, to name but a few. The arrival of a Long-billed Dowitcher, coincidentally at the same time as a Great Northern Diver, somehow sent shockwaves through the disparate Bedfordshire–Hertfordshire birding scene. Even I got to hear about the birds by way of a telephone call from a distant birding acquaintance. The buzz of excitement across the local bush telegraph was unprecedented: I just had to make the laborious Sunday afternoon bus trip to Tring to catch up with two species that I had never seen before. Both birds had taken up temporary residence on Wilstone Reservoir, which required a good two-mile walk from the nearest bus stop, and the would-they-still-be-there nerves remained until I could make out the comforting sight of a small crowd of observers gathered on the bank, obviously engrossed in the aquatic prowess of the diver as it disappeared under water for long periods in its pursuit of small Perch. When the diver completed its fishing forays, it would take a few moments to preen its immaculate, scaly plumage before drifting across the reservoir surface like a stately ocean-liner.

It was another long walk to the opposite side of the reservoir to join a small queue to enter the reservoir's hide, a somewhat primitive construction if my memory serves me well, but located strategically next to the widest muddy margin preferred by small flocks of waders. Several Common Snipe were present and, I have to be honest, what I could only identify as another 'snipe-like bird' with an almost equally long bill and nondescript, greyish plumage. This was obviously the dowitcher, although with only a few cursory illustrations to compare it with in my limited bird book library, I had to rely on the other more experienced observers present to explain the identification criteria. In theory, the dowitcher had surpassed the Minsmere Little Egret as the rarest bird I had ever seen. The fact that I had seen it in the late afternoon, when it was largely a silhouette, meant the experience was somewhat stilted. That said, the dowitcher was to prove a pivotal point in both my birding and journalistic careers. Walking away from the bird, I met up with an old sporting adversary from my school days. I had played football and basketball against Peter Marshall on many occasions. He was an accomplished midfielder with a neat touch, but I never dreamed that when we tackled each other as rivals on a football pitch or basketball court that we both harboured a love for birds. A friendship was instantly created that lasts to this day.

The next morning I told the boss of the news agency how I had seen two unusual birds at Tring and, with his instinctive nose for news, he told me to 'bash out a few paragraphs and put it all round'. I duly obliged and soon the telex was telling the world how 'birdwatchers were flocking to Tring to see two rare birds' as I was being dispatched to St Albans Crown Court to witness more tales of criminal activity and human failings. A solitary paragraph, in those days of Fleet Street opulence worth five pounds in lineage fees, appeared in the *Daily Telegraph* the following day. This was my first article to be published about birds and, in many ways, it was a much more pleasing experience than looking at the dowitcher's silhouette in the fading light.

The late 1970s segued into the 'Thatcher Years', with economic boom and bust, crippling unemployment, Alan Bleasdale's harrowing *Boys from the Blackstuff*, mullet haircuts, and my acquisition of a driving licence and membership of the RSPB local members group. My first outing with them was on 22 March 1980, a date that I have arbitrarily chosen, in the manner of British royalty, as my official 'birdwatching birthday.' Anniversaries play a big part in journalism, giving an excuse for a retrospective of any event, and I felt it would be a good idea to use such a platform to get serious about my fast-developing interest by creating a 'year dot' as a launch pad to new glories. Returning from that first local members' group winter outing to Walberswick, with its Snow Buntings and roosting Hen Harriers, I decided to start my whole birdwatching career afresh by giving my bird logs the once-over; subscribing to *British Birds* magazine and, equally important, buying a decent pair of binoculars.

By now, those Prinz £19 specials were feeling their age. Chipped, water-stained and slightly out-of-true, they had served me well for a little over a decade. It was time for a make-over and so I kitted myself out in a new birding jacket, my first pair of green wellies and also a pair of 8x30 Carl Zeiss Jena Jenoptems, cut-price optics with a popular following among birdwatchers on a budget. Frustratingly, they were packed inside a duffle bag when I learned one of the key lessons of becoming a proper birder: always keep your bins accessible. The following month I joined the local members' group on its coach trip to one of the most beautiful parts of England, the RSPB's Nagshead reserve in the heart of the Forest of Dean, a place where Pied Flycatchers, Wood Warblers and Common Redstarts abound. On the journey, somewhere close to Thame, with the entire coach party engrossed in conversation, snacking or snoozing, a sleek-winged bird appeared at eye level no more than 20 yards from the coach. My eyes flickered as the shape shuffled on fast-beating wings. It was a flight action I had seen somewhere before, but where? In an instant, it disappeared with a few more vigorous flaps of its rapier-like wings. Then it dawned on me: Alpine Swift, a bird I had seen as a youngster on a family trip to the Spanish Costas. I was about to call this rare wanderer from the rocky slopes of the Mediterranean to the massed ranks of bird group members, then realised I would be opening myself to ridicule, if not scorn. Who would believe me: an Alpine Swift in deepest Oxfordshire? Long gone, stopping the coach on a busy road to check for the bird was out of the question. I closed my eyes and dreamed about Pied Flycatchers.

The early 1980s should have seen my birding and reporting taking equal second place to fatherhood, but somehow I managed to keep all three juggled, building my lifelist to incorporate most of the scarce breeding birds of southern England, including such exciting species as Dartford Warbler, Nightjar and Hobby, and also getting my first casual shifts on national newspapers. Weekend shifts on the *News of the World, Sunday Mirror* and *Daily Star* bolstered our modest family income and provided first-hand experience of the blood-draining requirements expected by those hard taskmasters that run the frenetic national news desks. My chance to join Fleet Street's finest came in May 1982, when one of the news editors from the London office of the *Daily Star* suggested that I apply for a reporter's position at the newspaper's Manchester base. In those days, Express Newspapers had offices in Great Ancoats Street that were almost identical to its famous glass-fronted 'Black Lubyanka' in Fleet Street. The idea of working 'oop narf' did not go down too well with my family. I'd only been north of Birmingham on three occasions, each time on a school trip, and the thought of faggots, mushy peas and chips and gravy were far from appetising. A 300 per cent increase on what I was earning as a freelance, however, seemed worthwhile compensation. The only drawback about applying for the job was that interviews were being held in Manchester and I would have to make my own way there – as things were a little tight financially at home, the petrol costs to Manchester and back seemed prohibitive.

Petrol prices did not stop me from going birdwatching to Milton Keynes' Willen Lake the following Sunday morning with the hope of seeing a Temminck's Stint, which was taking a well-earned rest on the long flight north to its tundra breeding grounds. Looking for a tiny, sparrow-sized sandpiper the colour of damp gravel in acres of, well, damp gravel was proving a fruitless task for the small posse of observers. One of the keen local birders decided to drive off and call Nancy's Café, the world famous eaterie on Norfolk's so-called 'Birding Riviera', which in those days was the epicentre of the twitching world. The ashen-faced individual returned a few minutes later and began turning the air blue with expletive-enriched adjectives. A censored précis of what he had to say revealed that a Marmora's Warbler – a tiny inhabitant of Mediterranean garrigue, and a species that had never been seen in Britain before – had taken up territory on a South Yorkshire moor. It was, without doubt, the most sensational bird news of the year, and listening to the Milton Keynes birders making arrangements for an immediate trip up the M1 seemed as incredulous to me as if they were planning a Moon shot. I sloped off home, a mere 20-mile drive, rueing the sedentary nature of my birdwatching and wishing I was a real twitcher.

Although I had never been a twitcher, and my rarity-barren lifelist paid testament to the fact, inside I was suddenly going through all the emotions that real rarity-chasers put themselves through, sometimes on a daily basis. I was mopey, miserable and my appetite had withered in ratio with my temper. Watching all those excited faces making plans to travel north to see a bird that I had only rudimentary knowledge about, I decided that this was the way I wanted to birdwatch. Playing the dutiful family guy was the way I had to live.

Apart from looking up Marmora's Warbler in my Peterson, Mountfort and Hollom field guide, and also re-reading Eddie Watkinson's *Guide to Bird-watching in Mallorca* – the place we had spent our honeymoon, without seeing Marmora's Warbler (although the subspecies there has since been split as a separate species, Balearic Warbler). Any thought of seeing the South Yorkshire Marmora's Warbler for myself had faded from my mind. The next day I went to work at the news agency and over a cup of coffee was reading about the weekend's FA Cup Final which was featuring my team Tottenham

Hotspur against Queen's Park Rangers. I had somehow managed to get my hands on a ticket, which had helped to ease the pain of missing the warbler. Browsing the *Daily Star*, a cunning thought of Baldrick proportions came to mind: why not ring the newspaper in Manchester and request an interview? A quick check of the road atlas confirmed that I could drive up the M1, cross over the Pennines, call in to see the warbler and then attend an interview with the news editor after the early evening deadline. I broke the news that evening to my wife that the *Daily Star* was anxious to see me and that a salary four times my current pay cheque was on the table. For Annie, the thought of moving to Manchester was as unsettling as emigrating to Australia, but she acquiesced and I made arrangements to travel north on the Wednesday. There was no mention of the Marmora's Warbler.

Wednesday came and I headed off in my best suit – the one I wore for my wedding still fitted after six years – clutching a collection of newspaper cuttings I had written for the national newspapers and also my trusty Jenoptems, together with the other addition to my birdwatching arsenal, an Optolyth 30x75 telescope. An early call to Nancy's Café confirmed that the warbler was still *in situ*, and so I began the long drive north with the help of a few basic directions scribbled in a reporter's notebook. Three or so hours later I was pulling into a lay-by, where the tell-tale sign of cars splattered with birdwatching stickers such as 'birders do it for a lark' were confirmation that I was in the right vicinity. Vicinity was to prove an apt word. I had little idea of how far I needed to walk. Looking somewhat incongruous in my interview suit, shiny shoes and best white shirt, and with my binoculars gripped in my hands rather than in their customary position hanging around my neck – I did not want to mess up my neatly tied Windsor knot – I set off across the South Yorkshire moor with the pearl grey skies giving no hint of what weather lay ahead.

By early afternoon, the lucky souls who had already 'connected' with the warbler were making their return journeys along the moorland path that was already beginning to bear signs of heavy footfall. For a dyed-in-the-wall southerner, the unprepossessing atmosphere of bleak, heather-coated moorland with its tufts of cottongrass and *Juncus* were a reminder of one of the worst periods of my life, reading Emily Brontë's altogether depressing *Wuthering Heights* in third-form. Still, the thought of a Mediterranean rarity, albeit one with a drab slate-grey plumage, waiting to brighten the unforgiving landscape drove me ever forwards as the yards turned to furlongs and then to miles. Cheery faces heading in the opposite direction raised the spirits with their comments of 'what a bird' and 'it's showing so well,' which were a great pick-me-up as the walk began to take its toll. I was perspiring and thirsty, and my shiny shoes were beginning to take on the colour of the local geology. Then disaster, a misplaced step left me tumbling into one of the boggiest bits of the inauspiciously named Mickleden Clough. The knees of my charcoal-grey pinstriped suit were coated with mud the colour of mulligatawny soup. I was not giving up, though. After what seemed like an age, I finally found myself in a steep-sided gritstone valley, 1,400 feet up in the Pennines amid a gathering of a few dozen folk dressed in Barbour jackets and with stout boots – sensible wear for walking on the moors. A forest of tripods supporting expensive telescopes was focussed on a particular patch of heather on the eastern rim of the valley. There was no sign of the bird.

By now I was getting hungry. The skies were darkening, my 6pm interview was getting ever closer and the warbler, in the finest tradition of Latin lifestyles, was taking a siesta. Some beautifully amber-toned Whinchats and a solitary male Ring Ouzel, birds that I rarely encountered back in my native Bedfordshire haunts, were some compensation, and when a Red Grouse cackled before exploding into flight, I began trying to convince myself that the 'yomp' – at the time, the Falklands War was at its height and the word meaning an arduous walk had crept into everyday parlance – had been worthwhile. I knew, however, that if I left the moor without seeing the warbler I would be bitterly disappointed. And then, like an operatic diva, it was there, dancing on the breeze 20 or so feet above the ground, twittering its weak aria to an appreciative audience.

Marmora's Warblers, named after the Napoleonic War general turned naturalist Alberto Ferrero La Marmora, perform their ostentatious song-flights as a way of proclaiming and protecting their territories from interlopers. That this bird had decided to stage the ritual almost 1,000 miles north of its regular nesting grounds in the Corsican maquis, the first of its kind to attempt this venture, made its sky dance all the more alluring. I watched, listened and enjoyed. Occasionally, it would tumble back to a vantage point where I could study its delicate features and subtle tones. The overall impression was of a bird very much like our native Dartford Warbler, yet wearing a suit a few shades lighter than my own, perhaps the tone of a cuckoo. What accentuated its beauty were the contrasting tones of its beady, blood-red eye and orbital ring and ochre-coloured legs. For some reason, the bird reminded me of a Confederate Army officer, a dandy doomed never to find a mate on this windswept northern moor, but flamboyant and brazen to the last.

I saluted the bird as it scurried into the tangled heather and made my way back to the car and my rendezvous with fate. More mud and grime collected on my person as I stumbled along the path, some of it washed away by a short but ferocious squall, yet this time the walk back was basked in the satisfaction of having seen the warbler, which acted like a trusty staff as I picked my way through puddles and potholes. The drive along the A628 over the Pennines into Manchester remains a blur, such was the high of my first real twitch, and even though the rush-hour traffic and trying to find a parking spot produced hazards and tensions to match the warbler quest, I arrived for the interview with a few seconds to spare. What impression I made in a suit so heavily mud-spattered that it could easily have provided camouflage for an army sniper, I never discovered.

'We've filled the vacancy,' were the news executive's few curt words. 'Thanks for coming, there's always the next time.'

Life, I concluded, was an oxymoron: the sweet memories of the warbler; the antithesis, the harsh realities of modern journalism. I headed back south, this time down the M6, thinking that birdwatching held more of a future, more uplifting moments, than being a reporter. I had begun to hatch another cunning plan.

The Best of Days, the Worst of Days

Well, she laments, sir, for it, that it would yearn your heart to see it.
Her husband goes this morning a-birding.
—William Shakespeare, *Merry Wives of Windsor*. Act III, Scene V.

Only the memories of the Marmora's Warbler fluttering above the purple heather kept me awake on the long drive back from Manchester. The euphoria of seeing the first 'mega-rarity' of my birdwatching career had built up unwarranted expectations about the job interview and, like the exquisite little warbler of the moor performing its song-flight, I had come tumbling down to earth. Realising I was too young and inexperienced to join the ranks of Her Majesty's National Press, my mind turned to other ways to boost a career that seemed destined to remain as a humble regional freelance journalist on the fringes of the action. Wherever my thoughts wandered, they always returned to birdwatching. It was in my blood and although family and work commitments, along with a lack of hard cash, meant that I would never join the vanguard of the twitching movement, I convinced myself there were ways that I could make a contribution to the birdwatching scene. Somewhere near Keele Services it dawned. It was simple, it would be fun and, most of all, the idea would satisfy the burgeoning desire to become, dare I say, a fully fledged 'birder'.

Some may think of it as a matter of semantics, but there are tangible distinctions between being a birdwatcher, birder and twitcher, although back in the early 1980s the issue was very much clouded and words like ticker and lister were also commonly used parts of the ornithological lexicon. Indeed, other names used over the decades to describe seekers of rare birds have included the decidedly Edwardian-sounding descriptions of pot-hunter, tally-hunter and tick-hunter. The wonderful *Bill Oddie's Little Black Bird Book* went some way to explaining and clarifying definitions but arguments regularly arise today, even among friends, over how they like to be described.

Twitcher is easy. These are the battle-hardened storm-troopers of the bird world made up of guys (even in these days of equal opportunity, it is still largely a male pursuit) who can drop everything at a moment's notice to rush off and see a rarity found by someone else. They see no shame in spending a small fortune, risking wife and limb dashing across the country, sometimes two or three countries because Irish birds are also fair game, to have a momentary rendezvous with some tired, lost, even moribund, waif from distant climes.

R.E. Emmett described the etymology of the word twitcher at length in the following letter to *British Birds* in 1983. It goes to some lengths to explain that even in post-war Britain, the rare bird bug had bitten deeply:

'Twitcher' is actually a John Izzard–Bob Emmett word which was coined in the middle 1950s to describe our good friend Howard Medhurst, alias 'The Kid'. Birdwatching transport was very much a two-wheeled affair in those days. John Izzard and his girlfriend, Sheila, rode a Lambretta, whilst Howard rode pillion on my Matchless. The Lambretta had a unique luxury built into it: a back-warming, lap-warming dog, 'Jan', which used to travel jammed between John and Sheila. There was no such creature comfort on the Matchless; on arrival at some distant destination, Howard would totter off the back of my machine and shiveringly light up a cigarette. This performance was repeated so regularly up and down the

country that it became synonymous with good birds, and, as we all felt
a slight nervous excitement at the uncertainty involved in trying to see a
particular bird, it became a standing joke, and John and I would act out
a nervous twitch to match Howard's shiverings. This led us to describe a
trip to see a rare bird as 'Being on a twitch'. Inevitably, this led to the
term 'twitcher'. It was our association with the Portsmouth Group in the
New Forest that extended the term into more general use. In the late
1960s, it became a derogatory term to describe unscrupulous tick-hunters
(and as far as I am concerned it still is). It is pretty safe to say, however,
that Howard Medhurst was – in the nicest possible way – the original
twitcher. R.E. Emmett

(Reproduced by kind permission of *British Birds*)

In the mid-1980s, I was still proclaiming myself a birdwatcher – as
mentioned, in my language, the term had morphed into one word by
dropping the hyphen or space – but I was in a majority of one. 'Birder'
had certainly caught the imagination of even the hardcore proponents
of the pastime. The difference between a birder and twitcher was
popularly summed up by the phrase: 'birders find – twitchers follow'.
Put simply, birders prefer to go looking for their own birds, dredging
their home patches or visiting well known reserves and migration hot-
spots to uncover lurking *Locustella* warblers or skulking *Sylvia* warblers.
Even devout twitchers prefer calling themselves birders, as not only is
this a more socially acceptable moniker, but also because many top
twitchers are indeed top bird finders. Back in the early 1980s, my one
man campaign to stop the word 'birder' becoming part of the wider
birdwatching vocabulary fell at the first hurdle with an opinion column
I wrote for *British Birds* under the headline 'A Case for Birdwatching.'
Even my friends, now self-proclaimed birders themselves, thought I
was mad for writing the following rant:

America has a reputation for exporting the gimmicky and the unwanted:
bubblegum, skateboards, citizen-band radio and now – definitely the
worst – that damned word, 'birding'. Only recently has birdwatching been
afforded the privilege, particularly by such watchdogs of our language
as the National Press, of becoming a single word, not split into two or
separated by a hyphen. No sooner does that happen, however, and
everyone starts calling themselves 'birders'. To compound the matter,

anyone lunatic enough these days to describe himself as a birdwatcher
is greeted with the same reaction from the birding fraternity as if he
proclaimed in loud words: 'I am a dude.'

Birdwatching, as a word, may be criticised for being too bland a
description for today's esoteric pastime. No serious birdwatcher simply
watches birds. Perhaps it is for that reason that the birdwatcher has
become an endangered species, especially when good arguments for the
usage of birder are put forward by the likes of Bill Oddie: in his hilarious
Little Black Bird Book, he advocates his preference for birder, saying it has
a certain 'ruggedness.'

Maybe he has a point. A birder, before the Americans resurrected the
word from Shakespeare's *Merry Wives of Windsor*, was a hunter who
ruggedly braved the elements to kill anything that flew. In my view, that
is a good enough case against the horrid word.

For such a beautiful and omnipotent language as English, it is a
travesty to resort to Americanisms. Modern ornithology evolved in
Britain. It is only fitting, therefore, that the collective term we call
ourselves should be the one that derived in Britain, namely birdwatcher.
If we continue to bend towards transatlantic phraseology, how long will
it be before the British list contains Gray Wagtail and Rose-colored
Starling?

(Reproduced by kind permission of *British Birds*)

The effort I put into writing that piece, however much I was pilloried
at the time, was not wasted. Penning an opinion column for *British
Birds* magazine was to help me with the project I had dreamed about as
I took on a fresh supply of caffeine at the Keele Services on that long
drive south from the interview. While that memorable pilgrimage to
Minsmere, arguably the greatest of all the RSPB reserves, was a teenage
awakening to the wonders of our native bird life, my somewhat epic
adventure to the Marmora's Warbler stakeout in the Pennines was a
wholly different experience. It was covert in its inception as there was
no way I would have been given a 'visa' to travel to what seemed like
the other end of the country ('using all that petrol,' to quote my
wife, 'to see some tiny sparrow'). It was also foolhardy jeopardising a
potential job interview. What impression had I made on a national
news editor by turning up looking like Worzel Gummidge? But how
exhilarating was that moment when the Marmora's Warbler took

flight? Surely, if I had been left with such vivid mind's eye memories, scores of others had enjoyed similar experiences in their lives? Why not record them for posterity in one book? The great names in birdwatching all writing about their best day in the field? It would be a bestseller.

A few years later and the idea that had its genesis on the long drive home reached fruition to become *Best Days with British Birds*. The book was written in co-operation with the magazine and co-edited by Dr Malcolm Ogilvie and myself, and although it never quite made it to the top of sales charts it is still thought of fondly by all those who have read its eclectic blend of bird stories. Today, in fact, it often sells for more than its original cover price on Amazon.

For me, though, the idea of the book was a conduit to meeting all kinds of folk, all of whom held much greater standing in birdwatching's social structure. These were the people who had dedicated their lives to gaining knowledge about birds in all their glory, whether from a field identification angle, as an academic challenge or simply because they enjoyed spectacles and happenings that most of us only dream about. There were names such as Peter J. Grant, Keith Vinicombe and Ian Lewington, pioneers who were standing at the frontier of bird identification; there were greats from the previous generation such as Guy Mountfort and Bruce Campbell; there was 'über-twitcher' extraordinaire Steve Webb; top photographers such as Richard Chandler and David Cottridge; artists in the shape of Hilary Burn and John Busby; the legendary Chris Mead, and, of course, Bill Oddie.

Cold-calling, corresponding with and interviewing a line-up of more than 30 leading figures ensured that I not only created an address book of key birdwatching contacts but also that I began to move in the 'birdy circles' and was soon being invited to publishing drinks parties and other social functions. The fact that I remained a newspaper hack, albeit that I was a freelance and not aligned to any title, always left me on the fringes, but warm friendly characters, particularly the late Peter Grant, ensured that I became part of the fold through friendship rather than any birdwatching skills or talent on my part. This inclusivity bolstered my determination to become more active on the birding scene. I made every effort to embrace the pastime that was fast becoming a lifestyle in all its glories. Rare birds such as Cream-coloured Courser and Naumann's Thrush graced my hurriedly expanding checklist. Trips to Minsmere, Cley, Dungeness and Portland Bill were monthly rather than annual events. My Bedfordshire county list began to rival some of the stalwarts of the local scene with sightings of Blue-winged Teal, Ring-necked Duck, Collared Pratincole, White-winged Black Tern, Wryneck and Great Grey Shrike. When the shout went up that a 'goodie' (a bird, not Bill Oddie) had been seen somewhere within the Bedfordshire boundary, I started getting calls from any number of fellow keen county-listers.

My journalism was following the same steady course. I had survived the Falklands War – the thousands of column inches dedicated by the national newspapers to the South Atlantic conflict meant there was no space for more parochial news and sent many freelances into financial crisis – and there always seemed to be some incidents, court cases or gossip that I could sell on to red-top dailies or the Sundays. The summer of 1984, however, was to prove a defining moment. A series of burglaries with a disturbing sexual element to their motive began to be recorded in a small triangle of countryside on the Bedfordshire, Buckinghamshire, and Hertfordshire borders. One ended in a cold-blooded, but thankfully non-fatal, shooting. Without a positive link between the incidents, the stories remained small news items on the local radio and regional television. The grouping of the crime scenes got my wannabe detective brain working: were they linked? I approached the police with my theory only to discover that a covert operation was underway. The police had discovered that the attacker would break into homes, build himself a lair out of the occupants' furnishings and then wait for the householders to return before subjecting both men and women to unspeakable horrors. With a 24/7 operation to snare the attacker in full swing, the last thing the police wanted was press publicity. I agreed to maintain a news blackout.

When the attacker changed his *modus operandi* and began to strike over a wider area, I was called by the police and asked to circulate the story nationally. It sounds clichéd now, but one of the first things I did was nickname the assailant 'The Fox' because of the cunning way he built lairs inside his victims' homes before launching his increasingly sadistic attacks. Fleet Street reacted to the story spectacularly. Over a period of two months it was rarely off the front pages. 'The Pack' – the name given to Fleet Street journalists on tour – invaded South Bedfordshire *en masse*. Dozens of reporters wanted dozens of angles. With my colleagues at the local news agency, we kept them supplied with the inside story until the day the red-tops splashed 'Fox Snared' on millions of editions. As the Fox's victims tried to heal their deep psychological wounds, the police celebrated a textbook multi-force operation to catch their man and the assailant was beginning a life sentence, offers of work on Fleet Street came my way. Within a year I was a full-blooded crime reporter working for Eddie Shah's new title, *Today*.

The one agreement I made with my family as I set off on the first morning of my new job, wearing a smart suit and a wide, enthusiastic smile, was a promise to curtail my birdwatching. Even during the so-called 'Fox Hunt', there had been lots of opportunity to take a breather at Tring Reservoirs or Ashridge Woods and wind down by watching waders or listening to the calming strains of a Wood Warbler. Sixteen-hour days working the London 'crime beat' meant there would be little time for county twitches or days out at the coast with my circle of pals. Their life lists continued to grow; I had bylines by way of compensation.

Over the next three years, holidays abroad with the family became the only way that I had time to go looking for new birds. Package tours to Mallorca, Crete, the Spanish Costas and Italy produced encounters with colourful European Bee-eaters, noisy Black-winged Stilts and spectacular Black Vultures. Two or three hours in the field before family breakfasts over a two-week period most probably equalled the same amount of time I could dedicate to bird finding during the rest of the year at home. A week spent debriefing a retired Scotland Yard detective living in Spain about his gang-busting arrests gave me plenty of time to visit salt-pans near Alicante during spring migration and meant that my Euro list was flourishing while my British one had entered a long period of dormancy.

Working as crime reporter for *Today* and later the *News of the World* gave me an eye-opening view of the human condition. Tabloid clichés remain the only way to describe sadistic child killers, evil terrorists, crazed gunmen and dangerous gangsters. I worked on most of the big murders and terrorism cases of the late 1980s. There was the Jeremy Bamber case, the Brighton bombing, Brink's-Mat robbery and the Hungerford massacre. I was one of the first two national journalists inside Hungerford on the day that Michael Ryan went berserk and killed 14 innocent people before turning the gun on himself. I hid in a shop on Hungerford High Street as the shots from his semi-automatic Kalashnikov-type rifle were still ringing out over the Berkshire market town. Another assignment saw me in Luxembourg when detectives from the world famous Flying Squad recovered priceless diamonds stolen during the Knightsbridge safe deposit robbery, the biggest crime of its kind ever carried out on British soil.

In 1989 I got the opportunity of a job move that was to have a profound effect on both my career prospects and eventually my birdwatching. The *Daily Star* was looking to restructure its news desk and the great *News of the World* investigator Gerry Brown recommended me for the job of assistant news editor. The final interview for the post was conducted by another great Fleet Street character, *Daily Star* editor Brian Hitchen, a tough, no-nonsense journalist who had been around the block more times than a lost taxi driver. I was invited to his immaculate office overlooking Blackfriars Bridge, noting the Union Flag that stood proudly in the corner and the quizzical glint that shone in his eye. I waited for his first question.

'Have you got any hobbies?' was his opening gambit. A strange choice of question for someone noted as a ruthless interrogator.

'Er, birdwatching,' I muttered hesitantly.

A few Fleet Street hacks play golf, some enjoy yachting, but back in the 1980s many found the best way to spend their social hours was swapping stories in the wine bars and drinking dens of EC4.

'So what bird would you like to see?' Mr Hitchen continued questioning.

'Er, an albatross,' I replied, thinking of its literary connections through Samuel Taylor Coleridge's *Rime of the Ancient Mariner* and also because the famous Black-browed Albatross which had returned year-after-year to Scotland in search of a mate had vanished that spring. The chances of seeing another one in British waters seemed highly remote.

'Why an albatross?' the editor looked at me with his piercing blue eyes.

It was a question that set me regaling a story of unrequited love, intrigue, despair and hope. The Black-browed Albatross, affectionately known as 'Albert Ross' to a legion of twitchers, had been making an annual pilgrimage to the gannetry at Hermaness – the northernmost tip of Unst, which is the northernmost inhabited island in the Shetland group – since 1972, without ever finding a mate. Attempts at wooing one of the unpaired female Gannets on the island were always going to leave poor Albert frustrated and looking sad and crestfallen, a feature accentuated by his dark eye-markings.

Another angle to the story made the stalwart of countless Fleet Street scoops widen his eyes.

Because long-winged albatrosses are birds of the southern hemisphere, where powerful gales propel them on epic ocean-going adventures, any bird flying too far north is inviting disaster. Crossing the doldrums, the band of equatorial calms where light winds prevail, could leave an albatross becalmed or, if it did traverse the Equator in unusual weather conditions, the bird would be forever trapped in the northern hemisphere. Albert Ross's tragic tale had Mr Hitchen punching his fist with gusto.

'What a story. We must run it,' he enthused. 'When can you write it?'

A hearty handshake in his vice like grip and I was hired. I was the assistant news editor of the *Daily Star*.

'An Excuse for More Tits in the Paper...'

I think a newspaper should be provocative, stir 'em up,
but you can't do that on television. It's just not on.
—Rupert Murdoch.

News that Saddam Hussein's airborne commandos had arrived in the heart of Kuwait City on 2 August 1990 heralded a new chapter in world history as well as providing my induction of seeing a national newspaper on a war footing. The indomitable Brian Hitchen led from the front. A former paratrooper, he had a wonderful patriotic fervour and overwhelming passion that 'Our Boys' on the frontline must be supported at all costs. This duty of support was not confined to the courageous men and women of HM Armed Forces. The *Daily Star* sent its own team of reporters and photographers to cover the Gulf War from all angles. Journalists were embedded with the RAF, Royal Navy and Army, and also in Tel Aviv and Baghdad. Reporters flew on RAF refuelling missions and had to live in constant fear of Iraqi Scud missiles. As one of the news desk team, my role was collating their dispatches, watching news feeds from around the world and making sure that our reporters got the support they needed. Orders came down that the 'war desk' would run 24/7 until victory was declared, and with intelligence chatter suggesting that Saddam had chemical or biological weapons to unleash, the tension in the news room was always high, often stressful. If ever my future grandchildren ask me what I did during the Gulf War then I would have to be truthful and say that I nearly got the sack – and it was all because of birds.

As coalition forces first gained air supremacy and then unleashed a massive armoured onslaught in the so-called 'Mother of all Battles', a hard-pressed Saddam was left committing one of the worst environmental crimes in history in a fit of manic pique. On 21 January 1991, in a misguided attempt to stop US marines making beach landings, Saddam ordered 400 million gallons of oil to be dumped into the Persian Gulf by opening the labyrinthine network of pipes connecting the Kuwaiti oil fields to refineries. Oil wells were also set ablaze and so as the skies went black from clouds of billowing, sickly smoke, the warm waters of the Gulf went the same colour under a tide of crude. For wintering seabirds it was a disaster. Images of doomed Black-necked Grebes and Socotra Cormorants looking like glossy black dinosaurs as they struggled in the glutinous seas were among the saddest images of the entire conflict. Tens of thousands of birds perished.

When the first television pictures of the carnage were broadcast I was on late evening duty and took a call from a publicist offering to send over high quality still pictures of the carnage at sea. The conversation went something like this:

> Publicist: 'We have pictures of the ducks that you may have seen covered with oil.'
> Me: 'It's so awful watching those poor birds suffer. But by the way, they are not ducks they're Shags.'
> Publicist: 'Oh, what's the difference between a duck and a Shag?'
> Me: 'Er, come round here and I'll show you... (I laughed out loud)!'

I then proceeded to give, as it turns out, a hugely inaccurate lecture on seabird identification. I was later to discover the oiled birds were in fact Socotra Cormorants, not European Shags. To be honest, such a birding *faux pas* would have been mortifying if my friends had found out at the time, but what happened next was all the more humiliating. It's every journalist's nightmare to make the pages of *Private Eye's* 'Street of Shame' or the *UK Press Gazette's* 'Dog Eat Dog' columns. Invariably it means some errant hack has been involved in scurrilous behaviour, drunkenness, debauchery or other nefarious activities, or sometimes the whole lot.

My mention in Gulf War dispatches began with one of the Fleet Street gossip columns, asking: 'Is the *Daily Star* taking the Gulf War seriously?' The article then went on to quote my conversation with the television publicist near verbatim. Within minutes, I was the talk of the newsroom and my boss, the news editor, who was not known for his sense of humour, put me on a fizzer, as they say in military circles. The suggestion that a member of the *Daily Star* news team was not taking a conflict that was costing British soldiers' lives seriously was about as grave an accusation that could be made against a staff journalist. The news editor paraded me one-two-one-two down to Brian Hitchen's office, waving the offending gossip column article in his hand like an irate Neville Chamberlain. Rather than stand to attention inside the editor's office, I was ordered to wait outside while the news editor entered to read out the charges. I expected to be shot at dawn or worse – told to leave the office with a black bin liner and the contents of my desk drawers. Seconds later, the news editor came out, not saying a word. The matter was over. Brian Hitchen understood me well enough to know that I had the utmost respect for what our troops and reporters were doing. To be honest, knowing his own impish sense of humour, I am sure he had a good chuckle at my quip.

Brian Hitchen went on to edit the *Sunday Express* while his deputy Phil Walker took over the reins of the *Daily Star*. He too was a people person and I remember him introducing himself on his first day in the office and the question of birds came up. His eyes widened. A smile creased his face. He was birdwatcher, too. What's more, he had a cottage on the North Norfolk coast and over the coming months he would regularly give me updates of the rarities he had seen at migration hot-spots such as Holme and Titchwell. Phil and his wife Sharon, a former college colleague of mine, also enjoyed many an exotic holiday abroad and he would return from his travels extolling the credentials of Trinidad and Tobago and a host of other tropical paradises.

Our mutual love of birds once brought a morning news conference discussing the serious issues of the day to a standstill as a male Peregrine Falcon whizzed past the *Daily Star* offices on Blackfriars Bridge. The Peregrine, we soon discovered, was roosting on the giant brick chimney stack which today holds centre place at the Tate Modern. With a surfeit of pigeons, London was long ripe for colonisation by this most spectacular of raptors, and from our office vantage point, we regularly saw both male and female falcons quartering the skies outside the building before taking their luckless prey to the top of the chimney stack to devour. Other members of staff would often look on wide-eyed and speechless as Phil and I talked about the latest bird sightings or the details of an RSPB press release before getting down to discussing the serious issues of the day. For all our common interest in nature, I was left dumbstruck when he approached me one morning in late October 1994 and asked if I would like to write a birdwatching column for the newspaper. I gave an instant one-word reply: 'Fantastic.'

At the time, my birdwatching was enjoying a renaissance. I was writing the monthly bird club feature for *Birdwatch* magazine and had also become heavily involved as Honorary Secretary of the Bedfordshire Bird Club. Working as an on-the-road reporter had made concerted birdwatching nigh impossible. The job always came first. I had heard of birdwatching friends being sacked for pulling flankers to go on a twitch – there are only so many grandparents' funerals a grandson can attend. Equally, being 'ill in bed' does not make a very good excuse when you are seen on the evening regional news expounding the virtues of a mega-rarity! I could never find time to twitch, but working on a busy news desk with its long 11-12 hour shift rota system meant guaranteed set days off. I had volunteered to work regular Sundays so that the day off in the week would give me time to go birdwatching. It meant that I could rekindle the regular outings with the so-called 'Wednesday Club' that I had enjoyed so much time with in the mid-1980s. Built around a small group of Dunstable birders, including Rob Dazley, Johnny Lynch, Pete Marshall, Andy Whitney and Paul Trodd, the group had assembled with almost metronomic regularity to go on a full-day excursion once a month. Sometimes, we would set off in pursuit of a rarity – a venture that had seen the 'club' travelling as far north as the Lake District to see a Spanish Sparrow. More often it would be a case of a car-load of us descending on Titchwell or Cley for a general mooch. Over the years, the club's collective tally of birds must be closing in on the magic 400. Phil Walker's invitation to write a weekly column meant that birds seen on these wonderfully enjoyable Wednesdays out would provide plenty of material for my scribblings.

The first *Daily Star* birdwatching column appeared in the paper's TGIF (Thank God It's Friday) section on 11 November 1994. Deciding on a name for the regular article had been left to one of the team of talented sub-editors whose puns and snappy headlines were regularly winning awards on Channel 4's popular *Big Breakfast* show fronted by Chris Evans. The bird column would prove fertile ground for the subs' imaginations over the coming years, with such classic headlines as 'Egrets, I've had a few...' and, in the true spirit of feeding birds in winter, 'Lard's out for the Tits', a play on a rather risqué soccer chant of the day. There were several candidates as a title for the column but 'Strictly for the Birds' was chosen for its simplicity and for the feel of exclusivity it created, especially as the editor decided to announce its arrival on the front page.

'Strictly for the Birds! Britain's 1st Newspaper column for Twitchers, Page 37' – the prominent front-page blurb told the *Star's* 'army' of two million readers. There was also a photograph of yours truly peeking above my binoculars in what looked like a tropical paradise, although the portrait picture had been taken in a postage stamp-size patch of bamboo which lined the steps leading up to the editorial offices on London's Blackfriars Bridge. The maiden article had been designated an entire page all of its own and was heralded with a blockbusting introduction or 'standfirst', to use newspaper speak. Looking back now, this little bit of flag-waving was a work of tabloid genius – in your face, bouncy and alluring to the reader. Trying to entertain non-birdwatchers as much as drawing in birdwatchers who did not take the *Daily Star* was, of course, the column's *raison d'être*. The short introduction read like an advertisement for a soft drink or a new chocolate bar:

> Forget soccer and angling! Bird-watching is the big participation hobby of the 1990s. Whether it's chasing around the country looking for rarities, or watching blue tits in the garden, there's something for everyone. Stuart Winter, the Star's Chief Twitcher, has all the latest for fanciers.

Hand on heart, I cannot remember writing any of this humiliating claptrap and, years on, I still quake with embarrassment that my name appeared under the word 'soccer'. It is one word that should be *verboten* in an English newspaper. We invented FOOTBALL. It's our national game and we gave it to the world. American college girls play 'socca' – real men play football, not footie, not soccer, but F.O.O.T.B.A.L.L. The fact that the subeditors hyphenated birdwatching was also galling, but it would have sounded pedantic to complain. However, being described as 'Chief Twitcher' was something I would live to regret along with describing fellow enthusiasts as 'fanciers', but more of that later.

The column's maiden story appeared under the headline 'Twitch and Shout' and detailed some of the rare sightings made during the early days of November 1994. Below is the article in full, reproduced to not only give an idea of the tenor of the piece and its tabloid language, but also to show what excellent birds were around to give a fanfare to the new column.

What a week! The rain that turned Guy Fawkes' Night into such a damp squib certainly set off some birdwatching fireworks. The warm, southerly rain clouds also spread devastation across the Continent – but they helped create one of the most explosive birding weekends. There were a string of reports about birds that should have been thousands of miles from Britain, but somehow had managed to get sucked into a weather system that left them dotted along the East Coast.

Pride of place goes to an elderly woman who telephoned local birders in Leicestershire to tell them she had seen a hawk in her garden, and a 'funny little robin' with a blue tail. When the experts checked, it turned out to be an elusive red-flanked bluetail, one of the most romantic and sought-after birds on the British List. It should have been wintering in the warm, tropical forests of south-east Asia rather than the south-east Midlands.

In the Shetlands, the first little bustard to turn up in the UK for six years was followed by an equally unusual pine bunting. Farther south, a pied wheatear was spotted in Teeside.

But the real focus for last weekend's twitchers was East Anglia. The spectacle of four red-rumped swallows over Titchwell RSPB reserve, Norfolk, ranks as the biggest count of the species in this country. Nearby, a desert wheatear – a bird likely to have strayed from the Middle East –

was holding court at Cley-next-the-Sea. A Pacific or possibly White-rumped Swift was also seen in Norfolk on Tuesday, and a short-toed Lark was seen at Cliffe, Kent, on Wednesday.

As they say, it's an ill wind that blows nobody any good.

The article page also carried a 'Quick Peck' – a small 'nib', or news-in-brief, which stated:

A rare Blythe's [sic] pipit attracted one too many pairs of interested eyes yesterday. It had been thrilling twitchers at Landguard, Suffolk, until a hungry kestrel got in on the act...

Connoisseurs of fine bird literature reading my first efforts were no doubt left spluttering over their original John James Audubon's double-elephant folio editions of *Birds of America*. To start, the way bird names flutter from being proper nouns with initial capitals to being in lower case must have confused the readers. There were pine buntings and red-flanked bluetails but a White-rumped Swift and then, to confound everyone, a short-toed Lark! Consistency in a newspaper comes from its stylebook, but stylising bird names to this day gives me headaches. My basic rule of thumb is if I am writing for a 'bird publication' I cap up names, if I am writing for a newspaper I use small letters. Scientists continue to argue over this issue. The RSPB has taken the decision to use lower case bird names in its publications; the BTO prefers initial capitals.

How my first article managed to hedge its bets by using capitals and lower case willy-nilly is lost in the sands of time. My early dispatches were dictated from home to telephone copy-takers who would often listen to the reporters' efforts and – quite often justifiably – decide to correct grammar, house style and even totally re-write it when it read awfully. It would be easy for me to blame the copy-takers, a common practice among old-time reporters who always tried to pass the blame for their failings on to others, but I take full responsibility for that first error-laden report. I also admit the mistake in calling the ill-fated pipit a Blythe's rather than a Blyth's. I must have been thinking about the beautiful, award-winning Hollywood actress and environmentalist Blythe Danner, star of *Meet the Fockers*, *X-Files* and *Will and Grace*, who also happens to be Gwyneth Paltrow's mother, rather than Edward

Blyth, the Victorian zoologist and pharmacist who travelled widely across India and gave his name to the Blyth's Reed Warbler, Blyth's Leaf Warbler and Blyth's Hawk-Eagle. No doubt it was the tabloid training – we were always told to look out for the celebrity angle!

Apart from the teething problems over bird names, the column went down well with both the editor and the readers. I told a few fusty critics who wrote in to the newspaper to point out at style inconsistencies that if scientists argued over bird nomenclature, they had to show a little patience with a new column. Congratulatory letters came in from several northern aficionados of the newspaper who became regular entrants to the bird quizzes I set and who showed a deep knowledge of birding. More surprising was that the column got a plug in both *The Independent* newspaper and also the *UK Press Gazette* trade magazine.

Under the headline 'Winging it', *The Independent's* Talk of the Trade column declared:

> Are the tabloids going soft? The *Daily Star's* latest shot in the circulation war is neither scandalous royal scoop not political sleaze but ... a column on bird-watching. That's birds of the feathered kind (although presumably, the scantily clad Starbirds will retain their place in the paper).
>
> Every Friday, Stuart Winter, a 'self-confessed twitcher', will bring us the latest from the world of the tit and warbler, as well as 'the human side of the hobby'.

Where the 'self-confessed twitcher' description came from I was never to find out. The newspaper had billed me as 'Chief Twitcher', but that was far from being a personal confession. Indeed, for someone who was slowly acquiescing to the increasingly popular term birder instead birdwatcher (one word, no hyphen, had become my ever shrill clarion call) to be described as a self-confessed rarity-hunter was very much a moot point. But it was a broadsheet; what do they know?

If the twitcher versus birder/birdwatcher issue was my only gripe with the Indy's piece, the article that appeared in the *UK Press Gazette* was a wholly different matter. Under a nest photograph of a White Stork feeding two chicks, the trade magazine ran the following caption:

> If you can tell this from butter, you can get a job advertising margarine. If you can tell it apart from a plastic bag, contact the *Daily Star*...

The somewhat cryptic message was alluded to in the main article.

> The *Daily Star's* new column for twitchers, that rare breed of man who will go to the ends of the earth to see a rare breed of bird, is being written by Stuart Winter, No 3 on the newsdesk.
>
> In common with Phil Walker, Winter, now being billed as the *Star's* Chief Twitcher in his Strictly for the Birds column, is an avid birdwatcher.
>
> So when the *Star* picked up on what a big hobby birdwatching has become in this country, of interest not only to twitchers but also to the little old lady who feeds sparrows in her back garden, he was spotted as the man for the job.
>
> Winter is so enthusiastic, say colleagues, that he once spent a whole Saturday afternoon training his binoculars on a possible trophy sighting in a supermarket car park.
>
> His quarry turned out to be a plastic bag.

Now, if I was a sensitive soul, I would have been instructing libel lawyers. Like all journalists, the *UK Press Gazette* scribe had taken two and two and made five. To start with, it was not a White Stork but a Night Heron and, secondly, it was not in a supermarket car park but beside a lake overshadowed by one of the country's leading landfill sites. In respect of accuracy, the true story went like this. A Bedfordshire birder had discovered the Night Heron roosting among the dense willow and hawthorn scrub at the western end of Brogborough Lake, and the news was quickly disseminated around the county's grapevine. So by the next morning an expectant posse was lining the lakeside, all optics trained on the spot where the bird had last been seen. As dawn turned to morning, one of the sharper-eyed members of the crowds noticed some greyish bulk inside the distant tangle of hawthorn branches. The shout went up and the telescopes' high-powered zooms were focused on one spot. Seconds turned to minutes turned to hours. There was little action from the blob but there was talk of wing movement and the occasional stretch. Patience remained a virtue for all until finally one of the awaiting crowd volunteered to take a closer look at the bird to get absolute confirmation. After a long walk and a scramble through the near-impenetrable scrub, a figure emerged the very moment the 'Night Heron' disappeared. It was obvious why when suddenly the volunteer began waving a supermarket carrier bag of a well-known brand above his head. The once-white bag had obviously seen better days as it had faded to a very drab shade of grey. The same shade as a Night Heron's upperparts.

There was one more line in the *UK Press Gazette* article which caused even more merriment. Before the genesis of the bird column, a so-called 'nipple war' had raged between some of the rival red-top tabloids, resulting in a proliferation of, let's say, amply shaped young women appearing on news pages. Phil Walker, whose sense of humour matched his love of nature, gave the *UK Press Gazette* the unequivocal reason why he had introduced the bird column to the *Daily Star*: 'It's the only way I can get more tits in the paper.'

Those that can, Twitch

Amicus verus est rara avis.
A true friend is a rare bird.
—Latin phrase.

Being reclassified from one genus to another is an occupational hazard for birds, particularly in these days of mitochondrial DNA analysis. Even common birds are prone to suddenly finding themselves being hurtled from one scientific grouping into another because of something that has happened in a test-tube. Take the humble Blue Tit. In virtually every bird book I own, dating back to my prized set of Witherby's *Handbook of British Birds* to the truly superlative first edition of the *Collins Bird Guide*, the Blue Tit's Latin name is given as *Parus caeruleus*. Recently, however, it has had a scientific makeover. Advances in genetics mean that the cheeky little fellow who pillages peanuts from feeders the length and breadth of the land goes under the much grander, but more difficult to spell, name of *Cyanistes caeruleus*. I know exactly how the Blue Tit must feel because I had to undergo my own reclassification once I began writing my newspaper column. 'Twitcher', I definitely was not, but 'birdwatcher' – with or without a hyphen – became an all too unwieldy word to use to describe like-minded people who preferred getting their adrenalin rushes from covering their local patches rather than chasing rarities from Mizen Head to Hermaness. So in November 1994, almost 10 years to the day after my polemic in *British Birds* in support of the words 'birdwatcher' and 'birdwatching', I reluctantly became a 'birder', a birder very much in envy of twitchers.

Twitchers get a raw deal. To start with, twitching is hardly a sexy word to describe many of the high-spending, fast-travelling and highly knowledgeable proponents of what amounts to a sport. Secondly, offer National Lottery funding to go twitching to any group of birders who can neither afford the cost nor the time to go gallivanting around the country in pursuit of rare birds, and their home patches would be forgotten in an instant. If George Bernard Shaw was still alive today I am sure he would take one look at the birding scene, rub his beard and ruminate: 'Those that can, twitch; those that cannot, complain.'

The number of people I've met on field trips, leading bird tours abroad or bumped into at the Bird Fair who complain: (a) 'I am not a twitcher' and then (b) 'I don't like twitchers' makes me think that they protesteth too much. There are things that make you moan about twitchers. Some I have met over the years have smelled a bit, but after a long weekend without a shower, sleeping in a car and feeding exclusively on beans on toast, curries and burgers, then even someone with a colonic irrigation fixation would begin to hum. Twitchers can also talk too much. There is nothing worse than being in a company of twitchers reminiscing over past glories. 'I've seen a Pallas's Warbler every year since 1979' or 'I saw it an hour ago but I want to see it again to check the primary projection' are not the things you want to hear while in a crowd waiting for one of those teasingly elusive sprites to make an appearance in a gale-blown patch of coastal shrubbery.

One particularly anal, to use a pun (which will become clear below), fixation I have noticed among some twitchers is their obsession with creating lists of sightings with increasingly bizarre criteria. A 'life bird', meaning one that the observer has never seen before, is something to be savoured in all its glory. County birds and year birds are self-explanatory as many twitchers keep both county and annual lists. Garden lists are quite admirable. It is when we get to people tallying records of birds they have seen on television, while popping behind a bush to relieve a call of nature or, I kid you not, keeping a so-called 's*** list' of rare birds seen defecating, then we are entering the world of white coats, big hypodermic syringes and jackets that fasten at the back.

Finally, although these twitching foibles are by no means a complete list of bizarre behaviour, there is one undeniably infuriating trait that some rarity-hunting protagonists do exhibit: a tendency to revel in one-upmanship of any form. Among the acts of trumpet-blowing I have endured over the years are such banal boasts as 'that was my 17th Lesser Yellowlegs' or 'that wasn't even new for my year list' or, what really rankles, 'my girlfriend's not even interested in birds and she has got a British list of more than 400!' That said, we must admire anyone who hears about a rarity on some distant archipelago and immediately begins arranging epic light aircraft quests or boat crossings with the same aplomb as a military strategist. Trips to Shetland, Orkney or the Outer Hebrides, especially when they have to be arranged one after the other during a prolific run of rarities and particularly when there is never a guarantee of 'connecting' with a bird, are incredible leaps of faith or simply mug punting. Mortgages, family commitments, careers and, perhaps, commonsense, mean that most lovers of birds can never become twitchers. The lucky ones that do are left with wonderful life memories and a lot of collateral damage.

Early Strictly for the Birds columns were an endless testimony to the stamina, resolve and also luck of the nation's twitchers. One week I told the story of RSPB contract ornithologist Jeff Stenning who, using a lottery metaphor in deference to the new game from Camelot that was obsessing the nation back in 1994, had scooped the jackpot by discovering Britain's second-ever Grey-tailed Tattler while carrying out a seaduck survey at Burghead, near Elgin, Grampian. The tattler, a Redshank-sized shorebird hailing from eastern Siberia that is named after its babbling call, may have a somewhat nondescript plumage, but its presence on the official British List had become the stuff of legend. Jeff's discovery came almost 13 years to the day after Britain's first tattler had turned up at the RSPB's Ynys-hir reserve in Dyfed, but the news had been kept secret because of the pressures of congestion and parking at the remote site. In true newspaper exclusive tradition, Jeff's story had an incredible twist: he had been one of the lucky people who had been involved in discovering the first tattler in 1981!

Rare birds have provided the inspiration for many of my weekly articles, from the *Daily Star's* very first Strictly for the Birds right through to my current-day *Sunday Express* 'Birdman' columns. My own news sense was mirrored by the twitching community as a whole when it nominated its choices of favourite rarity encounters to celebrate the Golden Jubilee of the British Birds Rarities Committee. The summer of 2009 was a season that saw such mouth-watering rarities as the dazzling Blue-cheeked Bee-eater grace our shores, but it also saw the so-called 'Rare Men' mark 50 years of assessing rare bird records by helping to set the score straight on a debate that has preoccupied many people on long twitches or 'after match' wind-downs in such legendary birding bars as the Bishop and Wolf on St Mary's or the George and Dragon at Cley-next-the-Sea. Just what is the best rarity ever? One can only imagine the number of pints consumed by those arguing the comparative merits of Suffolk's Macqueen's Bustard in 1962, the Nutcracker invasion of 1968, the unexpected Marmora's Warbler that provided my first twitch or the incredible scenes the residents of Maidstone in Kent witnessed when a Golden-winged Warbler from America took up residence in a supermarket car park in the town during the early months of 1989. To help draw a line under such contentious issues, *British Birds* magazine conducted a poll, inviting readers to vote for the Top 30 Rarity Events of 1959–2008, and the results were published in the journal's August 2009 edition. The poll threw up some surprising results and the full Top 30 is shown below.

Top 30 Rarity Events of 1959–2008:

1st = 1998: Slender-billed Curlew in Northumberland

1st = 2005: Belted Kingfisher in Staffordshire, Yorkshire and Aberdeenshire

3rd 1989: Golden-winged Warbler in Kent

4th 1989: Red-breasted Nuthatch in Norfolk

5th 2003: Black Lark on Anglesey

6th 2006: Long-billed Murrelet in Devon

7th 1989–94: Swinhoe's Storm-petrel in Tyneside

8th 1990: Ancient Murrelet on Lundy

9th 1962: Macqueen's Bustard in Suffolk

10th 1996: Cedar Waxwing in Nottingham

11th 2008: White-crowned Sparrow in Norfolk

12th 1976–77 and 1977–78: Wallcreeper in Somerset

13th 1993: Red-flanked Bluetail in Dorset

14th 1982: Varied Thrush in Cornwall

15th 2007: Yellow-nosed Albatross in Somerset

16th = 1990: Pallas's Sandgrouse on Shetland

16th = 1999: Short-toed Eagle on Scilly

18th 1982: Marmora's Warbler in South Yorkshire

19th 1975: Yellow-bellied Sapsucker on Scilly

20th 1987: Philadelphia Vireo on Tresco, Scilly

21st 2007: Pacific Diver in North Yorkshire

22nd 1972–95: Black-browed Albatross on Shetland

23rd 1968: Nutcracker invasion

24th 1983: Tengmalm's Owl in East Yorkshire

25th 1966: Brown Thrasher in Dorset

26th 1972–84: Steller's Eider on South Uist, Outer Hebrides

27th 1975: Siberian Rubythroat on Fair Isle, Shetland

28th 1982: Common Nighthawk on Scilly

29th 1959: Dusky Thrush in Durham

30th 1963: Pied-billed Grebe in Somerset

Out of this enthralling list, nine of the so-called 'happenings' have occurred since I began writing my columns in the *Daily Star* or, more recently, the *Sunday Express*. Most of them gave me acres of copy to file.

For my first 'super twitch' story, I focussed on the way Kenneth Clarke, the then Chancellor of the Exchequer, had taken time off from fiscal policies and safeguarding the nation's bullion reserves to go looking for some birding gold – the Cedar Waxwing that graced Nottingham in early 1996. My article, published in the *Daily Star* on 1 March, revealed that the Chancellor had more good fortune combating inflationary influences and balancing public spending than finding one small North American songbird among the 10,000 Bohemian Waxwings that were estimated to have arrived that year. Although I never got to speak to the Chancellor directly, one of his backroom staff was quick to point out a policy statement on his behalf. My article read:

Chancellor Kenneth Clarke did not let the Scott [arms to Iraq] rumpus, Ulster peace crisis or the economy get in the way of one of his real loves last weekend ... birding. Back in his native Nottingham, he joined one of the biggest gatherings of birders in recent years, hoping to catch a glimpse of what is likely to prove the bird of 1996 – a wayward Cedar Waxwing.

Unfortunately, the quarry, a North American woodland resident, proved too elusive. But Mr Clarke did see the flock of 500 of the more common, but equally beautiful Bohemian Waxwings which have invaded from Russia. Back at work, the Chancellor waxed lyrical about his experience to his Parliamentary Private Secretary, Peter Butler. And in true Lobby fashion, Mr Butler had a pay-off line after talking to me.

'Please don't say the Chancellor is a twitcher,' he insisted. 'He describes himself as a birdwatcher.'

That's somewhat touchy for a politician who has been described as 'portly' and a 'piglet' in Parliamentary profiles. But you must admire a busy Cabinet minister who can balance the affairs of state with some good old rarity-chasing.

The remainder of the article put the arrival of the Cedar Waxwing into context compared with other rarity happenings, and pointed out its status as only the second record of its kind in Britain. The previous Cedar Waxwing had been recorded on Noss, Shetland, in 1985. What made the Nottingham bird so memorable was that it was found in a busy residential part of the city and was seen by thousands of birders, and also many ordinary folk going about their everyday business. Only a few people who looked for the bird missed it, including the Chancellor and yours truly, but that's another story.

The case of the Druridge Bay curlew still sticks in the craw of many twitchers to this day. Officially, the Slender-billed Curlew found on the Northumberland coast in the late spring of 1998 was one of the last authenticated records of a bird now thought by some to be globally extinct. That very fact, along with simmering arguments over the curlew's plumage and structure, still rankle. Some sceptics demand a review of the record, while those who saw the bird are only too happy to have ticked it. Whatever the dispute, the curlew was promoted to Category A of the British Ornithologists' Union official British List in January 2002. How long it will remain there is open to conjecture. Although I never travelled to see the bird, my article in the *Daily Star* on 15 May 1998 hinted at the controversial nature of the record in the early days. I wrote:

The doubting Thomases who failed to make the long trek north to see last week's 'runt curlew' must be cursing their luck. On the other hand, the few hundred believers who travelled to the Northumberland coast must be congratulating themselves on securing the tick of the century.

Only a few sceptics were convinced enough to make the journey after the odd-looking bird was tentatively identified as a Slender-billed Curlew – perhaps the last of its species. Thankfully, some of the country's most respected birdwatchers were among the trippers.

And through their expertise several of the Slender-billed's important fieldmarks were picked up. The sceptics were left cursing their luck as the bird's identity was unravelled over the birding hotlines. Sadly, by the time it was unmasked as a first-summer female, it was too late for thousands of twitchers. The bird vanished from Druridge Bay last Friday.

The Isles of Scilly are without doubt the most popular few square miles of rarity-finding territory in the kingdom, with perhaps only Shetland rivalling their magnetic powers in drawing in the unexpected and spectacular. Scilly veterans will chew the fat over the classic years and regale tales of encounters with such megas as Yellow-bellied Sapsucker, Philadelphia Vireo and Common Nighthawk. If ever there was any doubt about the islands' reputation, one golden spell in the autumn of 1999 will live long in the memories of all those who were there to experience the sight of a majestic Short-toed Eagle spreading its wings over the beautiful, rugged Scillonian landscape. Amazingly, Tim Cleeves, one of the key protagonists in the discovery and identification of the Slender-billed Curlew, was also in on another unexpected find when a large raptor was spotted flying over St Agnes, its pale underparts making it look like a large Osprey. Something was not quite right, though. It looked too large and strong and there was a distinctive breast band. Once its full suite of diagnostic identification marks was noted, the shout that went up from the delighted finders would echo around the islands for the next four days and summon a continuous stream of twitchers. From the mainland they came in their hundreds to watch the eagle in all its glory as it took up temporary residence on St Martin's. The fact that its arrival coincided with a succession of 'megas' that autumn made writing my weekly dispatch all the more easy. Under the headline 'It's the Scilly Season', I wrote on 12 October:

> The Isles of Scilly have stormed back to their rightful position as the
> place for twitchers to get their kicks. Crowds, rucks and rare birds have
> come back to haunt the isles once again. For the past three years Scilly
> has seen a slow dwindling of its autumn invaders. The lack of real
> 'megas' in recent times had seen many birders opting for trips abroad
> in late autumn. Then pagers started bleeping mega alerts:
>
> Mega...Siberian Thrush over Gugh...
> White's Thrush on St Agnes...
> Short-toed Eagle on St Martin's!
>
> As only the second twitchable Siberian Thrush in Britain, it would
> have been the star bird on Scilly of the past decade. But while the
> Siberian Thrush was playing hard-to-get under a mile away a distant
> cousin was equally elusive. The White's Thrush was so shy that a 'flush'
> was organised to drive it into the open – splitting the birders with claims
> of harassment. However, as the row went on, arguably Scilly's best bird
> of all time showed up. The first ever Short-toed Eagle seen on British
> soil came from nowhere. Over the weekend, the eagle with its six-foot
> wingspan attracted a huge number of birders. When you consider all
> this, you can see why the Scilly Season will stay on twitchers' books for
> many years to come. But birders arriving yesterday to see the eagle were
> left disappointed.
>
> Conservationists were planning to rescue the bird due to fears it
> would starve to death as the Short-toed Eagle's favourite food is snakes
> – creatures not found on Scilly. But the eagle simply soared to 1,000 feet
> and headed out to sea. Hopefully, it will have the energy to make it to
> France and the long journey south to its wintering grounds.

Three years after the Short-toed Eagle dared to make it into British
airspace, another mythical species was creating history on a cliff top at
the RSPB's South Stack reserve on Anglesey. The Black Lark held a
special place in British ornithology long before its arrival on 1 June
2003 due to its formal removal from the British list in the wake of the
Hastings Rarities scandal. Sixteen species, including Slender-billed
Curlew, Grey-tailed Tattler, Calandra Lark and Brown Flycatcher,

were tainted with suspicion of fraud because of the dubious activities of one George Bristow (1863–1947), a taxidermist and gunsmith from St Leonard's-on-Sea, who purportedly made the princely sum of £7,000 selling the skins of rare birds to wealthy ornithologists. The provenance of the birds gathered by Bristow has long remained a mystery, however, of the 16 species erased from the record books, a total of 14 have subsequently been readmitted after arriving in the UK naturally.

In his recent book *Rare Birds: Where and When*, Russell Slack describes the Black Lark's appearance on Anglesey as 'one of the ornithological events of recent years, stimulating many a dormant twitcher to take to the road' and goes on to explain how its occurrence helped convince the authorities to accept a previous record from Spurn Point, East Yorkshire, dating back to 1984.

Russell, who was then the voice of BirdGuides, was the first person I spoke to before filing the following *Daily Star* dispatch dated 7 June 2003:

A crowd that would delight an average Nationwide football league club this week greeted one of rarest birds ever to touch down on British soil. Thousands of twitchers from across the country huddled together on the windswept, grassy cliffs of the RSPB's South Stack Cliffs reserve to catch sight of the legendary Black Lark.

Its arrival comes almost a century after this mythical denizen of the Russian steppes was caught up in one of the most sinister episodes in the history of British ornithology. In the early 1900s, up to 13 of these starling-sized birds were shot or captured along the south coast, yet the records were eventually dismissed as a hoax. It became known as the Hastings Rarities Affair.

But while none of the army of twitchers who trudged along a clifftop pass on Anglesey to watch the lark feeding on an area of burnt grass doubts this bird's authenticity, its arrival has raised a few questions. One theory put forward for the lark's appearance is that it may have hitched a ride on an Asiatic freighter *en route* to Merseyside and jumped ship in the Irish Sea.

Although rare birds have regularly turned up in Merseyside, courtesy of its container port, a recent series of other rare bird arrivals across Europe may help solve the mystery. Europe has been awash this week with far-distance stragglers from one of the remotest parts of the world. The sighting of a Turkestan Shrike in Somerset, a Rock Bunting and an Eastern Olivaceous Warbler in Denmark, and a Trumpeter Finch in Holland could be connected with the Black Lark's appearance in Wales. All these birds could have originated from the barren, arid steppes east of the Caspian Sea, an area that has recently suffered from traumatic weather systems.

Rarity chasers believe that a major climatic event could well have sent the lark and the other vagrants hurtling westwards to northern Europe. Russell Slack of BirdGuides, the country's leading internet bird news provider, said: 'It has been an incredible period for rare birds in northern Europe, the highlight for British birders being the arrival of the first authentic Black Lark.

'I travelled to Anglesey to see the lark and it looked very much at home feeding on the grass clifftop.'

He added: 'Although some say it may have come from a passing ship, it's very unlikely that it could have arrived by that means.

'The nearest open water to its breeding ground is the Caspian Sea – and that is landlocked. Unusual weather patterns in that part of the world are the more likely cause of it turning up, along with a number of other very rare central Asiatic birds.'

Another good friend of mine was involved in the story of another recent mega-rarity to find itself on the British Birds Rarities Committee's jubilee list – Pacific Diver. This is a species whose arrival may have long been predicted, but which caused something of a stir when it was identified on a late winter's day in 2007. This was because it was discovered on a reservoir near Harrogate, North Yorkshire, rather than the windswept Cornish coast or a remote Hebridean island. How the bird, a close relative of our native Black-throated Diver, arrived in Britain, thousands of miles from its native haunts in the Alaskan and East Siberian tundra, will no doubt be discussed and understood as more sightings amass. The sterling efforts of Martin Garner and John McLoughlin in not only identifying the Yorkshire diver, but also explaining to the wider birding community what plumage and structural features to look for, helped to bring about a number of subsequent sightings of this evocative bird. Martin and I built our friendship trawling the rubbish tips of Bedfordshire looking at gulls during the early 1990s, and he has gone on to become one of the foremost identification experts of his generation. When news of the Pacific Diver surfaced, he helped me to compile my report published in the *Sunday Express* on 4 February 2007. I wrote:

Stately, elegant and donning a stunning necklace – it sounds like the Countess of Cornwall and her headline-grabbing appearance across the Atlantic last week. But while the paparazzi's cameras were focusing on Camilla's stunning gems in New York, another type of 'necklace' has been causing a stir among British birdwatchers.

The distinctive dark neck markings on a mysterious bird found on a fishing lake in deepest North Yorkshire has not only helped solve its identity but also made ornithological history. A long-time friend of mine, Martin Garner, one of the country's foremost authorities on field identification, and another bird ID expert John McLoughlin, announced the arrival of the first confirmed Pacific Diver to reach Britain last Monday.

They confirmed its identity after noting all the key diagnostic features of a species long expected to arrive in the UK, but whose indistinct markings would confuse even the most experienced birdwatcher. Pacific Divers are closely related to our native Black-throated Diver, a sleek water bird that breeds on a few remote Highland lochs. Around 200 pairs nest in Scotland and, in winter, their numbers rise to about 700 birds with arrivals from Scandinavia.

Divers are extremely cumbersome on land, but their serpentine-shape, however, makes them the most adept of all water birds. In their varied breeding, winter and juvenile plumages, Black-throated and Pacific Divers are very similar and were 'split' as different species by leading authorities only as recently as 1993.

Despite regularly turning up on America's Eastern Seaboard, the fact that both species are difficult to separate in field conditions meant the Pacific Diver remained an unlikely contender for acceptance as a new British bird.

Indeed, one record for the Outer Hebrides remains on the pending file. But thanks to Martin and John's efforts it should now be accepted by the appropriate records committee with ease. Martin and John had visited the Farnham Gravel Pit site, near Harrogate, early last week after news filtered out about the mystery bird and soon they were confident it

was showing all the subtle field marks of a juvenile Pacific Diver –
including its subtle head shape and dark flank and neck markings.

Martin said: 'The bird shows all the classic signs of a Pacific Diver.
If it's not, then it means it is impossible to identify them in the field.'

Looking back, only three of the top all-time rarities which occurred
while I have been writing my columns failed to be immortalised with
my ink. Following their discoveries, they either delighted large crowds
of twitchers or just a few lucky individuals. The reasons for their
omission from my columns are more down to my ineptitude rather
than any question of the birds lacking charisma or historic notoriety.
I would like to say that like some other birders I dismissed the arrival
of the Belted Kingfisher on 1 April 2005 as an April Fools' prank. The
bird certainly led birders a merry dance as it went on a national tour
with guest appearances on the Staffordshire and Worcester Canal at
Milford, Staffordshire, and Eastrington Ponds Nature Reserve, East
Yorkshire, before finally settling at Peterculter in Aberdeenshire,
where it became a recluse and was never seen again. Such was the
incredulity at the initial sighting that BirdGuides issued the following
notice on its website: 'Staffordshire Belted Kingfisher – Finder is
considered reliable and has stated this is not a hoax.'

Looking back through the archives, the reason I never mentioned
the kingfisher was that I was writing about the dearth of Swallows and
had come across an incredible story of how locusts had swept across
Mauritania. They destroyed everything edible in their wake, including
the green sward of the national soccer stadium and the presidential
gardens, and by doing so robbed migrant birds of verdant refuelling
stations on their long flights north.

Both the Long-billed Murrelet that turned up in Devon in
November 2006, and the Atlantic Yellow-nosed Albatross of the
summer of 2007, turned up during periods when my column had been
dedicated to specific stories, one giving details of a project to protect
the Aquatic Warblers of Poland, the other congratulating *British Birds*
– publishers of the top rarity events report – on reaching its centenary.
Missing out on big stories, be it major international events or the
occurrence of a mega-rarity is always galling. Journalists need to report
from the frontline; they want to witness live events, speak to
the newsmakers and listen to the people whose lives are tossed around

by the winds of destiny. Just being there is the essence of great journalism. Often it means being literally in the firing line. Sometimes, however, good stories can fall into your lap.

A Black-and-white Letter Day

A letter is a joy of Earth – it is denied the gods.
—Emily Dickinson (1830–1886).

Of all the rarities I have seen, of all the manic twitches I have witnessed, indeed, of all the stories I have written about rare birds creating history or causing commotion, one event stands out in my time as a birder and journalist. It is not a tale of some long-lost species being rediscovered, or of birders performing incredible acts of human endurance to get their tick. Neither am I directly included in the story. I never saw the bird in question, nor did I make any attempt to see it. In truth, its occurrence was not deemed worthy enough to be included in the prestigious list of rarity events witnessed over the past 50 years. However, and this is a big however, opening a reader's letter on a cold December morning shortly before Christmas 1996 brought warmth to the heart and joy to the soul. I get many letters from readers. Some ask what books or binoculars I recommend, most ask for tips on feeding their garden favourites or how to get rid of pesky squirrels. Sometimes they include photographs of 'mystery birds' – usually common species such as tits with beak deformities or House Sparrows in a state of leucism (a pigment deficiency that turns plumage a milky colour). In winter I get letters to inform me that gardens are being graced by Fieldfares, Redwings and, occasionally, even Bohemian Waxwings, visitors from Scandinavia anxious to replenish their body reserves on fruit-rich berry bushes. Summer inquiries are almost invariably about how to help 'lost' fledglings. One inquiry will forever hold pride of place in my in-tray. It was a letter notifying me that a lady from North Wales had seen a bird of such significance that it went on to make news in all the birding publications.

Before revealing the identity of this mystery species, and also the reasons why its occurrence was so exciting, I would like to emphasise that I have not got all my birding thrills through the mountain of mail that arrives at Express Newspapers. Indeed, of those fabled birding events of the past six decades, I managed to catch up with four of the legendary birds and failed, for a variety of reasons, both bizarre and mundane, to connect with several others.

The part that the Yorkshire Marmora's Warbler played in my career development has already been explained. There have been several mega-rarities over the years that were already engrained in my psyche before they even turned up. After seeing them in the bird books I had pored over in my youth, they seemingly rose from the pages to activate the hunter-gatherer twitching gene that exists in all birders when the species finally came to grace our shores. There was no way I was going to miss the Cream-coloured Courser that turned up near Southend in 1984, the Sociable Lapwing on the Isle of Sheppey in the autumn of 1998, or the two Slender-billed Gulls that also arrived in Kent the following year. These iconic sightings for me no doubt adorn the notebooks of each and every member of twitching's higher echelons. Stodmarsh's American Coot and a Blackpoll Warbler at Bewl Water have been other welcome Kentish additions to my British life list, as have Norfolk sightings of Sardinian Warbler, Pacific Golden Plover and Black-winged Pratincole. The so-called 'Birding Riviera' that runs from Holme next the Sea to Cley next the Sea has also produced some of my best 'self-found' birds such as Laughing Gull and Pectoral Sandpiper. There have been many happy run-ins with scarcities and even rarities in Wells Woods or on Titchwell's teeming wetlands. Portland Bill, Dungeness, Minsmere and, of course, my native London and adopted home county of Bedfordshire, have all seen exciting encounters with great birds. Names such Bee-eater, Hoopoe, White-tailed Eagle and Red-footed Falcon, and even 'birders' birds' such as Hume's Warbler and Naumann's Thrush, lend my sub-400 British list a degree of credibility. By now you may be seeing a pattern emerge – one where my so-called British list has a finite geographical range contained within the boundaries of south-east England. Let me say at the outset that this is not due to any aversion to the Midlands, the North, Scotland or Wales, but simply a dislike for long-distance driving, a predisposition to travel sickness and never quite having the time to make plans for journeys that last more than two hours. This explains why three of the four legendary megas that I have had 'communion' with were all occurrences below the Wash–Severn divide. Communion with a bird is a wonderful term that I regularly borrow from the famous American birder Pete Dunne. Pete, Mr Cape May to many of the Brits who have made a pilgrimage to America's famous migration hot-spot at the southernmost tip of the New Jersey seaboard, is a writer of wonderfully spiritual birding stories, a talent that helps to explain how his moments of grace with wildlife, be it birds or mammals, are described in such a way that they are like having sacred encounters.

My moment's connection with the Red-breasted Nuthatch that took up residence in Wells Wood in the winter of 1989–90 was hardly spiritual, or even an encounter in the true sense of the word. It lasted all but a split-second, a fleeting glimpse as the stubby little character that had miraculously arrived on the English east coast after crossing the Atlantic whizzed overhead on shuffling wings. I had driven to Wells-next-the-Sea as much to test-drive a new car as to see the diminutive nuthatch, but once inside the dark, forbidding coastal forest, many an hour was spent traipsing through the aromatic litter of pine needles and cones, head held continuously upwards at an obtuse angle trying to detect the bird as it foraged with a marauding tit flock in Holkham Meals.

The following extract from *British Birds*, written by British Birds Rarities Committee chairman Rob Hume and British Ornithologists' Union Records Committee chairman Dr David Parkin, shows that even writers of official publications of record can get excited by totally unexpected events:

> ... People descended on Holkham Meals in their hundreds to see the bird. Indeed, it developed into one of the largest gatherings of birdwatchers so far seen in the UK, a situation not helped by the narrowness of the paths, the elusive nature of the bird and the desperation of a few observers literally fighting for a better vantage point. Some people visited eight or more times without seeing it at all, and many needed a second or third attempt before catching a glimpse. For others, however, it performed remarkably well. By listening for its distinctive call, or by following the tit flocks, or by simply waiting in a favoured spot for the nuthatch to appear, many people were able to see and photograph it during its stay of several months.
>
> (Reproduced by kind permission of *British Birds*)

Four years would pass before I would again feel the adrenalin-fuelled excitement and reassuring camaraderie of another mass birding event.

The Red-flanked Bluetail is a denizen of the dense taiga forests that stretch from Finland across Siberia to Japan. This charismatic wanderer, with its blue-tinged plumage, has won a special place in British birders' hearts, mainly due to its historic rarity and, I would assume, also its robin-like demeanour. The bluetail's mythical status was enhanced because most of the early records following its first appearance in Lincolnshire in 1903 were invariably on remote Scottish islands. A grand total of 12 birds in 90 years was scant reward for the thousands of birders who had looked longingly in their field guides at the gaudy male bluetail, bejewelled in cobalt and subtle apricot tones, and dreamed of finding one on the mainland. It was the day before Halloween 1993 when the dreams became reality. Well-known bird artist Mike Langman was taking a pre-lunch walk with his family and fellow birder Neil Morris in Dorset's picturesque Winspit Valley when an unusual 'robin' was spotted perched up in an ivy-clad tree. As it flew off, displaying a tell-tale flash of blue, the birding alarm bells were sounded. Despite early incredulity, the bird flitted back to display its full ensemble of colourful field marks and another birding legend was born.

My rendezvous with the bluetail came a day or so later. I joined the thousands of pilgrims to marvel at a bird that all of us had been marvelling at in a two-dimensional bird book format for years. The publication a few months earlier of Lars Jonsson's lavishly illustrated *Birds of Europe*, with its wonderful painting of the bird that perfectly captured its 'jizz', had only helped to enhance its 'most wanted' status within the birding community.

The bluetail, to be honest, barely qualifies as being a European breeding species. I have subsequently seen them on their Finnish pine forest breeding grounds, a thin strip of mosquito-blighted taiga where the gaudy males sing their ethereal Woodlark-like songs under the midnight sun. On that cool November morning in a steep-sided coastal valley awash with warm autumnal colours, the fact that it was silent and in subdued first-winter plumage never diminished the experience for the assembled masses. Time and again, the bird would flit among the low-level vegetation like a burnished coppery leaf caught on a breeze. Then it would rest, turn and give a tantalising view of its Biro-blue rectrices. The crowd cheered. I joined them.

If only this remarkable event had happened 12 months later. What better way would there have been to launch my newspaper column than with one of the great historic twitches and one that I had been there to savour? I would have to wait nearly 15 years to be in the grandstand seats when one of the truly memorable twitching events took place. It was worth the wait.

The most recent rarity event to make the *British Birds* fabled 'Top 30' was the arrival of a White-crowned Sparrow in one of the most widely publicised and talked about birdwatching occasions in history. Photographs of massed ranks of telescopes, their owners shivering and quivering in the biting cold of the Norfolk New Year, were given display-page coverage in all of the tabloids, with headlines screaming: 'Couple besieged by 1,000 birders after rare sparrow lands in garden!' and 'White-crowned Sparrow boosts local tourism.'

If ever a bird wanted to settle somewhere to generate optimum attention, then choosing a sumptuous house with a walled garden close to one of Cley-next-the-Sea's most celebrated watering holes was a wonderful choice. While the sparrow, a gaudy bird resplendent in its black-and-white 'headgear' and warm battleship grey underparts, fed happily on seed put down by the householders, the twitchers could warm up in the nearby Three Swallows public house after enduring long shifts waiting for the bird to appear. And did it make people wait.

Three- or four-hour stints were not uncommon as the sparrow went walkabout and birders were left stamping their feet to stop toes getting frostbite. When it did arrive, it was greeted like a Broadway star with 'oohs' and 'aahs' and even a round of applause on occasions.

By the time the sparrow had made its last curtain call, the bucket left out to collect donations from contented birders had been filled with more than £6,300 for the village church restoration fund, and a promise that the bird would be remembered for posterity in a new stained-glass window.

To keep the showbiz metaphor going, the weekend after I had enjoyed the sparrow show I decided to write my column in the *Sunday Express* in a style fitting for the festive season. Oh, yes I did...

The day was turning into a pantomime. Huddled ranks of birdwatchers in their expensive weatherproof clothing, with even more expensive optical equipment, shivered with stoic patience awaiting the star attraction. For more than a week the American visitor had performed for the crowds – today he had stage fright. Or was it Norfolk's notoriously fickle weather finally catching up with all the theatrics?

January on East Anglia's 'costa del twitching' can serve up a dank, dismal coldness that saps the strength and twists the mind, hardly a place for the nation's most famous rare bird to put on a show.

Nothing though, was going to defeat this audience. And so for hours they waited. Even the quick wit and ready repartee of such gatherings was vanquished by the communal gloom and despondency. Every so often, a flickering Dunnock or an inquisitive Robin caused a flutter. Binoculars would be held aloft in unison, all focusing on the 'centre stage' – a gravel drive garnished with birdseed fit for a superstar from across the Pond.

And this was some superstar.

Only three White-crowned Sparrows had been seen in Britain before the bird's surprise appearance on 6 January 2008. With its regular virtuoso matinees, thousands of delighted twitchers had made a New Year pilgrimage to Cley-next-the-Sea for a momentary glimpse of the bird and a celebratory tick on the checklist.

Then I arrived. It must have known I was coming. Having got a 'ticket' for a seat in the gods, courtesy of a donation to the local church restoration fund, I joined the throng and waited, first with patience, then forbearance and finally in a self-induced torpor.

As my mind drifted to all the other failed twitches I had endured – the five-hour wait for a Siberian Rubythroat, to name but one – the thought of a warm duvet and hot mug of coffee kept me sane.

Like an automaton I would raise my binoculars every time a bird settled on the path, only to grimace with disappointment as the image focused into a Chaffinch or House Sparrow. But then, at the very moment I was contemplating retiring to the local hostelry for brunch, came the familiar panto cry: 'It's behind you…'

With whoops of glee, the crowd did an about-turn and lapped up every detail of this most flamboyant of star-spangled birds with its pink bill, zebra-striped head and slate-grey breast. Even Christopher Biggins could not compete with this kind of celebrity.

By the time Cley's celebrity sparrow had come to the end of its run, the bird had become one of the most watched and photographed rarities in history. I for one went back for second helpings. Yet for all the razzamatazz of the national newspaper and birding press headlines, its fame pales compared to arguably the greatest rarity of all time. If there was such a thing as birding's equivalent of the *X-Factor*, then the winner by sheer popular demand would be 'Sammy the Stilt'. There can hardly be a birdwatcher in the country that did not focus his binoculars, take a few 'digi' shots or even pose up with Sammy tiptoeing around in the background. This gangly shorebird with bubblegum-coloured legs and eye-catching pied plumage took up residence at the RSPB's flagship Titchwell reserve in the early 1990s and went onto hog the 'what's about' bulletin board for the next decade. Black-winged Stilt is an official British rarity – less than 250 have occurred in this country since the end of the Second World War – and every sighting requires a description that has to be collated by the British Birds Rarities Committee. Though some years can see a handful of birds overshooting their Mediterranean breeding grounds to take up temporary residence in the UK, stilts can be remarkably elusive and they often don't hang around for long.

Sammy was a show-off, though. His reliability as an easy tick made him a favourite with tens, perhaps hundreds, of thousands of birdwatchers, from manic year-listers to families enjoying a day out at the coast. Whatever the weather, and remember that Titchwell can get awfully cold in winter for a Mediterranean species such as a stilt, and equally, no matter what other rarities were about, every visitor to the reserve always took time out to see Sammy. Some days he rummaged on the brackish saltings, other days he paddled in the reserve's freshwater sector. But despite the lure of an autumn migration south, Sammy always remained loyal to Titchwell after settling there in 1993. For those fascinated by keeping an annual tally of sightings, no New Year was complete without stopping off at Titchwell to track him down. His striking plumage meant he was easy to pick out among the myriad of other shorebirds – a remarkable testimony to his longevity considering the frequency of Peregrine Falcon sorties over the reserve. When Sammy finally went 'missing believed dead' there was a general feeling of sadness among the birding community. For arguably the most famous, and certainly the most watched, bird in twitching history would no longer be there to brighten up those drabber days on the north Norfolk coast with that striking plumage and those preposterous legs. His passing moved me to write an obituary in the *Sunday Express* on 31 July 2005 under the headline 'Alas, poor Sammy, I knew him well...':

There can be few birds in history that have deserved a fully-fledged obituary but Sammy the Stilt was no ordinary feathered creature. In his long and active life, Sammy became a friendly, familiar figure to virtually every birdwatcher in Britain.

With his striking black-and-white plumage, needle-sharp bill and outrageous bubblegum-pink legs, Sammy was difficult to miss. This ability to stand out in a crowd meant that an estimated half-million people have been delighted with his John Cleese-like funny walks around the RSPB's Titchwell reserve on Norfolk's north coast these past 12 years.

Indeed, his status as the 'most watched' bird in history would be a fitting epitaph on his gravestone – if only we knew where poor Sammy finally curled up his extraordinary toes. Black-winged Stilts always create excitement when they arrive in the UK from their breeding grounds around the Mediterranean, as Sammy did late in 1993.

Typically, stilts are birds of shallow salt-pans and coastal lagoons, where they noisily squabble alongside flamingo flocks and equally lanky egrets. Only about four birds turn up in Britain each year and this is why Sammy came to prominence. In the competitive world of year listing, 'ticking off' Sammy in the first weeks of January became an event as important as spotting the first Swallow or hearing a spring Cuckoo.

Whether there were flurries of snow or a howling northerly, Sammy would be there, often tip-toeing in water on the very point of freezing over. The sight of him braving frosts and passing the day with plovers and waders from Siberia and Greenland, when he should have been enjoying the sunshine of the north Sahara, must rank as one of the most incongruous sights ever on a British nature reserve.

But for all his stoicism in the depths of winter, there was no spring mating ritual to warm his lovelorn heart. Sammy's status as a one-off meant there was no Samantha to court, build a nest and raise fledglings. He tried to woo many unattached Oystercatchers with his bizarre mating display, but with those legs? No chance.

His romantic shortcomings, however, did not stop him becoming a pin-up. Nature magazines, the glossy pages of rare bird books and countless websites featured his handsome profile. Sammy was last seen on 21 May and his prolonged disappearance led the RSPB to post his death notice last week.

Yet life springs eternal and on the other side of the country there has been a happy event. Sammy's arrival and survival has often been quoted as evidence that our climate is slowly becoming more Mediterranean. This argument was supported last week with the news that a pair of Bee-eaters from Southern Europe had successfully bred in Herefordshire.

Sammy the Stilt has staked his place in history, but he is not the only rare bird to have had its own moniker. 'Elsie' the Lesser Crested Tern – the etymology of her name was a play on the initials L and C – took up residence on the Farne Islands during the 1980s. She spent many years looking for a mate, a seemingly forlorn venture for a bird whose nearest native breeding grounds are on islands off the North African coast. Somehow, the allure of a male Sandwich Tern made the long spring trek to the North Sea worthwhile and, after several years, she began breeding with her darker-billed suitor and raising hybrid young. In their inimitable style, the *Daily Star* sub-editors came up with the headline 'Love-hungry Elsie grabs herself a Sandwich' when I revealed the intimate details of her love story in the spring of 1995:

Broody Elsie, the Lesser Crested Tern, is certainly a rare old bird. She has been visiting Britain for the past nine years, but still hasn't found a male

Lesser Crested Tern to share her love nest. Instead, she's been billing and cooing with a Sandwich Tern. The odd couple have even managed to raise hybrid chicks.

Elsie, who gets her nickname from the initials LC (Lesser Crested), is a native of North Africa, but her trips over here make her the rarest breeding tern in Britain.

Many think Britain's rarest breeding tern is the graceful and swallow-like Roseate, a seabird whose future is far from rosy. Numbers of these beautiful terns with their subtle, pink-toned underparts have spiralled downwards in recent decades to the point where only 70 pairs now breed in the UK.

The destruction of coastal breeding areas and disappearing fish stocks have both taken a heavy toll on the Roseate.

News of Elsie's breeding success is featured in the latest report from the Rare Breeding Birds Panel. The report, covering the 1992 nesting season, shows that Roseate Terns managed a slight improvement in their breeding success on the previous year. That said, they're still the most threatened British species on the worldwide Red Data List.

Looking back through the archives, it seems that to be afforded a nickname a bird has to be both charismatic and enjoy longevity. 'Albert Ross', whose story played an important part in my appointment to the *Daily Star* news desk, is one such legend. From 1967 until 1995, lovelorn Albert patrolled the North Atlantic looking for a mate while his kinsfolk went about the process of propagating the species at the same latitude south. To the casual visitor, the remote outcrops and rocky promontories of the Falklands archipelago look very much like the rocky outcrops and remote promontories of Shetland. Albert was not to know that his internal compass was upside down and so, with his hormone-driven ardour at full speed, he set about trying to woo any Northern Gannet that caught his eye. It was not to be. His carefully crafted nests always went empty, and when he finally slipped off the radar almost 30 years after his arrival, birding had lost one of its most enduring characters.

Another durable character, certainly not as rare as Albert but almost as charismatic, was Cley's notorious heavyweight bruiser – 'George' the Glaucous Gull. His name was supposedly a play on the name of actor George Seagal (as opposed to George Seagull). No winter visit to north

Norfolk back in the early 1980s was complete without popping in and saying hello to George as a he patrolled the beach looking for anything edible to cram into his extraordinarily large crop. How many Little Auks had gone the same way as fish innards, seal offal or birders' unwanted cheese sandwiches is open to conjecture. Whatever the answer, finding food around the old beach car park was never a problem and this obviously helped George to live to a ripe old age. When George finally failed to return from his summer haunts on the edge of the Arctic pack ice, his place was taken by an immature Glaucous Gull with an equally ravenous appetite. As soon as it was obvious that this young interloper was going to become a fixture on the Norfolk birding scene, the wags began looking for a suitable name. They only had to look at the music charts and the legend of 'Boy George' the Glaucous Gull was born.

Of all the rarities I have seen and of all the birds I have ever sweated intros over, one in particular comes to the fore. I get an incredible sense of warmth from the story of a *Daily Star* reader who wrote to me in the December of 1996, thanking me profusely for an article about a trip to the Scilly Isles that coincided with a mini invasion of some extremely charismatic Yanks. Mrs Pat Thornton's letter arrived as I was putting together the following review of the year's birds.

This was the year that football came home and we seemed to say goodbye to Oasis every other week. But for me 1996 will be remembered as the Year of the Black-and-white Warbler.

It's not just because I added it to my British checklist after grabbing some brilliant views of this American dandy on the Isles of Scilly but because of a reader's letter. A few weeks after I returned from Scilly, I received a note from Mrs Thornton of Mold in North Wales.

'Thank you, thank you,' it read. 'You have solved a mystery for me.

'In your column was a picture of a Black-and-white Warbler. I saw one of these birds a few weeks ago on my daily walk with the dog. I had a chance to study it for a while then went home and looked through my bird book but to no avail. When I saw the picture in the Daily Star, I said to my husband, "That's it."'

It certainly was! After a telephone conversation with Mrs Thornton in which she accurately described the striking plumage and tree-creeping behaviour of the warbler, I passed the details on to the relevant authorities. This month the major birdwatching magazines published details of Mrs Thornton's find, which should now get official ratification. Her sighting on 1 October was the first of five Black-and-white Warblers recorded in Britain this year. Of all the rarities seen in the UK during 1996, these captivated the hearts of the twitching masses.

Besides being incredibly rare – the species is so charismatic that it has been adopted as the logo of the Bird Information Service – they always put on incredible acrobatic performances. After Mrs Thornton's bird, a second was spotted by a handful of observers at Beachy Head, East Sussex, before the crowds caught up with two more on Scilly during mid-October. A fifth was later seen in Norfolk.

Indeed, October proved to be a great month with a Northern Waterthrush at Portland Bill, the first-ever twitchable Great Knot in Cleveland and a sprinkling of goodies in the West Country.

The reason that receiving Mrs Thornton's letter was one of the highlights of my career was the sheer delight she had gained from seeing an unusual bird, and that I had played a small part in her joy. Engaging with the reader and informing them is one of my duties as a journalist. Helping a fellow birdwatcher along the way is one of the great things about our special pastime.

The Dips So Maniacs

Dip-a-Dee-Doo-Dah,
Dip-a-Dee-ay,
We're not seeing any birds today...
—Anon – Scilly, 1997.

Nature's forces are held in perfect equilibrium. For protons there are neutrons, for yin there is yang. Twitching, therefore, would not be the all-consuming passion it is without … 'the dip'. Dipping crept into my vocabulary after reading *Bill Oddie's Little Black Bird Book*. Without a car, without being on the 'grapevine' and without a life list, I simply had no concept of what it was like to miss a bird. I remember the envy of not seeing Johnny Lynch's Marsh Harrier that momentarily graced Dunstable Sewage Farm one day while I was away on holiday. I also remember a tinge of jealousy when Johnny later found a Shore Lark in Houghton Regis Quarry after I had been grounded for some school-boy misdemeanour. But these were misses, not dips. Note the subtle difference. If I had later attempted to see the birds and not seen them, I would have dipped. As I had no prior knowledge of them until they were long gone, they were simply history. Thus I was spared the feelings of 'disaster, calamity, catastrophe and misfortune' that are incumbent with dipping. Is that overdoing the emotional stuff? Well, look up the word 'heartbreak' in *Roget's Thesaurus* and those are the dreadful synonyms that equate with having a broken heart, a sensation suffered by all those who miss out on a rare bird. It was Bill Oddie who equated dipping with such feelings of dread. In his brilliant section on explaining birding's glossary, Bill defines the verb 'to dip out' as failing to see the bird you want to see. He then goes on to explain: 'This is the experience a twitcher most dreads, and it is sheer heartbreak.'

Bill, who confesses to being an expert on dipping out, tells of the horrors of filming a TV series in Cornwall and between breaks hopping over to Scilly on several occasions only to miss out on Sharp-tailed Sandpiper, Paddyfield Warbler and a Pallas's Warbler in quick succession. With most chronic or acute cases of dipping there are usually aggravating symptoms and, to compound Bill's woe, it turned out that the Paddyfield Warbler had been trapped and ringed with a net once owned by him, while the Pallas's had turned up at a spot where he had previously been having his packed lunch. These would be perfect exam-condition examples of dipping to use in any essay on the language of birding. However, in terms of the annoyance, frustration and feelings of melancholy endured by some poor souls, Bill got off lightly.

Even in my 'heyday' of twitching in the mid-1990s (not that there was much 'hey' and I certainly did not go chasing rare birds every day) I did manage some spectacular dips. I remember driving around the flat, open Fens one bank holiday with the children screaming and my wife pulling her hair out as I tried to catch up with a Greater Yellowlegs. The family day out under the notion of a 'sightseeing trip to Ely Cathedral' had begun with a sneaky call to Birdline to confirm the yellowlegs' presence and then some furtive deception to get my binoculars into the car without Annie seeing. It was when she came out with a 'you don't need a map – surely you know the way to Ely' that I knew I was in for trouble trying to find a 15-inch bird among one of the most featureless landscapes in the known world. The cathedral trip went down well, the kids absolutely loved the Little Chef, especially the lollipops they got for clearing their plates, and I got an obligatory nod of the head from my co-driver when I asked if it was 'alright to call in to see a rare American bird on the way home?' Three hours later we were hopelessly lost; the Little Chef meals had been regurgitated on the back seat and my wife Annie was at breaking point. The expedition was abandoned. I had dipped. It was 'heartbreak' all round.

Other dips duly followed to keep yin (jumping up and down after seeing a good bird) and yang (counting the bill for wasted petrol as well as facing family discontent) in a state of perfect balance. There were several trips to see Bonaparte's Gulls and Terek Sandpipers, but both species seem to have an aversion to my attentions everywhere they turn up. And there were also Bedfordshire county dips for Grey Phalarope and Purple Sandpiper, which I failed to see after so-called birding friends failed to call me (I know who you are and where you live).

Like the Chancellor of the day, the Right Hon Kenneth Clarke, I also dipped out on Nottingham's Cedar Waxwing in 1996 after an extremity-numbing cold day trying to pick a single North American interloper out of a flock of 1,000 Bohemian Waxwings – while avoiding nonplussed drivers almost coming off the road at a busy intersection where the birds were foraging on berry bushes. People would quite happily step out into the road to get better views of the waxwing flocks as they rested on rooftops. Fortunately, Nottingham's rush-hour motorists were more adept at missing the jay-walking birders than the birders were at making out the yellowish tones of the Cedar Waxwing's posterior from the rufous-vented Bohemians. On a dipping heartbreak scale, this venture only reached 'mild upset' level for two reasons. Firstly, my day had begun with a British tick, a splendid male Redhead (North America's answer to the Pochard) on a Nottinghamshire gravel pit. Secondly, as it was my first birding venture north of the Wash–Severn divide since the 1982 Marmora's Warbler twitch, I was technically out of my south-east comfort zone. By the mid-1990s I had revised my bird list to only count birds seen below the magic North–South Divide, but more about that in the next chapter. This has nothing to do with me being a dyed-in-the-wool, warm beer-drinking southern softie ... honest.

Other dips followed in ways that explore both the etymology of the term and also its semantics in ways that would keep a panel of fusty

English professors in research grants for years. For instance, a long drive through packed seaside traffic to see Britain's 'first' Western Reef Heron left a bitter taste in July 1998 when it was deemed that this potential long-distance wanderer from subtropical Africa was in fact most probably a Grey Heron x Little Egret hybrid. At least I had seen the bird and had come away from Stanpit Marsh, Dorset, unconvinced about its credentials as a Western Reef Heron by virtue of its size and shape. Therefore, in the true meaning of the word, it was not really a dip.

One tragic story of a twitch going wrong helped to assuage any personal feelings of disappointment. Hundreds of birders lined the banks of the River Witham on the outskirts of Sleaford on 2 March 1996 to see an imperious White-billed Diver patrolling the slow-moving waters with its ivory-toned beak cast snootily in the air. For many, the inland occurrence was a welcome opportunity to catch up with a bird that hails from the most northerly fringes of Siberia and Arctic North America. My column, dated 8 March 1996, takes up the story:

> Like hundreds of twitchers, I made hurried arrangements for my own pilgrimage to see this legendary bird. Virtually every one of the 100-plus British records of White-billed Diver this century has occurred on the lonely northern isles of Shetland or along the Scottish coast. The only previous inland record was in Manchester in 1987.
>
> But almost as quickly as the presence of this new visitor was announced, came the news that the diver had been accidentally hooked by a pike fisherman. Two hours later the news was even worse – the bird had died on a vet's operating table. Hundreds of horrified birders had watched helplessly as the diver first took the fishing bait and then fought frantically to free itself from the angler's line.
>
> The diver, perhaps driven inland after being slightly oiled in the North Sea, had grabbed at the dead bait, thinking it would be an easy snack. As soon as the bird swallowed the two sets of triple-barbed hooks, its fate was sealed. Although a vet later removed one set, the other barbs had embedded themselves deep in the diver's sternum and it died.
>
> Birders have laid no blame on the unlucky fisherman, and they even praised the way he carefully landed the bird rather than cut his line and leave it to a slow death.

Missing out on seeing the diver paled in comparison to the bird's sad demise. In fact, it was somewhat reassuring that I had abandoned my journey *en route* at the very moment the bird was being taken into care. Adding the unfortunate diver to my list of sightings, especially if it had been floundering in agony when I arrived, would have been cold-hearted and pitiless in the extreme.

Of all the dips I have endured, one did bring about feelings of pathos and rankle enough to leave me questioning the whole business of twitching, as well as the sanity of standing for hours in a field waiting to see birds that, like Godot, never come. To put this particular dip in context one has to understand the very currency of the species involved. Imagine every birdwatcher you've ever met telling you there is one bird they would like to see. Then, taking this wish list, you begin to browse your bird books and turn to the page where the bird in question stands out in all its full glory in its colourful breeding plumage. Then you read that it has only been seen once before on British territory, a lengthy 22 years earlier on Fair Isle. Suddenly, the brand new Rare Bird Alert pager you have just invested in begins flashing 'mega alert ... mega alert ...' You read the LCD screen and it reveals that this magical bird, the precious Siberian Rubythroat, has just been sighted on the Dorset coast and, even better, you are off work tomorrow. Best of all, the bird is a male and, according to some lucky observers, its eponymous ruby throat was still shimmering in the fading light when the bird went to roost at dusk.

My stars were in alignment, a lift was arranged and by 3am the next morning we were on the M25 and heading towards Osmington Mills, a coastal village between Portland Bill and Swanage, where the rubythroat would be waiting to delight and thrill like no bird before. When we arrived, the village was still bathed in darkness, but shadowy figures with the telltale shapes of tripods slung across shoulders could be seen moving in the murk. Voices were hushed, footfalls softened; a small army moved effortlessly towards the point of rendezvous. There was an overwhelming feeling of optimism, a condition that increased the sense of cheeriness and well-being despite the ungodly hour. Jokes were whispered and courtesies exchanged. As night became day, the huddled masses spread across a field of emerald and shaped themselves into a phalanx with all eyes focused upon a tangled area of undergrowth 100 metres away. Then we waited. And waited. And waited... Every flicker amid the distant tangle was scrutinised and discussed. Each Dunnock or Robin that dared to raise a wing came under the glare of a thousand telescopes. Whispers of 'what woz that' broke the stillness. Bramblings flew overhead without a mention. Over the passing hours blind optimism turned to hope to inertia to acceptance to disappointment to despair then, as Bill Oddie had warned, heartbreak. The rubythroat had gone. We traipsed back to the car without a word. Dipping, I had discovered, felt like Tottenham losing or Arsenal winning. It clawed away in the pit of the stomach like John Hurt's diabolical monster in Alien. Only when I returned home did the story of the bird's disappearance begin to emerge. It was one of subterfuge and treachery but, luckily, not murder. Under the headline 'Let's lamp the killjoys', my *Daily Star* column helped me to vent some spleen:

> Angry twitchers have come up with a novel use for the battery-powered torch. If you want a few clues think 'insertion' and 'orifice'. The reason: One of the most appalling events in birding history.
>
> Last Sunday the twitching grapevine almost went into meltdown as news broke that the first Siberian Rubythroat for 22 years had arrived on British soil. The rubythroat has become the most legendary bird on the British list, with the only previous sighting being a dowdy female found on Fair Isle in October 1975.
>
> That's why news that a male bird had been seen in a Dorset coastal valley sparked a birding gold rush. By early Sunday evening, the village of Osmington Mills had come under siege from about 200 twitchers who feasted on brilliant views as the bird preened and displayed its plumage.
>
> As the sun went down, the birders retired and the rubythroat went off to roost in an area of dense hawthorn and sycamore. Those unlucky enough not to see it on Sunday made preparations for the Twitch of the Decade the next morning. But what happened next has sent shockwaves through the birding community.
>
> In the pitch dark, at least two birders were spotted trying to find the roosting Rubythroat with flashlamps. Birds have a defence mechanism when disturbed – they fly off. Hence, next morning when an estimated 1,000-plus birders, some from as far away as Scotland, assembled, the rubythroat had vanished. We may now have to wait another two decades

before the birdwatching community can tick the Rubythroat off *en masse*.

I doubt if anyone who spotted this week's bird by flashlamp will have the courage to claim it – for fear of receiving a torch enema.

That was my worst dip. It hurt but I got over it. For many other twitchers, dips have been more heartbreaking, certainly more expensive, and sometimes even dangerous. One group of frontline twitchers found themselves at the centre of an air-sea rescue in November 2000 when a fishing boat carrying them to South Uist to see Britain's first Long-tailed Shrike – a distant wanderer from central Asia – suffered a gearbox failure and began to drift helplessly. The dozen frightened twitchers, who had paid £75 a head to charter the boat, were eventually saved after HM Coastguard mounted a rescue operation. A helicopter was scrambled, a lifeboat dispatched and the beleaguered birders, some of whom were suffering the effects of seasickness, were eventually towed safely back to port.

Scotland has featured regularly in my accounts of top birders suffering from bad doses of the dips. My third ever column, on 25 November 1994, told the story of Steve Gantlett's ill-fated trek to Fair Isle to search for one of the most enigmatic birds ever seen on British soil. The headline summed up the story perfectly in three words: 'The Little Bustard!' The article explained why:

A twitcher's life is littered with tales of epic journeys made in vain. The habit of missing a good bird has even coined its own phrase – to dip out. Those in search of a rare migrant will happily travel halfway across the country, only to find the bird has flown. The sight of grown men crying into their field guides is not a pretty one.

I've had my fair share of dips, but mine are minor league compared to top twitcher Steve Gantlett's amazing trek. Steve went on an epic expedition in a bid to spot an elusive Little Bustard, a species missing from his impressive 483-strong list of sightings.

It all began with a phone call from a contact reporting that the first 'tickable' bustard for years had been seen on Fair Isle. Bustards have become increasingly rare in their natural habitats in Spain, Portugal and the Eastern European steppes. To see it, Steve needed to travel more than 500 miles from his home in Norfolk. For a Little Bustard, it seemed worth the effort.

Steve explained: 'The idea was to make the flight from Aberdeen to Shetland the next morning. I drove through the night with a car-load of mates and arrived with plenty of time for our flight but the news was not good. That morning the bird had not been seen.

'It seemed we had missed it, so we began the long drive home. A few hours later we then heard it had been seen again. We did a U-turn and headed back to Aberdeen to catch a flight. Finally we got to Shetland and made arrangements to hire a helicopter to Fair Isle. But the weather was bad. When things finally got better, there was no sign of the bustard. It had gone!'

This is the kind of dip which all twitchers suffer at some time, some with alarming regularity.

Tales of epic star-crossed twitches dating back more than a decade may help accountants to understand the mathematics of failed birding campaigns – internal flights, car hire, boat charters and motorway service station sandwiches are hardly cheap – but they will not explain the psychology of the high-spending mentality of the rarity hunters. Costs of flights to far-flung parts of Britain and Ireland are often steep compared to the budget airline prices offered for trips to the Mediterranean or other popular Continental destinations. It would be far cheaper for a group of friends to fly to Madrid, hire a car and clock up sightings of both Little and Great Bustards, throwing in Calandra Lark, Lesser Kestrel and Roller, than it would be to get to some of the more remote Scottish islands. But that's not the point. If you have a British list, if you cherish and nurture it as an old woman may spoil her cat or a miser his gold coins, then nothing is going to get in the way of that all-important tick.

Mark Golley, a well-known Norfolk birder, spent a small fortune in the autumn of 1998 missing a bird which, if seen, would not officially count today. The Daurian Starling that beckoned has never been accepted by the birding authorities as a truly wild bird because of the suspicion that it may have escaped from captivity. A handsome bird with a purplish sheen on its back contrasting with ashy-grey underparts and pied wing-markings, the starling had taken up temporary residence in the village of Balnakeil, close to Cape Wrath, and about as far north as you get on the British mainland. For Mark, the lure of a Daurian Starling meant flying from Norwich to Aberdeen and then embarking on a four-hour drive across the breadth of Scotland. The starling departed before the twitchers arrived, leaving Mark's wallet £350 lighter. To add insult to injury, during their time in the Highlands Mark and his companions came across a magnificent Saker Falcon hunting rabbits on the coastal moorland. And although weather conditions would have been perfect for a truly wild Saker to have arrived from eastern climes, the bird was stained with the same odour of 'escaped bird' as the starling.

All manner of obstacles can create a dip. Sometimes the bird conspires against the twitchers by flying off before they arrive *en masse*. On other occasions the twitchers arrive in time but the provenance of the bird is called into question. Species such as Red-headed Bunting never get accepted, wherever and whenever they arrive, because so many are kept in captivity. In some instances the credentials of long-staying rarities are queried, and in other cases birders have failed to make a journey at all because news from the scene says that the bird's ID is questionable. However, those most spectacular dips, those that bring smiles on the faces of rivals and generate rancour in the hearts of victims, invariably involve serious cases of misjudgement.

Martin Garner is one of the most respected identification experts in Europe but even he cannot escape the curse of dipping. He explains:

'It was 1982 and I was a full-on 19-year-old twitcher – young, free, single and slightly loopy. In those days, I was keeping company with the likes of Tim Andrews, then likely to become the youngest British birder, at the age of 21, to have seen 400 species in Britain.

'We were game for anything, so when a Greater Yellowlegs turned up at Blennerville, County Kerry, in April an action plan was put into effect. It meant going from Hertfordshire to London, picking up Keith Lyons (infamously known as 'Dipper' – I should have guessed), and then driving five hours to Fishguard.

'After that, we had a three-and-a-half hour ferry crossing, had to hire another car and then drove for five more hours to Blennerville.

'I don't remember much about the overnight journey, except a noticeable slowing down in Southern Ireland as we traversed the country, punctuated by the occasional standstill when tractor drivers nattered to local farmers on country lanes.

'We finally arrived around 15 hours later, leaving us with a grand total of three hours to locate and observe our quarry. It was make or break time. Surveying the tidal, marshy inlets, we opted to divide duties with me heading westwards and Dipper and Tim going east.

'Two hours later and there was still no sign of the bird. Then, ten minutes before we had to leave to make our connections back, Dipper and Tim had views of a yellowlegs in flight, going away.

'They were elated but I was gutted. Our time window had maxed out and we had to leave. The long journey home was uneventful, only interrupted by the occasional delighted cooing of two happy birders and the grumbles of one not so happy.

'Typically, a Surf Scoter I had wanted to see at Rosslare also failed to show, meaning I had double-dipped.

'It was only when I arrived back home did the event take dipping into an all together new dimension. Tim telephoned me the next day to say that there had also been a Lesser Yellowlegs at Blennerville that weekend and, as both he and Dipper were not sure of the species they had seen, they could tick neither!

'Fast forward to 12 October 2007. I arrived on Foula to be greeted by the ever-exuberant Ken Shaw and compatriots to be told they were looking for a yellowlegs species which they had seen the previous day in a howling north-westerly.

'The photos they had taken were later to prove that the bird was a Greater Yellowlegs. And, of course, I never saw it. Given the identification challenge that some Greater and Lesser Yellowlegs created, even in very recent years, what species was (or were) present in winter 1982 at Blennerville remains a mystery. And by the way, I still haven't seen Greater Yellowlegs in Britain or Ireland. Maybe one day my healing will come.'

Paul Stancliffe, stalwart of the British Trust for Ornithology's media office, tells a story of how romance and birding are often incompatible bed-mates, and how attempts to reconcile the two can sometimes end with disastrous consequences. Having planned a move south from his Nottingham birthplace in the late summer of 1985, Paul thought that he would make a romantic gesture and arrange a weekend getaway with his then girlfriend at the seaside. Like any true birder, he mused over venues for such a starry-eyed break – and chose north Norfolk. Cley, with its windmill, cosy pubs, big skies and breathtaking landscapes, seemed just the place to warm a female heart. Halfway through the weekend of traipsing round the boardwalks and along the heavy-going beach, it had become apparent that there was a seismic difference between their ideas of a romantic August Bank Holiday break. Birding was abandoned and the lovebirds settled for lunch in nearby Sheringham.

You can still hear the irony in Paul's voice when he speaks about his 'lovely day out.' As evening and the long drive back to Nottingham beckoned, Paul drove back along the coast road. Something seemed to be stirring.

Paul picks up the story:

'When we drove through Salthouse, I noticed a group of birders looking out over the saltings between there and Cley. As I slowed to see if I could see what they were looking at there was a big sigh from the passenger, which said it all. I carried on my way.

'The following week was spent preparing for my move south and so a call to Nancy's café, the nub of bird news in those days (remember that pagers and mobiles were still in the future), didn't even feature on my list of things to do.

'Two weeks after the August Bank Holiday, I finally found time to go birdwatching at what I decided would be my new local patch, Hengistbury Head. It was here that I bumped into one of the local birding stalwarts and, as we were talking, he told me there had been a Little Whimbrel in Norfolk over the Bank Holiday weekend. What's more it had spent its time in the Cley area.

'The subsequent report in *British Birds* outlined what this amazing bird did during its 11-day stay in Norfolk, including spending the day on the rough grazing marsh between Salthouse and Cley on Bank Holiday Sunday.

'Suddenly, the penny dropped, albeit a long time after the event: this is what the group of birders that I drove past were watching! And to think I almost stopped.

'To add insult to injury, I had already dipped the Glamorgan Little Whimbrel, which was the first British record of the species, on a twitch from Nottingham three years earlier, arriving there on the day that it left. This too was August Bank Holiday.

'My girlfriend and I went our separate ways soon after my move to

Hampshire. Do I blame her for missing the Little Whimbrel? You bet I do. Well, her and August Bank Holidays.'

Of all the dips in all the world, one stands out for its pure piquancy of failure. Think World Cup, false dawns, a Land of Hope and Glory and then ... the Germans (or the Portuguese) and the dreaded penalty shoot-out. For Chris Batty, one of the driving forces of the Rare Bird Alert pager service, England's World Cup campaign to qualify for the 2002 finals in Japan was to leave him holding his head in his hands. My report in October 2001 told his story:

Unlucky Chris Batty must have been the only Englishman alive who never cheered when David Beckham's free kick sailed gloriously into the net. As World Cup euphoria was gripping the nation last Saturday, poor old Chris was feeling as sick as the proverbial manager's parrot. His latest twitching venture – the last month has seen him criss-crossing the country on a string of futile twitches – has ended in failure. Again.

Chris was among an intrepid band who had foregone the torture of Old Trafford to endure even more masochism on the trail of an elusive Grey Catbird on Anglesey. The catbird – the first twitchable record of this North American garden bird – had been playing cat-and-mouse with hundreds of birders as it lurked in thick gorse bushes. Then, at 4.45pm on Saturday, Chris, who had just clocked up his third day waiting for his quarry, heard a cheer echo around the RSPB's South Stack Cliffs reserve.

He dashed towards the jubilant crowd, thinking that the catbird had finally reappeared. Unluckily for him, the whoops were coming from delighted twitchers who had just heard about Becks's crucial equaliser against Greece. And while the nation was able to look back at a successful, if lucky, World Cup qualifying campaign, Chris could only ponder more misses than England's stuttering forwards.

The past month has seen him clocking up thousands of miles travelling between Norwich, Shetland, Northern Ireland and Wales on the trail of the best collection of rarities for years.

Most of them have avoided Chris. Admittedly, he saw a Pallid Harrier on Shetland, a Stilt Sandpiper in County Down and a Green Heron in Lincolnshire, but over the same period he lost out on two

Pallas's Grasshopper Warblers, a Thick-billed Warbler, Isabelline Wheatear, Siberian Blue Robin and the catbird.

Chris said: 'I spent hours waiting for the catbird. You can imagine how I felt when I heard this roar only to discover it was birders cheering England's equaliser.'

Why I am not huffin' for a Puffin...

Ninety calories per serving and you wouldn't eat puffins?
What's more tempting than that?
—Dieting website.

I have a confession: I have never seen a Puffin. I have seen raptors in their thousands soaring over Israel's Negev Desert and I have been thrilled by hummingbirds in tropical South America. I have spot-lamped nightjars on the African savannah and I have marvelled at albatrosses in the South Atlantic. I even travelled to Yorkshire once to see a little grey warbler from the Mediterranean. Puffins and I, however, have never seen eye to eye. And, hopefully, we never will do. Well, not quite yet. When I say 'puffins', I specifically mean the Atlantic Puffin. I have gone to sea off the Pacific coast of North America to look for the grand Tufted Puffin with its bulky black, seafaring demeanour and bright orange bill. I would drop everything at a moment's notice to see a Horned Puffin on its nesting grounds in

Arctic Alaska. I have even seen some of the Puffin's more distant relatives such as the diminutive Little Auk and the preposterous-looking Rhinoceros Auklet. But the Atlantic Puffin, a.k.a. the Sea Parrot, Tammy Norrie, Little Friar, Old Bottlenose or Parrot-billed Willy, to name but a few of its aliases, is a bird that remains as tantalisingly distant as the Slender-billed Curlew or Great Auk in my orbit.

Before I get accused of *fraterculaphobia*, please let me explain. I have nothing against Puffins. They are cute, charismatic little fellows, small in stature and big of character. They can do amazing things with fish in beaks the colours of the rainbow. Puffins may be challenged in the flight department with those little stubby wings, but put them on a grassy cliff top and they strut and preen with the same panache as catwalk supermodels. There must be millions of people who have done a touch of star-spotting with Puffins. I wager all those tourists who travel to the Farne Islands or Skomer don't think of themselves as birders or twitchers when they go looking out for Puffins to freeze frame for posterity on their little compact digital cameras. No, what they are really doing is superstar gazing, and the Puffins they capture striking a pose are the bird world's equivalent of A-list celebrities. The only difference is that they have fishy breath. One only has to look at the way Puffins exploit their image rights to understand this star quality: tea-towels, T-shirts, cuddly toys and jewellery are sold by the lorry load at tourist shops from Scilly to Shetland in honour of the creatures. They have even got their own publishing company!

Let me at this stage point out that this is not a diatribe against the Puffin. We've already agreed they are cute and cuddly – that's if you desire to have your nails trimmed to the first knuckle with those pincer-like beaks – as well as being captivating and charming. In my dinner jacket and with, let's say, a more portly status of recent years, I may well look like one from certain angles (Please note: I do not have webbed feet and my nose is in proportion with the rest of my body). Equally, I have nothing but respect for anyone who has ever taken a seaside holiday in Cornwall, Wales or Scotland and raved about their encounters with Puffins. They are truly creatures to write home about. Millions must have either written or received postcards telling of audiences with these endearing little fellows. Little wonder that 'Pope' was one of their 17th century names. With such history, such folklore, and also because of their choice of breeding grounds – surely Britain's seabird cities are the most awesome of all our natural wildlife spectacles – I will be as bold to say that all serious birders in Britain, indeed, anyone who has binoculars and a field guide will have made some effort to see the Puffin somewhere in the UK. Then there's me.

So what have I got against Puffins? It's a long story, so let me paint the background. I was born in London's East End and then moved to a sprawling overspill council housing estate in South Bedfordshire when I was barely out of the pram. Luton is about as far as you can physically get from the sea in the UK, and although Dunstable Sewage Farm, my favourite teenage haunt, pulled in occasional shorebirds, alcids are hardly renowned for inhabiting settling beds or smelly, dishwater-coloured sewerage lagoons. With both parents working for Vauxhall Motors and with me being an only child, our family was lucky enough to be able to afford package holidays abroad in the late 1960s while our neighbours were travelling to Cornwall and Devon or even Scotland to brave the vagaries of the British summer. So at least they got their fill of Puffins, be it taking photographs or splashing out on Puffin paraphernalia. By the time I had begun noting my sightings in an old school exercise book and collecting points in my 'I-Spy' book of birds, the notion that I had never seen a Puffin began to dawn. Still, it would only take a school trip to the seaside and I would be able to get my fill of these cheeky little mariners and get the T-shirt, or so I thought. School trips to Paignton, Devon, came and went without any Puffin encounters. A school trip to the Lake District secured an incredible sighting of a Golden Eagle – still my only British record of the species – as well as an afternoon at St Bees Head where there were Razorbills but no Puffins. Geography A Level took me into the very heart of the Puffin's dominion – the island of Eigg – but, once again, there was to be no sign of the P-bird.

The 1974 Scottish field trip turned into one long birdwatch after our geography master decided that we would not have to submit any coursework from our stay but take a map-reading paper as an alternative. Long days were spent walking over wild moors and around spectacular lochs where Red Grouse grumbled and divers wailed. Black Guillemots, otherwise known locally as 'Tysties', would show off their diving skills in the clear waters of Eigg's harbour at Galmisdale. Manx Shearwaters would visit the island by night and Willow Warblers would sing by day. One morning saw the school party boarding a fishing vessel to sail to the nearby isle of Muck. It was a beautiful spring day and, with one of my birdwatching school pals, we headed off to the northernmost point where, we were told, Puffins nested. It is the only time of my life that I have intentionally gone looking for Puffins, but the warm afternoon and the previous night's camp fire activities with cans of 'heavy' both took their toll and rather than birdwatching I took a cat nap. By the time I awoke, Muck was coated in a heavy grey mist, the fishing boat could not dock and our school group had to sleep in a barn without supper. Next morning, the teacher negotiated a deal with a crofter whereby his now famished students would pick potatoes in return for breakfast – a bucket of salty porridge and bacon. It was the best meal of my life. Scotland's hospitality ended there. On the return journey to London I was head-butted, wrongfully arrested after being mistaken for a Glasgow Rangers hooligan and had a brick thrown at me. I vowed never to step north of the sanctuary of Hadrian's Wall again. Thirty-five years on I have kept my promise but, in doing so, my British birding range has been truncated, and my chances of seeing a wild Puffin seriously impaired.

Even after my birding renaissance in 1980 and the overhaul of my life list, Puffins were an embarrassing bogey bird that I kept quiet about even among my closest circle of friends. Of course, all birders have bogey birds. For top twitchers, they are the birds that put in once-in-a-decade appearances when trips to Antarctica or Kazakhstan have been arranged. Less frenetic souls have their bogey birds, too. The Aquatic Warbler, an eastern European denizen of sedge-rich marshes, appears annually in Britain but is so furtive that many enthusiastic list-keepers wait years before ticking it off. Hawfinches, Lesser Spotted Woodpeckers and, sadly, the fast-disappearing Willow Tit take a lot of finding and someone taking up birding today could wait a few years before seeing all three. Capercaillie, Crested Tit and Scottish Crossbill are three species that require a visit to Scotland. You might need to spend hours looking out to sea to see Sooty and Balearic Shearwaters and to brave London's traffic for an encounter with the exotic Ring-necked Parakeet. Fortunately, going on monthly excursions to Norfolk, Kent or the south coast with the Wednesday Club – our group of pals that have been birding together since the early 1980s – and fitting in occasional twitches saw my list pass through the 350 barrier without the appearance of the Puffin. It began to take on a new aura: from bogey bird to a contorted badge of honour. I finally came out.

At first, my closest friends thought I was mad ... or lying. Nobody could believe that I had never seen a bird that so many non-birders had seen. Not only had all my friends seen Puffins, but their wives and children had too. When I began tour-leading, one well-known birding figure asked me never to tell his clientele about my Puffin deficiency. When people did find out, I went on the defensive, declaring that I wanted to see a Puffin when the time was right. Exactly what this would entail remained vague but if I was planning to make this a life challenge, it needed to be a big adventure. With this in mind, I decided to let the world know about my case of 'Puffinitis' in the Strictly for the Birds column of 29 June 1998. Under the headline 'Why I am huffin' and a-puffin' I wrote:

What would you consider to be the most recognisable British bird? Blue Tit, Robin, Blackbird, Barn Owl? Yes, they're all well known, but I would bet 99 per cent of the population could tell a Puffin from a hundred paces. In fact, I bet this cocky little seabird with its rainbow-coloured beak has been seen by most of the country on holiday or trips to the seaside. This is why I have always kept schtum about my bogey bird when twitchers talk about needing Corncrake for their 300th tick or Aquatic Warbler for their 400th. It's a bit like if you are still a virgin at 45 or that the closest you've got to overseas travel is visiting the exotic food sections at the supermarket... Naff or what?

Things have got so bad that I've told my birding mates to tell me to close my eyes during autumn seawatches just in case one whirrs past and spoils their chance at a cheap jibe. Why I have managed to avoid the Puffin – there are around 900,000 in the UK, a tenth of the world population – has a lot to do with me being a southern softie and having a hatred of boat trips.

Puffins breed almost exclusively around our northern and western coastlines. The largest colonies are found on remote islands. The nearest significant breeding colony to London is at Bempton Cliffs in Yorkshire, a long hike of 200 miles. Without making a pilgrimage to see them waddling around their clifftop nesting warrens, beaks dripping with sand eels, the only other way to see them is striking lucky during a stormy seawatch in Norfolk or Cornwall. Thanks, but no thanks.

Why I am not huffin' for a Puffin

I've braved a few October trips to the Scilly Isles, where a cottage industry makes everything from Puffin tea cosies to Puffin brooches in celebration of the archipelago's small population. But by this time of the year, the birds have left for their winter holiday haunts far out in the Atlantic. I guess I'll eventually catch up with the elusive little blighter and I often dream about an intrepid expedition to the Arctic to see them alongside such legendary birds as Brünnich's Guillemot and King Eider.

Until then, I have one excuse for my failure: Puffins are not really birds, they're fish! It's a little known fact that in medieval times the Church declared them to be fish so they could be eaten by protein-starved Scottish crofters during Lent. And who the hell wants a fish on their checklist?

Tell someone that a Puffin is really a fish and watch their reaction. It is my favourite dinner party conversation stopper. Friends are always picking my brains for the latest Fleet Street gossip, the stories the newspapers dare not print about errant royals, showbiz celebrities or professional footballers. It's then that I throw my Puffin curveball into the conversation.

'Did you know that the Puffin is really a fish?'
I stand back and watch.
'Puffins: Fish?'

Friends' faces wrinkle with incredulity before the thought process kicks in. You can see them picturing Puffins torpedoing through the seas and an air of acceptance takes over their demeanour. They think again, and always say the same thing:

'But they can fly!'
'Never heard of flying fish?' I respond.
More furrowed brows and more questions.
'Haven't they got feathers? Don't they lay eggs?'
'Haven't they got stubby, little legs?'
'Yes, yes and yes. But they're still fish,' comes my reply.

As a final act of kindness I put them out of their misery and tell them how Puffins were decreed to be fish by early papal edicts so that they could be eaten on Fridays and during lent. Puffins were often a mainstay for remote island communities around Britain and, along with Barnacle Geese, were thought of as fish rather than poultry. Eating beavers' tails was given similar dispensation by the church. Puffin is still regularly eaten in Iceland and in the restaurants of Reykjavik it is served up under the name of 'lundi' – a clue to how Lundy Island in the Bristol Channel got its name from Norse invaders. It is said to taste 'rich and gamey' and is best served smoked or lightly grilled. At 90 calories per helping they are most probably a highly nutritious source of protein, but I prefer my poultry courses to be poultry and my fish to be fish (although since writing this I have become a vegetarian).

After years of being embarrassed about my Puffin paucity I finally came up with a plan to put to good this glaring omission in my list of life experiences, and one that would not entail eating Puffin as some strange kind of penitence. What about a sponsored Puffin quest: a worldwide odyssey to see all the world's 23 species of auk and, as a final act reverence to little Tammy Norrie, I save him until last?

Today, Mission Puffin is still in the early stages. The strategy has been worked out like a synchronised battle plan, it's only the logistical nightmare and time-devouring elements of the operation that need to be resolved. Some day hence, when everyday commitments allow, I will get a message that a small squadron of baby Puffins have been colour ringed – to allow easy identification in the field – at one the key breeding colonies around our coast. As the baby Puffins, or *Pysja* to use the Icelandic name, mature, I begin my global journey to see and, hopefully photograph, all its close relatives. I will be working to a strict deadline. For I hope to see all the other species of alcid before the young Puffins return to their cliff top nurseries to become parents themselves. I will have two summers to complete my mission. Young Puffins rarely return 'home' during the first calendar year of their lives. Research has shown that as many as one in four opt to settle in new colonies. Mortality rates are also high for the young birds, which spend much of the first 20 or so months of their lives far out in the Atlantic where they are at the mercy of winter storms and mountainous seas.

While the Puffins mature, I will begin my first journey around the Pacific's 'Ring of Fire', visiting the remote Siberian cliffs and Asiatic islands where 19 of the planet's alcid species breed. I hope to admire the majestic head adornments of the Tufted Puffin and coo at the sparrow-sized Least Auklet. If I am very lucky I may get to smell the tangerine aroma of Whiskered and Crested Auklets. Both these species have glands that produce a citric scent that either acts as a way of attracting mates or driving away parasites. The second stage of the adventure will see me in waters I have ridden before. Pelagic voyages off the Californian coast have already provided me with exciting views of Pigeon Guillemot, Cassin's and Rhinoceros Auklets and Marbled Murrelet, but I long to reacquaint myself with these West Coast specialities, as well as both Craveri's and Xantus's Murrelets which occur in more southerly waters off of Mexico. Fortunately, Atlantic Puffins, as their name suggests, do not occur in the Pacific. This means that it will be possible to 'clean up' the world's alcid family to pave the way for a spectacular denouement by finally coming face to face with a Puffin, one of my specially ringed birds, on some remote Scottish island.

To ensure that this final encounter is not tarnished before the final act, my life has deliberately been a Puffin Free Zone for the past decade. Not seeing a rare bird because you've 'dipped' is an occupational hazard for the twitcher. Not recognising a bird because of an identification issue is something that all birders face. Actively avoiding a particular species is an act of madness. First, it requires a geographical bias to your birding; hence, 99.9 per cent of mine has become restricted below the Wash–Severn dividing line. Any attempt at seawatching has to be confined to the safe waters of the north Norfolk coast where Puffins, thankfully, are rare. Fortunately, seawatching sessions in Cornwall, the Isles of Scilly and Kent have been conducted during seasons when the Puffins have left our coastal waters. Whenever there is a risk of a 'Puffin incident' I have one tactic: facing inland. My Wednesday Club associates have often been left nonplussed at the sight of their thin line of telescopes pointing out to sea at Dungeness or Titchwell, while mine is turned 180 degrees facing inland. In August 1999 when thousands of people flocked to Portland Bill, which had been billed as one of the best coastal locations to see the total eclipse, there was such a risk of a Puffin confrontation that I mooched around inland while my friends appreciated the finer details of Balearic Shearwater plumage until the sun-starved skies made it too dark to see. Finally, Puffin aversion has also had serious implications for my life list. Anglesey's long-staying Black Lark is one bird I would love to have seen had it not been for the risk of members of the island's healthy Puffin population pushing themselves into view.

There is one footnote to my Puffin escapades. As I sit writing this chapter, there comes a report of a Tufted Puffin photographed at Faversham Creek on the Kent side of the Thames Estuary. To celebrate the Tufted Puffin's arrival, I wrote the following report for the *Sunday Express* on 20 September 2009:

As two merchant ships were cutting through the frigid seas of the fabled Northeast Passage last week, was another mariner making the same historic journey? Climate change has opened the once impenetrable icebound waters over the top of the world, allowing shipping to take a short cut through once perilous seas. The commercial fallout from this new shipping lane could be huge. Without having to pass through the Suez Canal, vessels will be able to cut journey times and reduce fuel bills during the summer months when the seas above Siberia are open.

Arctic seas free from ice could also have a massive impact on bird movements. Sightings of Pacific species such as Glaucous-winged Gull and Long-billed Murrelet around the British coast in the last few years have already opened up the debate on whether these birds travelled westwards along Russia's northernmost coastline during the summer ice melt.

The sight of the most unlikely bird ever seen in British waters last week could be further, compelling evidence that Pacific birds, like commercial shipping, are now using the Northeast Passage to visit Europe. Kent birdwatcher Murray Wright had every reason to rub his eyes when a large puffin-like bird with a bright orange bill alighted on the waters of Faversham Creek.

Murray knew instantly what species he was looking at: he had seen Tufted Puffins previously on a birdwatching adventure in Siberia. But the idea of one swimming the salty waters of the Thames Estuary rather than those of the Aleutian Islands or Kamchatka was hard to believe. Fortunately, Murray managed to take a few photographs of the bird before it flew off never to be seen again. Still excited from witnessing the Bird of the Millennium, Murray told how he was with a group of fellow birdwatchers at Oare Marshes nature reserve looking at three Arctic Skuas when his attention was grabbed by a strange looking interloper.

He said: 'We were following the skuas, which were circling into the mouth of Faversham Creek, when a bird flew in the opposite direction through my binoculars' field of view. I got a rear-end look and it appeared all black. At first I thought it was going to be a scoter, but a glimpse of orangey-red towards the front had me thinking of a summer-plumage Puffin, which, in itself, would be a mega bird for Oare.

'Luckily, the bird dropped onto the water about 75 yards away and then it became obvious, even if still too incredible to believe, what it really was: an adult Tufted Puffin, an alcid from the north Pacific! I've seen the species in the wild in Siberia so identification was not a problem. The guys in the hide were already all on the bird, too. Panic ensued, but I managed to take a few record shots despite shaking uncontrollably. In fact, I still am!'

This is the first time a Tufted Puffin has been seen in Britain. There is one other European record of a bird discovered in Sweden in 1994.

One can only imagine the pandemonium if the bird had lingered. Thousands of twitchers would have revelled in the excitement of watching this long-distance seafarer bobbing in the waters of the Thames when it should have been on the other side of the world. And I, for one, would have been there, too. It's only Atlantic Puffins that I have a thing about ...

A Scilly Love Story

For years, the Scilly Islands languished as a tourist destination.
Not because they didn't have anything to offer,
but because Harold Wilson holidayed there.
—Max Hastings.

The fuzzy shadow of our helicopter cut a neat furrow across the towering waves 1,000ft below. Frothy crests were bucking and rearing and white glints of Gannet wings glistened whenever the milky morning sun broke through cloud cover. Land's End had become a fleeting memory. The inky darkness of the Atlantic looked as daunting from the sky as it must have done to the hardy souls being flipped and tossed on the fishing boats and merchantmen out on the open ocean.

'There's Scilly!' A voice blurted out over the heavy churring of the rotor blades. We had only been flying for a few minutes but out to the west the Atlantic was taking on a different texture, something darker and more solid – dry land.

'And that's where the Upland Sandpiper should be,' exclaimed another voice, referring to the hot news that had come over the bird pagers as we waited for take-off at Penzance Heliport. An Upland Sandpiper, an oddball of a shorebird from the prairies that breeds as far from the sea as any wader in North America, had been seen near Telegraph, a small settlement on the north-east side of St Mary's.

The helicopter's shadow continued to cut its trail, but now the sapphire seas were beginning to change colour: first there were the light azures of shallow water and then the colder tones of wave-drenched rocks before a carpet of lush green rolled out welcomingly beneath us. We could easily have been mistaken for the vanguard of an airborne offensive. Khaki-clad warriors, holding telescopes instead of M16 carbines, waiting for the green light to decamp the moment the chopper touched earth.

Go...go...go.

In one seamless operation, the helicopter's company decamped, each man ducking instinctively under blades that had come to a standstill. Backpacks were picked up and strapped on to impatient shoulders; 'scopes screwed on to tripod mounts with the precision of a bayonet drill. One quick look at a map that had been pawed and folded countless times in preparation, and our little invasion force – Rob Dazley, Don Green, Andy Whitney and myself – was ready for action.

Our 1995 Scilly campaign was the realisation of a long-held dream that through its length of conception, planning and final execution could only be thought of in terms of a military analogy. Years of expectancy, years of jealousy, had provided the driving force for the adventure; months of phone calls, reading and saloon bar conferences had helped synchronise our every step to the final touchdown on St Mary's. Army metaphors may seem crass for a weekend jolly to a jumble of rocks 27 miles off of Land's End. Holidaying families manage the same feat year after year. Locals do it daily. For our little band of birding brothers, though, our maiden visit was a final awakening, an initiation into one of the key rites of birding passage. It deserved a pageant, a ceremony.

My own Scilly aspirations had begun with tales from Baz Harding, a 1970s adventurer to this outpost in an age when every visit from the mainland seemed to make ornithological history. Baz had taken me on an early schoolboy trip to Minsmere, some time after he had found fame among birders for turning up Britain's first ever Scarlet Tanager in the Porth Hellick area of St Mary's. The discovery enshrined his reputation in the pantheon of top bird-finders and the details of his discovery not only graced the pages of *British Birds* but made excellent listening for young ears. A decade later, another stalwart of the Scilly season, Paul Trodd, would narrate similar tales of bird-finding, mentioning the names of North American and Asian species that were invariably confined to the appendix sections of my European field guides. Listening to his romantic accounts of seeing Rose-breasted Grosbeak and Common Nighthawk on the archipelago seemed as remote and unachievable as visiting the United States itself. Even the supporting cast of birds he mentioned, annual scarce migrants such as Little Bunting, Short-toed Lark and Rose-coloured Starling, were birds that I had never encountered. The autumn of 1981 was a classic Scilly year for Paul and I remember him and his wife paying a social visit to see our newborn daughter. As the women cooed over the baby, Paul regaled me with tales of rare birds at Lower Moors and on The Garrison, bracing boat trips to St Agnes and Tresco and the vibrant atmosphere of the Scilly 'night scene' when birders met up in the Bishop and Wolf to wax lyrical about the day. I remember looking down at my little bundle of joy and calculating that fatherhood meant it would be decades before I could afford a trip to Scilly.

Fourteen dream-filled years were to pass before I would set foot on the islands, but the overwhelming impression of that first instance as we left the helicopter was that it was exactly how I imagined it would be: meandering lanes; stone walls; patchwork bulb fields; swathes of bracken and bramble; big skies; small, stone-built cottages; few people; fewer cars – and birds. Not rare birds, not even birds that would make a Scilly veteran reach for his binoculars, but still lots of birds. There were House Sparrows and Robins aplenty and Blackbirds almost everywhere. There were also Swallows and House Martins, summer visitors that had long departed the mainland, and yet were still present on a little piece of England in mid-October. It augured well until we passed a group of birders with CB radios and the voice of an old friend filled the air...

'Upland Sandpiper now flying towards Cornwall. Copy!' The

unmistakable voice of Lee Evans came over the radio – 10-4 (loud and clear, in truckers' speak).

Lee has spent so much time on the islands over the years that he is almost a Scillonian. He was directing operations over the airwaves with his usual aplomb. Birders already on the islands had no doubt caught up with the Upland Sandpiper, but new arrivals were left with the ironic thought that the last helicopter to land at St Mary's Airport may have passed the bird in mid-flight. For us, it was our first bit of bad news since we had left home 30 hours earlier and had 'cleaned up' – to use a twitching term – in Cornwall before catching our flight from Penzance. A Red-eyed Vireo, a robust American songbird with head-markings seemingly fashioned from the stripes of Old Glory, had emerged from the mist at Sennen to provide a perfect induction to the world of Nearctic rarities. Nearby a drake American Wigeon and Pectoral Sandpiper added more flavour to the menu of stateside rarities.

If I was an artist, then the mid-1990s would have been my 'American' period. I had become obsessed with all-things transatlantic: the food, the politics, the cult of celebrity and *Baywatch*. I had even learned the rules of gridiron football. The British press has always had a fascination for American news stories and events that would be ignored if they happened in France or Germany. Liaising with our correspondents in New York and Los Angeles was a key part of my job on the *Daily Star* and meant that I got a daily briefing on big stories such as the O.J. Simpson case and the Oklahoma bombing, as well as all the 'Tinsel Town' tittle-tattle. A fascination with late-night US soaps, the humour, wit and philosophy of Homer J. Simpson and a growing awareness of the American birding scene and its eye-catching birdlife had only stoked my desire to cross the Pond. Birding on the hoof, sampling doughnuts and skinny lattes while marvelling at brightly coloured wood warblers seemed to me like a lifestyle honed in heaven. Family holidays to Disneyland were not enough. Trips to Cape May, the capital of US birding, and adventures in California's wilder reaches duly followed. I was even invited to take part in the rather grandly named World Series of Birding – a 24-hour 'twitchathon' – by friends I had made in New Jersey.

While American birds in America were wonderful, the lure of seeing tiny Yankee warblers on British soil had become too much of a temptation to miss. Even though spending a week on the Scillies was not much cheaper than flying to New York, the sheer thrill of admiring a bird that had braved 3,000 miles of open ocean to arrive on our side of the Pond had become the key driving force behind this October adventure. Before leaving London for my first visit to Scilly in October 1995, I filed this dispatch for the *Daily Star* in anticipation, hope and super-charged excitement:

> The Yanks are coming! These latest invaders might not be over-sexed or overpaid – but they are certainly on their way over here. Luckily, this is a welcome invasion, one which could result in the birding highlight of the year.
>
> The advancing hordes are American songbirds, scheduled to be heading down Mexico way for the winter. Hurricane systems across the Atlantic and the mixed-up weather responsible for our current Indian Summer are producing the right conditions for a real birders' bonanza. Just how creatures weighing a few grams can make 3,000-mile non-stop flights across the Atlantic illustrates the tremendous power of cyclonic weather systems.
>
> These conditions catch birds heading south along America's Eastern Seaboard in deep depressions and then send them hurtling on the high-speed jet-stream towards Europe. Unable to feed or head back to their original course, the birds only have 48 hours of natural energy to make landfall. Thousands, perhaps tens of thousands, perish. The lucky ones touch down on the first piece of European soil they see – Scilly. These remote islands on Britain's west coast make a perfect stopping-off point for exhausted birds that have crossed the Atlantic.
>
> Next week, I'll be on the archipelago with hundreds of other twitchers, hoping to see some of the most exciting birds on the British list. Mid-October has become the traditional time for the country's top listers to migrate themselves to birding's 'treasure islands', 27 miles off of the Cornish coast. Rarities such as Scarlet Tanager, Magnolia Warbler, Upland Sandpiper, Common Nighthawk, Wood Thrush, Rose-breasted Grosbeak and Philadelphia Vireo have turned up on Scilly in the past.
>
> Birders can usually count on half a dozen or so gems each autumn. But on exceptional occasions there's a positive gold rush. Both 1975 and 1985 were excellent years on Scilly and offered a mouth-watering range of American land birds. For some inexplicable reason, exactly a

decade on from the last 'big year', we are in for another record breaker.

Early October has already produced a Northern Parula, three Red-eyed Vireos and a Yellow-rumped Warbler. By the end of next week there could be as many as 2,000 birders on the islands of St Mary's, Tresco, St Agnes and St Martin's. Predicting what you will see on Scilly is one of the fun things about birding. I am just predicting one of the best weeks of my life.

With Lee's voice giving CB radio news updates of the Upland Sandpiper's speedy exit from Scilly airspace, the celebratory tones of the column seemed all too premature. Scilly had failed at the first fence. The Swallows that clicked and buzzed overhead seemed to be laughing. Even the Chiffchaffs were having a bit of a *hooet*. A case conference was called and we decided to amend our plans about spending the first day on St Mary's and chance our luck on neighbouring Tresco. Tickets were bought at the quay to take us on one of the many gigs – the small open-topped boats that criss-cross between the islands – for an afternoon's birding on the island famous for its subtropical plants and wild, rugged heathland.

A half-hour later we were in a land time had forgotten. Legend suggests that Tresco was Lyonesse, the so-called 'land across the sea' where King Arthur was laid to rest. Apart from the striking palm trees, the exotic South American, African and Australian plants, and the careful crafting of the splendid Abbey Gardens, the island exists in a time warp that could easily be either post-Second World War or post-Roman. The rumble of car engines is absent; the hubbub of mainland life forgotten. Birdwise, however, Tresco is abuzz. The Great Pool's large expanse of freshwater and the statuesque pine and broadleaved trees dotted around its perimeter provide sanctuary for waterfowl and leaf-loving songbirds alike. Only when a rare bird comes to rest in this idyllic setting does the island's tempo increase. Before heading to Scilly I had made mention of the presence of a Yellow-rumped Warbler on the island, and within minutes of stepping off the gig we were drawn to a spot of willow scrub where three dozen or so birders were huddled into a scrum. Working out the geometry between where their binoculars, 'scopes and cameras were pointing drew me to one particular willow. A flicker of movement amid the browning autumn leaves and then a quick twirl of the binocular focus wheel and I was locked on to the warbler as it worked ceaselessly in the pursuit of insects, trickling through the foliage as if it was a falling leaf itself. Every time it took flight, the small crowd swooned at the sight of the sunshine yellow rump markings from where it got its name. Many Americans still call this species Myrtle Warbler, a far more imaginative name than the rather prosaic Yellow-rumped, and although it is by far the commonest wood warbler on US soil, this dazzling sprite – D.I.M. Wallace described it as the 'butterfly bird' when he saw one at the same spot in 1973 – is a real five-star dandy in Britain with less than 30 sightings.

Marvelling at the endurance qualities of a bird that had braved the high seas and brutal winds of the Atlantic on a gram or so of body fat can be quite meditational until the shout goes up about the presence of another bird. A call of 'Ortolan' brought me out of my transcendental state and I was directed to a small olive-toned bunting scrambling about in a patch of fallow ground yards from my feet and totally oblivious to the attentions of a growing number of birders satiated with views of the Yellow-rumped Warbler. The Ortolan was another new bird for me in Britain and was as delectable to watch, with its subtle head markings and pink bill, as, so I am told, it is to taste, but more about the epicurean qualities of Ortolans in a later chapter.

A successful search of the Great Pool for an American Black Duck, a swarthy, nondescript American cousin of our dear Mallard, confirmed that Tresco's benevolent nymphs were indeed smiling upon us. We began making our way back to the jetty for the return boat trip, but not before the occasion got to me. As I had done 25 years before at Minsmere, when I mistook a Cuckoo for a Merlin, I made another howler with the same embarrassing consequences. A rustle of bird movement in the dense path-side bracken, a hint of rich foxy-browns and grey tones and a mouth working independently of brain led me to yell: 'MEGA!' Tresco's peaceful idyll was shattered in an instant. Birders behave like the best pointer dogs on such occasions, freezing as if they were playing the party game of sleeping lions, not daring to move until the quarry breaks cover. We waited; I got more excited. My memory banks were in full search mode. Somewhere in the dark recesses of my mind I knew I had seen the bird before. The combination of colours made me think Song Sparrow, another North American passerine but much rarer than even the Yellow-rumped

Warbler. I waited for my moment of glory, willing the mystery bird to come out into the open, perhaps provide a little song. We waited. Tension grew. I orchestrated a bank of pointing binoculars towards leaf movement that was becoming ever more pronounced.

'There!' From out of the jumble of decaying ferns came a recognisable foxy brown and grey shape – a Dunnock, one of the commonest birds on Scilly. A collective, disappointed 'umph' filled the air and I could feel metaphorical knives between the shoulder blades.

One wag leaned across and whispered in my ears: 'Bad case of premature exclamation, son. You should get it treated!'

I kept quiet on the return boat trip to St Mary's and the walk back to our digs. Even the appearance of a diffident Wryneck out in the open failed to loosen my tongue. The first rule of birding on Scilly had been learned painfully: 'Be swift to hear, slow to speak.'

The quotation comes from the Bible (James 1:19) and the parable of the Dunnock was to become the basis of an article a decade later in the *Sunday Express*, written to highlight the growing conservation concern for this nondescript but fascinating bird.

Nothing gets the adrenalin pumping or the imagination running as wild as birding on the Isles of Scilly. This windswept archipelago is a magnet for rare birds from the world over. Yanks and Sibes – American wood warblers and cuckoos as well as Asiatic buntings and thrushes, to name but a few – draw in thousands of twitchers to witness the autumn spectacular. But birding in the gaze of so many prying eyes can have its down moments, as I once discovered to my cost.

Calling out 'mega' – the top category for a rarity – in earshot of fellow birders earns applause when it's right and derision when wrong. I once got it wrong: big time. Scouring the undergrowth on Tresco, I was suddenly confronted by a small, skulking songbird with a striking head pattern. The combination of foxy red and slate grey plumage convinced me I was looking at an American Song Sparrow. My whoops of joy were silenced all too quickly.

'It's only a bloody Dunnock,' a gruff voice admonished, 'don't wet yourself, lad.' Suitably chastised, Dunnocks remained a mute subject with me for a decade, but not for much longer. Sadly, it is now all too rare itself. This nondescript garden bird has become a priority conservation target of the Government because of its dramatic decline. Since 1970 numbers of the race '*occidentalis*' – a subspecies confined to England, Wales and eastern Scotland – have fallen by 26 per cent.

This worrying trend means that the Dunnock, along with two other declining garden birds, the House Sparrow and Starling, are being made the subject of Biodiversity Action Plans (BAPs) and thus gaining much greater conservation resources. Survey work, particularly in the BTO Garden BirdWatch, has given an insight into the worrying plight of the Dunnock.

Much is still to be discovered about the Dunnock and the causes of its decline. Indeed, only recently has the sordid private life of this little bird come to light. Females mate with two males, while some males take up with two females. Inter-relationships between three and four males are not unknown. This has done nothing to help its breeding because females are subordinate and often forced out of hospitable garden feeding areas into the country during harsh winters with high mortality rates.

Mike Toms, BTO Garden BirdWatch organiser, told me: 'Our rarest species attract the most attention, either from the media or from targeted conservation action. However, the large decline in populations of more common species, like Dunnock, House Sparrow and Starling, are also worthy of attention. It is through the efforts of volunteers in long-term monitoring that we have been alerted to the declines and this has prompted their inclusion on the new Government list.'

Learning, the hard way, to hold my tongue in the company of hardened twitchers was all the more ironic because the only reason I was on Scilly was to speak. Although the Scilly dream had tantalised for years, it was an approach by a television production company that had helped to facilitate my visit with friends who were already locked into the dream. An hour-long Channel 4 documentary called *The Twitchers* was focussing on the October 'Scilly Season', and besides interviewing many of the annual stalwarts they had wanted my personal take on proceedings as Fleet Street's 'birding reporter'. Once on the islands, co-ordinating meetings with the film crew became a nightmare as the rarities came thick and fast. The day after the Yellow-rumped Warbler came the lure of Red-throated, Richard's and Tawny Pipits at St Mary's Airport, along with a possible eastern race Yellow Wagtail. A Short-toed Lark was also in the vicinity, enjoying the open grassy perimeters as if it was at large on a vast swathe of steppe. Apart from being filmed for a three-second scene which showed me climbing on to one of the gigs, my services were not required by the crew again that afternoon. This allowed more time for birding, a few pre-dinner drinks and later a visit to the Porthcressa Inn, a well-known watering hole whose cellar bar had become enshrined in Scilly folklore as the location for the evening 'log call'.

In the early 1980s, David Hunt had established the inn as the evening meeting place for the twitching hordes to swap notes and call out their sightings. The flurry of rarities each autumn became a source of national news and I would speak regularly with David from my freelance agency office in Bedfordshire and get the latest rarity bulletins to be sold on to the national newspapers. One night in October 1983 David telephoned me at home breathless through laughter rather than birding exertion.

'We've got a Cliff Swallow here, Stuart,' he said excitedly, emphasising that it was not only the first time this North American migrant had ever been seen on Scilly, but anywhere in the British Isles.

'It gets better, though. You will not believe this...' he paused to increase the dramatic effect.

'It was found by Cliff Waller,' he burst out laughing. 'There's your headline: 'Cliff Waller finds a Cliff Swallow'.'

More laughter.

Although none of the nationals took up David's offer of a free headline, the story did make a few paragraphs in the dailies and that was the beginning of small cottage industry for us both. Tragically, David was killed in a tiger attack in India in February 1985, without us ever meeting face-to-face. One of his last acts was to write a chapter for *Best Days with British Birds* about a September morning out with Bill Oddie and some other pelagic stalwarts in which they got breathtaking views of Leach's Storm-petrel, Sabine's Gull and Long-tailed Skua from a sharkers' boat off of the islands. His love for birds, particularly those on and around his beloved Scilly, was strikingly evident and he always promised to make my first visit to the islands a trip of a lifetime. It is a regret that he was not there to show me around when I paid my first visit a decade later.

Without a doubt, David would have been one of the stars of the show in the 1995 television documentary that provided my 'visa' to the islands. The British Film Institute says of the *The Twitchers* in its

111

archive notes: 'The documentary film follows an eccentric band of people who spend their lives chasing rare birds; they are called twitchers because of the way they twitch with excitement at the prospect of seeing a new bird.' What wonderful understatement. Far from being a genteel documentary version of an Ealing Comedy, the film was cutting edge and racy and its stars were seen as dynamic larger-than-life characters with both big personalities and big bird lists – rather than quaint eccentrics plucked from a bygone age.

For the production crew, Scilly was the perfect backdrop to not only get 'up close and personal' shots of the main protagonists – Chris Batty, Lee Evans, Dick Filby and Keith Lyons, to name a few – but also to incorporate enough dramatic licence to make the overall story really work. I was invited, in my position as a national newspaper columnist, to give an overview of proceedings in a short filmed interview. For my bosses back in London, this was seen as a perfect opportunity for some free publicity for the *Daily Star* and so I was allowed to join my birding friends from Bedfordshire on their first-ever sojourn to the islands. We've all heard the Hollywood adage about never working with children or animals, but I bet in film studios across the world birders are also regarded as production Jonahs. Each time I was supposed to meet up with the crew there always seemed to be a good bird to see and interviews were postponed on almost an hourly basis, and although my friends and I were filmed getting on and off of the boats, time was running out for a proper sit-down chat in front of the camera. On my penultimate day on the islands, the film-makers suggested that I should meet up with them at the one annual event that always manages to pin down the twitching masses to one location – the annual Birders versus Islanders football match. This fixture, engrained in both Scilly and twitching folklore, pitches the locals against the fleet-footed skills of the visiting birders. For the locals, the game takes on an almost international feel. With the islands' league comprised of just two teams who met weekly to fulfil an entire season's fixture list as well as a cup competition, the opportunity to see fresh faces on the pitch, such as acclaimed bird artist Ian Lewington swapping his paint brushes for goalkeeping gloves, invariably drew the largest crowd of the year.

As kick-off approached and the smell of liniment filled the air, the film-makers were allowed a little artistic licence to give the production a dramatic denouement. Chris Batty, who was then a 17-year-old lower sixth former skipping school to be on the islands so he could build up his already impressive British life list, was drafted into the team with the idea that he would get substituted after a few minutes to dash off and see a rarity. I was standing on the touchline, itchy-footed after permanently hanging up my boots the year before, with the idea of giving some kind of commentary to camera *à la* John Motson. For both Chris and I, there was an added frustration. While we were about to be filmed, news had come through of a Subalpine Warbler on neighbouring St Agnes, which we both wanted to see.

According to the storyline, Chris, who had taken to the field wearing his Rare Bird Alert pager, was supposed to suddenly dash off during the middle of play when news of a rarity was flashed through. Amazingly, as the cameras began to roll, a report came through of a possible Semi-collared Flycatcher – a bird that had never before been seen in Britain – being seen less than a mile away in the grounds of the Longstone Heritage Centre. Pandemonium ensued. All I can remember is the crew and most of the Birders' football team dashing from the pitch to the amazement of the Islanders' team. Minutes later, more than 400 pairs of binoculars were focusing on a rather nondescript *Ficedula* flycatcher flitting around a garden, and most of the frustrated observers cursing their lack of field experience with one of the trickiest of groups of European birds to identify. Horror of horrors, the documentary director turned to me and asked me to give a running commentary of the proceedings. Before I could speak, I was 'miked up' and the cameras were filming. I had to switch from Motson mode to the role of a roving BBC reporter on the frontline. Luckily, as the camera flitted between the masses, the elusive flycatcher, and me, I managed to remain non-committal on the bird's identity, concluding that if the bird was a Semi-collared Flycatcher everyone gathered would be ecstatic, but if it turned out to be a humble Pied Flycatcher there would be a feeling of mass disappointment. Luckily, I remained equivocal, a wise move bearing in mind that a Scandinavian flycatcher expert was somewhat scathing of the British birding community a few weeks later when he finally ruled on its identity. In a column headlined 'There Ain't No Flies on the Swedes' I reported the findings of the eminent ornithologist Krister Mild. I thought a football metaphor was appropriate having recently seen the England national football team humbled by the Vikings. I wrote:

Britain's twitchers are going the same way as our lousy footballers –
becoming sacrificial lambs for the Scandinavians. England's finest were
ceremoniously dumped out of the last World Cup by Norway and who
can forget turnip-head Graham Taylor's disaster in Sweden...

This week Swedish ornithologist Krister Mild declared that the
mystery Longstone flycatcher was of the much commoner Pied variety.
The verdict highlights the cool, careful and calculated analysis of a
problem that you would expect from a Scandinavian.

Krister wrote: 'I don't know why flycatchers like the Scilly bird are
always suspected to be Collared or Semi-collared if they turn up in
England. In Sweden, the bird would not even provoke a second glance...'

Luckily, when *The Twitchers* documentary was eventually screened on
a prime time slot on Channel 4, the shots of me in my Barbour
being evasive and ambiguous on the tricky question of flycatcher
identification stood the test of time. Indeed, a few experienced
twitchers who saw the programme were impressed with my ability to
remain oblique and ambivalent enough not to make a fool of myself.
Perhaps they were still trying to work out the continuity of the filming.
When the documentary was eventually screened, the football match
footage was dovetailed with the incredible scenes that greeted the
arrival of a Yellow-billed Cuckoo that had occurred several days later.
It made edge-of-the-seat viewing: crowds were shoe-horned into a
meandering, high-banked lane; local traffic was trying to pass. There
were shouts of 'you're driving on my foot' and the 'oohs' and 'aahs' of
excited twitchers as their telescopes focused on the sleek contours of a
North American cuckoo doomed to starve to death because of the lack
of its favourite food – hairy caterpillars – in late autumn. It was classic
Scilly, if seen through the lens of a television camera with an eye for a
good yarn. As they say in the newspapers, never let the facts get in the
way of a good story.

I was Bill Oddie's Body Double

Goodie-goodie-yum-yum.
—*The Goodies*, BBC TV (1970–82).

It was during one of the regular hosing-downs by my father that I first learned Bill Oddie was a birdwatcher. There I stood in the garden, everything waist down coated in a foul-smelling veneer of human effluent, while Dad sounded off about my ridiculous hobby and the scrapes it got me into with increasing regularity. Having to remove a layer of smelly sewage-farm settling bed with a garden hose was not his idea of fun. *The Goodies* was not his idea of fun either. He hated their corny slapstick humour and, in particular, he reserved his derision for Bill Oddie. Long-haired Oxbridge comedians were his nemeses. The schoolboy humour of the Footlights set was anathema to someone brought up in the heart of London's pre-war East End, when life was not just tough but about survival. He was one of 12 children living in a council flat in

Hoxton, arguably the most deprived of all East End neighbourhoods at the time. According to his birth certificate, my grandfather scraped a living as a 'scavenger' – an old Edwardian term for a scrap metal collector – and that was only when he was not in prison for running illegal betting rings. The travails of being dragged up by the bootlaces did not mean Dad never had a sense of humour, it was just that 'overgrown schoolboys with scruffy haircuts' did not make him laugh. Neither did standing outside in the near dark hosing me down and then having to fork out for new jeans and trainers every time I decided to take a shortcut across the sewage farm's settling beds.

'I read in the paper the other day that Bill Oddie bloke is one of you lot,' he moaned on one occasion. 'Bloody bird spotters are all the same – not got the sense they were born with.'

Finding out that Bill Oddie was a birdwatcher was brilliant news. As far as I was concerned Bill was the best one in *The Goodies*. He was the funniest, the funkiest – he never wore a collar and tie – and, a bit like me, he also got into the best scrapes. I felt a kindred spirit, perhaps even a sense of superiority. Yes, Bill may have confronted the 200ft-tall 'Kitten Kong', but I had nearly drowned in raw sewage trying to see a Pectoral Sandpiper.

Throughout the 1970s, Bill and his two sidekicks, Graham Garden and Tim Brooke-Taylor, continued to make hilarious television – the 'Bunfight at the OK Tea Rooms' was a work of comic genius – while I tried to perfect my own comic writing style on the sixth form magazine and later at journalism college. I was told to stick to hard news. I am sure there were lots of subliminal references to birds and birding in *The Goodies*, but it was not until I received a copy of *Bill Oddie's Little Black Bird Book* as a Christmas present in 1980 that I realised the high esteem in which W.E. Oddie, to use his proper ornithological nomenclature, was regarded by the birding community. His important role in the discovery and identification of Britain's first ever Pallas's Reed Bunting on Fair Isle in 1976 is a textbook example of how to combine fieldwork and reference book research to make a positive identification of a tricky species. The story is told at length in the Poyser classic *Birds New to Britain and Ireland*, and it conjures up wonderful images of Bill and other legendary figures such as Richard Richardson marvelling over the wayward straggler from deepest Siberia at the Fair Isle Observatory.

I first got a chance to marvel at Bill Oddie in the flesh in the early 1980s when I was invited to a book launch in London. I admit to being star-struck. Fleet Street's modern preoccupation with celebrity (or perhaps that should read obsession) is not a new phenomenon, well not among its reporting cohorts. Hacks love stars and I would defy any newshound not to be left in awe of the world's glitterati and beautiful people. We are like the readers we serve; when it comes to meeting someone you have only seen on a television or cinema screen you really do sense star shine. My recollection of the first time I met Bill has become hazy with the fog of time. I think it was at a party to celebrate the publication of Peter Harrison's seminal *Seabirds: An Identification Guide,* to which I had been invited after coming up with the idea of writing the *Best Days* book in conjunction with *British Birds.* All I can remember is that I kept staring at him as if he was some rarity blown in from afar and then being tongue-tied when I had a chance to speak to him.

The one upshot of meeting Bill was that he agreed to write a chapter on his 'best day' for the book. I was delighted. His agreeing to take part, especially as he was the best-known birder in the country, was a key to the project's success, yet because of my own ineptitude it almost ended in disaster. Due to a combination of diffidence and being somewhat spellbound by one of my favourite television stars, I gave Bill a wholly wrong briefing when he agreed to write up his account for the book. As one could expect from an accomplished writer, he took no time in producing a well crafted, neatly written account of his favourite day's birdwatching. I can remember it arriving in the post in a brown A4 envelope with a North London postmark and hurriedly opening it to see what kind of day Bill had decided upon. Would it be Scilly or perhaps Fair Isle? Could it be a day on location when he had taken a break from filming *The Goodies* in Cornwall or some other birding hot-spot? All too quickly it dawned that Bill had not written about his best day with British birds. Indeed, I had not heard of most of the birds he mentioned. Rather than a day on his beloved Hampstead Heath or the West Midland reservoirs where he earned his birding stripes, he had chosen New York. My stomach turned over. I realised I had not said it had to be a day's birding in the British Isles. Could I ask him to rewrite it? He was busy and had obviously gone to great lengths to write a 1,500-word chapter. Should I change the name and parameters of the book? No, it was being written in conjunction with *British Birds*. Before panicking, I sat down and read Bill's opening lines. They caught just the tone I was looking for – excitement, enlightenment, pure birding. They were also about to open up a whole new world for me, one which would eventually help me gain Bill's respect and plaudits and bring hours of joy. Bill wrote:

> In New York's Central Park, people get up to all sorts of extraordinary antics. There are joggers, roller-skaters, mime-artists, musicians, lovers, preachers, dog-walkers and horse-riders all, as the Yanks say, 'doing their own thing', with no sense of shame or embarrassment. Central Park also provides cover for muggers, rapists, junkies and assorted all-American psychopathic loonies. Outside daylight hours, most sensible New Yorkers wouldn't be seen dead in the park – unless that's what they already are – dead! A fair smattering of murders take place in the park, too.

The more I read, the more I was captivated by Bill's story of Central Park and its birds. There were birds I had never heard of such as Chipping Sparrows and Ruby-crowned Kinglets, and others that were just sketchy images in the European field guides of the day. Bill reserved his real excitement for the American wood warblers. During a period of 90 minutes he managed to tally 17 species, some with rainbow-coloured names to match their multi-coloured plumages and others described after their fieldmarks or habitat preferences. There were Common Yellowthroat and Black-throated Blue, Black-throated Green and Chestnut-sided Warblers. There were also Palm and Myrtle Warblers and Northern Waterthrush. Best of all was the monochrome Black-and-white Warbler, which Bill christened the 'Creeping Zebra Warbler.' When added to a supporting cast of four thrush species, three different flycatchers, five sparrows, two wrens, three vireos, tanagers, orioles, Sharp-shinned Hawk and Green Heron, Bill had not only written one of the steller chapters of the book, he had initiated me into the world of Nearctic birding. I dreamed of working my way through the Central Park's notorious Ramble – the overgrown shrubbery where good birds and bad people lurked – and sampling the delights of a spring dawn among the open lawns and towering maples and willows. It would take a decade for me to arrive in the Big Apple but it would be worth the wait.

The growing popularity of birding through the mid-1980s and into the 1990s has seen Bill become the smiling face of the pastime while his dulcet tones have provided the voice-overs for countless television commercials. It is a combination that has propelled him into superstar status among the birding community. No Bird Fair is complete without seeing Bill's distinctive form moving around the marquees or orchestrating proceedings at the celebrity game shows. His quick wit and eclectic bird knowledge make him the perfect compère for such events, but I have always wondered how he feels when he tries to mooch around the stands as nondescriptly as possible and every step is greeted with whispers and murmurs of 'There's Bill Oddie...' or 'Go on, you ask for his autograph.'

Although I got to meet Bill regularly at bird-related functions, I always sensed that I was a bit of an encumbrance. Perhaps he had heard me telling my children 'there's Bill Oddie, go and ask for his autograph' whenever I spotted him moving through the crowds. I cannot help myself. It's something, as a so-called trained people-spotter, that I am supposed to do. The cult of fame dominates the national press and invariably rubs off on its protagonists. Many a time I have been left star-struck with eyes bulging like some celebrity stalker after spotting the likes of Rod Stewart holidaying in Sicily or Paul McCartney carrying Christmas presents in London's West End. Indeed, my list of star 'ticks' well outnumbers my British birding life list. The Queen, Pope Benedict, Prince Charles, Princess Diana, Tony Blair, Margaret Thatcher, Sir David Attenborough, several Hollywood superstars, countless celebrity A-listers and more footballers than you can sign in the transfer window feature on my human checklist. Some I have chatted to, a few have honoured me with full-blown interviews, many were simply gawped at like I was a besotted teenager. Bill was always regarded as a good tick whenever and wherever I spotted him.

This slavish devotion to bathing in the reflected glory of others' fame must have left a bad impression when I finally got to meet Bill properly in the spring of 1998. Stephen Moss, director and producer of the *Birding with Bill Oddie* series, had invited me to join his crew on their quest to film the fascinating Neotropical delights of Trinidad and neighbouring Tobago. Phil Walker, the Editor on the *Daily Star*, had recently returned from the islands full of tales of colourful hummingbirds, tanagers and trogons, and he was willing to pay my expenses to join the BBC team (TV licence payers please note) if I wrote a feature about the trip. I needed no persuasion and met up with Stephen, Bill and the rest of crew at Gatwick. The moment I shook hands with Bill I sensed unease. Who could blame him? The idea of a Fleet Street journalist joining a BBC crew to write a sort of fly-on-the-wall, or should that be flycatcher-on-the-wall, feature about the making a television programme must be disturbing for TV folk. Newspapers rarely, if ever, return the compliment. That's why you never see documentaries about newsrooms.

So there we were. Me feeling uncomfortable because I felt that I was making Bill feel uncomfortable. Airport departure lounge small talk soon turned into awkward silence. Bill read a copy of *Mojo* – music of jazz origin – magazine and I crammed up on the islands' specialities in Richard Ffrench's *Guide to the Birds of Trinidad and Tobago*. Catching up with lost sleep, taking in a few in-flight movies and lots more field guide-cramming saw the flight literally fly by. Before I reached the songbird section, our flight was preparing for touchdown. Arriving at a foreign airport, particularly at a tropical location, is always an exciting time for the travelling birder. Well, once the baggage carousel has done its job and produced your suitcase with the lock intact. Outside, hirundines and swifts patrolled the early evening airspace, flying too high and too fast to make any positive identification in the fading light, especially with tired eyes and without binoculars. It only whetted my appetite for a spot of pre-breakfast birding the next morning around our base at the Pax Guest House on Mount St Benedict, where the BBC crew would be focussing on the plethora of hummingbirds attracted to the gardens.

With my body-clock out of sync and the cacophony of a tropical dawn chorus rippling through the guest house, I was up, showered and itching to walk around the grounds while it was still pitch black outside. For the first hour I had to make do with focussing my scope on the yellowish glow of Saturn, and in the pollution-free atmosphere high on a Trinidadian hillside, the planet's wonderful rings could be seen in all their glory. The distraction passed the time long enough for the first rays of sunshine to peek over the eastern horizon and for invisible bird shapes to begin morphing into silhouettes. Silhouettes they might just as well have remained. Even with the intense field guide cramming, I found the first hour or so completely confusing. Not only was I birding in a new country, but I had awoken in the planet's most diverse eco-zone to be confronted by an incredible range of new genera, new families and even new orders. Until you get a hook on a bird's jizz and also a few diagnostic field marks, identifying individual species can be a Herculean challenge. Walking round trying to multi-task by holding a field guide and sketching field notes with one hand and then holding binoculars in the other, it seemed that every bird I noted became the avian equivalent of a matchstick man with pointers to key identification features. One thing soon became clear: most of the dawn chorus overtures were coming from bright, sulphur-yellow thrush-size birds with distinctive black and white head-markings that appeared to be stationed on every available vantage point. Their rasping *kisskadee, kisskadeeeee* calls were a clue – they were Great Kiskadees, a tyrant flycatcher that breeds from South America across Central America and as far north as Texas. As daylight increased, another call began competing for dominance across the hillside. At first the shrill noise reminded me of a recently toilet-trained puppy desperate to relieve itself outside the house, but soon the source was traced to a fruiting tree where rival flocks of Orange-winged Parrots appeared to be squabbling over squatters' rights. They were my first wild parrots, not counting, of course, the garrulous Ring-necked Parakeets that have taken over most of west London and, for all their brilliant green finery, add little of the tropics to places like Chiswick, Roehampton and North Sheen. If you want to enjoy the incredible social interactions of the Psittacidae, do it somewhere hot and sunny. Parrots in Trinidad sure beat parakeets in Twickenham. With temperatures beginning to warm, buzzy hummingbirds began taking to the wing. The first Black Vultures started circling ominously overhead and the Bananaquits came out to play. Within seconds of seeing my first, it was obvious that they would become the most ubiquitous species on the island, a sort of cheeky sparrow but with Caribbean clothing, all bright yellows and greens and with a fine, decurved bill for sampling nectar.

Talking of Bills, another one came into view as I was trying to make out a vireo working its way through some dense foliage. Like me, Bill Oddie had also been keen to get some pre-breakfast birding in before the day's work filming began. It was obvious straightaway that he was a proper birder. He was performing the same balancing act – juggling a notebook that appeared to already hold a sizeable list of carefully sketched sightings and a pair of top-of-the-range binoculars. We exchanged morning pleasantries and spoke of our mutual enthusiasm about the quality of the birds around the Pax Guest House. The rest of that initial conversation is lost in the fog of time but, as with any two birders who meet and appear to be walking in the same direction, we joined forces and began pointing out bird movement overhead or in the hillside vegetation. Blue-grey and Palm Tanagers along with tiny Ruddy Ground Doves were duly picked out and written down in our respective notebooks. We enthused together about the wonderful velvety crimson tones of male Silver-beaked Tanagers and brilliant Yellow Orioles. Then it happened. Something brown and mouse-like flitted on to a dead snag deep in the under-storey. It reminded me of a Treecreeper in terms of size and colour tones, but was more upright in shape. The mystery bird turned, exposing the same distinctive upturned bill I had seen in the field guide.

'Bill, I've got something,' I called. 'Up there, on that exposed branch... I think it's a Streaked Xenops.' Bill got into position and got straight on to the bird. I glanced sideways and could see he was downloading its features.

'See its bill, er, Bill,' I hesitated. 'It's upturned, a bit like a Black-necked Grebe.'

Bill nodded his agreement and continued to take in details until the xenops vanished. As he began to make notes, I pulled out my field guide and showed him the picture.

'Well done,' he said. 'That's it. Definitely. Good bird, Stuart.'

I must have blushed the same colour as a Silver-beaked Tanager. Bill Oddie was congratulating me on finding a bird. Me! I could feel the warm glow of pride racing through my veins. Not only that, I suddenly sensed Bill's immediate acceptance of me as a birder. The slight air of unease I felt from him had vanished. Over the next hour or so our conversation was dictated by the birds we found and identified together. A Little Tinamou, a furtive ground-feeding bird that belongs to one of the most ancient living bird groups, was another good find that helped me underscore my birding credentials. There was nothing Bill needed to do to prove to me that he really is a top-notch birder.

Watching Bill find, analyse, identify and record birds in his notebook was textbook birding at the highest level. He gave me a master class lesson in vireo identification when I called a Red-eyed Vireo and he explained how it was the local *chivi* race, which is still regarded as a full species, Chivi Vireo, in some books. By the time our pre-breakfast walk had come to an end, I felt I was talking to a long-lost birding buddy, a feeling reinforced when he asked if I would like to meet up again the next morning.

After breakfast, work began for Bill. The production team had drawn up a tight itinerary to allow filming at Trinidad's eclectic array of habitats, ranging from the coastal mudflats at Waterloo to the spectacular views from the colonial veranda of the Asa Wright Nature Centre. As a casual observer and self-appointed 'bird finder' for the team, my job was a cinch, but for Bill there was the onerous task of making sure every scene got the approval of director/producer Stephen Moss and had plenty of birds, lots of action and faultless commentary. Watching Bill at work without ever needing a second take was as much a master class in television presentation as his earlier lesson was on vireo ID.

Over the following days I enjoyed some of the best birding of my life. Each morning would begin by meeting up outside the guesthouse and then walking circuits around Mount St Benedict. Our list brimmed with birds as colourful as their names: Golden-fronted Greenlet, Violaceous Euphonia and Blue Dacnis, to name a few. No walk was complete without spending time watching the manic comings-and-goings at the bird feeders. Here, the incredible Tufted Coquette, one of the world's smallest hummingbirds, would always grab our attention whenever it zoomed into view, choosing its moment carefully so that it could feed alongside bulkier species. Although dwarfed by the deliciously named Black-throated Mangos and White-necked Jacobins, the tiny coquette, with its rusty head-dress and gorgeous cheek plumes, never seemed fazed and simply zipped in, filled up on sugar water and then vanished in a blink. One evening, the crew descended on the famous Caroni Swamp by boat. Bill travelled alone with the guide while the production team followed behind, filming as his boat meandered through the dense mangrove forest. There was time to pick out a well-camouflaged Common Potoo and a sleepy Tree Boa coiled around a branch before we came to arguably the highlight of the entire shoot. The boatman positioned us so that the crew could film Bill from a distance as the swamp's most famous residents came in to roost. We did not have to wait long in the fading light until the first Scarlet Ibis came into view like a flying neon light. In the gloom, its vermilion plumage seemed to be powered by electricity and as hundreds more birds arrived, the scene took on the aura of the Las Vegas Strip at night. The experience must rank as one of the top ten things for any birder to do before they die and would have stolen the show had it not been for the next shoot. It was time for me to play Bill Oddie's body double.

The following article was written upon my return to London and published when the Trinidad and Tobago episode of *Birding with Bill Oddie* was broadcast a few months later. Hopefully, it not only encouraged readers to watch the programme but also gave a little insight into the making of a wildlife documentary and revealed what a hard-working and professional troubadour Bill really is:

Bill Oddie's face, reddened by the sun, glossed with sweat and tormented by pain began tensing with frustration. The tropical humidity deep in the rainforest and a nagging shoulder injury were bearable; Bill's irritation was about a film shoot going awry.

Deep below the towering hardwood giants, light was fading. The camera was in place, the sound was rolling but he had not seen his quarry. Bill, comic actor cum serious birder, had been brought to this secret place, Trinidad's very own Jurassic Park, to witness one of nature's eeriest spectacles – a nesting colony of Oilbirds in a dark, damp subterranean cavern.

This was to be the highlight of his new TV series for the BBC, a pilgrimage to see a bird so mythical and magical that its banshee cries and phantom wings have haunted Man throughout the ages. The film crew had gone on ahead and their hi-tech video camera peered out of the gloom watching Bill make his way down the meandering track towards the gaping hole in the rock face.

Cut! Director Stephen Moss wasn't happy. Neither was Bill. An over-officious guide was turning Bill's quest into a glorified tourist outing. It was more like a school trip to an oil refinery than a historic quest to see one of the world's most sought after birds. As the afternoon sun began sliding towards the west horizon, its fading light fragmented by the jungle canopy, the TV crew worked even harder than the forest floor ants to get their shots. The camera rolled once more. Bill picked his way through the tangle of roots and over the rocky slabs that littered the fast-flowing stream spewing into the cave.

From my watchpoint, I could see Bill commentating on his progress and Stephen nodding his approval. Minutes later, the team emerged smiling: a job well done. I will not give anything away but the Oilbird sequences will be among the highlights when the programme is shown tonight.

When it comes to colour, spectacle and sheer quality, any birdwatcher could do no better than visit the Caribbean islands of Trinidad and Tobago. Families like antbirds, woodcreepers, hummingbirds, trogons and parrots are all represented there. Then there are the Oilbirds – one of the bird world's oddities: nocturnal, fruit-eating and classified in a family of their own, they look like buzzard-sized nightjars with a 42-inch wingspan and shrill cry to curdle the blood: perfect television material.

What my article omitted was the part I played in this key sequence, and not so much because of my screen presence or acting skills, but because Bill is a proper birder. The production team could have easily settled for some clichéd film angles, following Bill and his guide as they entered the dark, forbidding cave and then using some archive material of the Oilbirds at rest. Not the BBC's innovative Natural History Unit and not Bill. The team wanted to capture Bill's emotions at that supreme moment when he finally got to see a new, iconic bird. Every birder knows that warm sense of joy and satisfaction when a quest is accomplished and a new bird finally encountered. Filming Bill at that precise moment inside the cave meant getting camera angles just so, a job easier said than done in a deep cave with a treacherous, guano-covered floor. One problem was that Bill did not want to mislead the viewers. If he was going to be filmed seeing the Oilbirds for the first time, he did not want to go into the cave before the shoot. Enter stage right, yours truly.

Stephen Moss suggested that I could play Bill, picking my way through the entrance boulders and down the precipitous throat of the cave so that the crew could experiment with lighting, sound and the position they wanted Bill to stand when he made his grand entrance. A half-dozen or so takes later and I was left feeling as shattered as Bill.

Walking repeatedly in and out of the cave had been arduous work but at least the cameras were ready for Bill. Action! The scene went like a dream. One take, one delighted Bill, and lots of red-eyed screeching Oilbirds. It was to prove the highlight of the programme. Of course, the footage of me entering into the cave ended on the cutting room floor. Being a few inches taller than Bill and, in those days a little slimmer, there was never a chance that viewers would be misled with second best. Anyway Bill's entrance was all the more sedate. He never got splattered with Oilbird poo when he walked in!

When I returned to the UK many birding and non-birding friends and colleagues were intrigued to find out what it was like travelling with Bill. I think it's fair to say that he did have a bit of a reputation in those days for being a 'grumpy middle-aged man', to use his words, and people love to hear juicy gossip, particularly about celebrities. Throughout the trip to Trinidad I was patently aware that I was a guest and that as a Fleet Street hack I might find some of the production team uncomfortable about my presence. To that end, I tried to constrain most of my conversations over dinner or during down periods to the subject of birds, particularly when speaking to Bill. Picking out the Streaked Xenops certainly helped to enhance my credibility with him and we continued our early morning birding sessions throughout the assignment. That said, before travelling with Bill, my impression was of someone who did not suffer fools lightly and, being someone who puts silliness and triviality high on the a genda, I always thought he felt I was a bit of an uncouth, talkative idiot. Years later, reading Bill's deeply touching and insightful autobiography, *One Flew into the Cuckoo's Egg*, my mind was put to rest. He wrote:

> Somebody once said about me, 'He doesn't suffer fools gladly.' That really upset me. I hate that word 'fools'. It's a horrible, cruel word. People aren't fools. I honestly have never thought of anyone I've known or worked with as a fool, but I fear there have been times when I have made someone feel like one. I don't mean to.

Lee Evans – my part in his Legend

Jealousy is the tribute mediocrity pays to genius.
—Fulton J. Sheen (American Roman Catholic bishop and broadcaster).

Genius is an overworked tabloid cliché. Any day you can pick up a newspaper and read about so-called football geniuses, musical geniuses or even child geniuses capable of using the TV remote and getting top marks on a PlayStation before they can walk or talk. There are animal geniuses, too: dogs that can moonwalk or juggle get more than their fair share of column inches in the national press, and it seems as if every other budgerigar can recite the national anthem backwards. While dictionaries describe a genius as 'somebody whose intellectual or creative achievements gain worldwide recognition', I much prefer the following definition: a talented person is someone who can do something ordinary people find difficult; a genius can do things a talented person finds impossible. Using this criterion, I have basked in the glow of meeting three true geniuses. The first was a schoolboy footballer whose skills and technique were so sublime that he could almost make the ball talk. Godfrey Ingram was playing in our under-16 team when he was 13 and went on to captain England Schools. One performance against the German youth team left the national team coach, Helmut Schoen, describing Godfrey as 'the next Pelé'. It was strangely prophetic. Although Godfrey never went on to play for the full England team, nor, in truth, a major top class European club, he did join the New York Cosmos in the mid-1970s and appeared alongside side such *galácticos* as Franz Beckenbauer, Johan Neeskens, Carlos Alberto and Pelé himself.

The second person who has always had the ability to astound me with acts of pure genius is Alastair Campbell, king of the spin-doctors and one of the most influential non-politicians in modern politics. Campbell's behind the scenes activities during Tony Blair's occupancy of Downing Street is writ large in the annals of modern British history, but what many people do not realise is that he really is a brilliant, no a genius, journalist. As a Fleet Street greenhorn, I sat close to him on Eddie Shah's revolutionary *Today* newspaper and would frequently be left spellbound at his ability to pick up a telephone, make a couple of calls, and produce a hard-hitting front-page story as first edition deadlines dawned. His contacts book was the envy of the office; his ability to craft a story masterful.

So who is the third genius? A scientist, perhaps, or an astrophysicist? Or what about one of those geeky technocrats who's made a few billion dollars designing a computer operating system that allows you to buy things online that you never really wanted? No, it is someone who goes birding rather a lot.

Mention the name 'Lee' and everybody who has ever travelled to see a rare bird will know who you mean without having to allude to a surname. This is normally something you can only do with Popes and Royalty. Elizabeth, Benedict, John Paul, Charles – we know immediately who they are. Think of Tony and Gordon and you could be talking about ladies' hairdressers. Harriet and Jacqui sound like a couple of drag queens. Even 'call me Dave' Cameron needs the Cameron bit for a proper introduction. Yet when you are talking about birding and Lee's name crops up there is never a need to mention the Evans bit.

If Bill Oddie is the most famous birder known to the public at large, then Lee Geoffrey Richard Evans is the best-known among the greater birding community. Over five decades he has grown from an enthusiastic schoolboy traipsing around sewage farms and watching Sand Martins at the RSPB's headquarters in Sandy, Bedfordshire, to become a one-man birding industry. He is controversial. Disliked by some and envied by many. He can irritate and infuriate. He can make even the most dedicated birders question whether they want to pick up their binoculars again if they dare to clash with him over a subject dear to his heart. He will take on the big boys of the RSPB and argue against government policy, and woe betide anyone who questions one of his identifications. Worse still, doubt one of his records and you will be up before the self-styled 'judge, jury and executioner' of British birding before you can say Slender-billed Curlew at Druridge Bay. He also has a fan club of those he has encouraged, nurtured, assisted in the field or simply pointed out good birds to during his long birding career. I am one of them. I am also lucky to have played a small part in the legend that is Lee Evans.

If by chance you are one of the few birdwatchers who has never heard of Lee – you may have been ringing on some South Pacific island since the early 1980s – then this will do as a potted field description:

Plumage: Lee has never been one of the green Barbour birding brigade. I have seen him in the field in suits (usually light-coloured), smart jackets and cagoules that looked far too flimsy for the weather conditions. A picture of him wearing a hip navy blue shell-suit with accompanying gold neck chain and labelled 'Ali Lee' has become one of modern birding's iconic images. Without a doubt his taste for certain fashion accessories is questionable. He has a penchant for white socks and has been known to wear a dangly earring. He lost an eye in a dreadful road accident in 1978.

Food: Never been seen to eat. Still incredibly trim for someone reaching middle age. October 2010 marks his 50th birthday. Food appears to be an unnecessary hindrance between driving to see a bird and then watching it. His long-term partner Carmel says he likes pizzas.

Behaviour: Obsessive. Lee is the living embodiment of the word fanatic. Some may say he lives, sleeps and eats birds. That would be wrong. He does not have time to eat or sleep.

Range: Anywhere with birds.

Migration: Lee travels more in a year than the average Arctic Tern.
He drives up to 63,000 miles in the UK alone and then there are
his foreign adventures, which add another 20,000 miles to his
gallivanting. His lifetime milometer must be close to clocking up
three million miles. He must have covered more square inches of
British soil than anyone in history and his passport has the look of
a modern Alan Whicker. He has seen more species in the Western
Palearctic than any living birder and has also found time to go
birding in Asia, North and Central America and Africa. The
incredible riches of South America await his arrival.

Vocalisations: Once quoted as saying: 'Birders are very sad really. They
include an assortment of weirdoes in cagoules and many drop-outs
from mainstream society. I can hardly talk, though, as you know
you are obsessive and have lost the plot when equally obsessive
individuals think that you are mad!'

Social behaviour: See below.

My first memory of Lee was pre-Christmas 1980. I was popping into
Luton town centre to do some errands. He was sitting in his Vauxhall
Cavalier Sportshatch, bedecked with birding car stickers and sun-strip,
as was the fashion of the day, waiting to pick up some friends *en route*
to see a Lesser White-fronted Goose at Slimbridge. The engine
was roaring. People were looking. The idea of not having family
commitments and racing across the country seemed so romantic. My
birding at the time was confined to RSPB weekend coach trips; here
was this young free spirit about to see a bird I had only seen in a field
guide. I felt jealous, an emotion that no doubt many birders have felt
when dealing with Lee over the years. That I knew Lee, or at least his
car, said something about his reputation within the local birding scene
when he was barely out of his teens. I am sure our paths must have
crossed in our youth as we both lived in south Bedfordshire and shared
the same mentor – Baz Harding – as well as both having what
amounted to unofficial season tickets at Dunstable Sewage Farm.
Surely, being a couple of years older, I never dismissed him as a
whippersnapper?

As my birding renaissance took shape in the early 1980s, so chance
encounters with Lee became more regular. Whenever a bird of any note
turned up in our home county of Bedfordshire, the best way to find it

was to look for Lee's car. As a Vauxhall design stylist, his vehicles were always the snazziest in Luton: bright colours; lots of racy extras, just the thing to look out for when driving down a country lane looking for an entrance into a wood or clay pit to track down some unusual finch or wader. That Lee would be at the site ahead of the Bedfordshire birding posse was an accepted fact. Even during in the early days of his twitching career, he was well connected into the national grapevine and it seemed that every bit of local gen would go through him before reaching the outside world. Indeed, if ever you wanted to know what was happening in the county, a call to his charming grandmother was the best way to find out.

'Lee's not here at the moment,' she would explain sweetly. 'He's gone to Tring to see a....'

Sometimes she got the bird names wrong, sometimes she came up with some really comical ones – I seem to remember she always had trouble pronouncing merganser – but Lee's Granny Win was only too willing to read out what was on the telephone pad to help others follow in his wake during those halcyon days before mobile phones and pagers. One such chase for a local rarity created the only conflict I have had with him. A Rough-legged Buzzard had taken up winter residence on Bedfordshire's Green Sand Ridge but was proving extremely elusive. The only way to see it was by trespassing. A bit of discreet hedge-jumping and barbed-wire fence limbo dancing duly brought the spectacular raptor into view. For me, the sight of the buzzard with its dark belly and distinctive tail pattern soaring elegantly over a pheasant shoot was worth any gamekeeper's wrath. As it was, I got two barrels from Lee. He was furious that I had trespassed. I stood my ground. I had trespassed on more sensitive sites in my duty as a member of Her Majesty's Press. Sneaking into a game copse was small fry compared to country estates owned by notorious East End villains. Lee and I went our separate ways mumbling rebukes, but within a week or so I was back in his slipstream looking for another rare bird and there was no mention of our tiff. Lee, I had learned, does not harbour grudges.

The promise of a career in Fleet Street, fatherhood, a hefty mortgage and all the other chains espoused in Jean-Jacques Rousseau's *The Social Contract* kept my birding well and truly fettered during the 1980s and into the 1990s. Lee's single-mindedness saw him enter the *Guinness Book of Records*. A determined, resolute mindset to keep ahead of the pack saw him give up his well-paid job and become a 'professional' birder. He also sampled life as a married man, albeit for a few months. His romantic misfortunes left *The Sun* with a scoop on its world famous Page Three, next to a topless beauty and under the headline: 'Birdwatch Champ's wife has flown.' How I felt sorry for Lee as I read how he had been ditched by his wife of 18 months because he was always chasing birds – feathered ones. Lee reportedly told *The Sun*:

> I think it's best for her to go. Being married has made me miss four rare birds. When the Philadelphia Vireo landed in Ireland I was trapped on the Scilly Isles with my wife. I'm totally obsessed by birds. If I don't get out and about looking for species I get withdrawal symptoms. I start twitching. I feel quite ill. She put up with me before we married. It's only since then that things have gone downhill.'

The article went on to say that the final straw came when Lee headed off to the Shetland Isles on successive weekends to see a Brünnich's Guillemot – only to find that the bird had flown. What impact the story had on Lee is something he has never spoken to me about.

The same year as his marriage breakdown also heralded another major change in his life. He left Vauxhall Motors to become a full-time birder. As Lee's professional birding career was taking off, my leisure time with binoculars was being forever squeezed between domestic duties and covering Old Bailey trials and the murky world of south London contract killings. For Lee, it meant being at the forefront of the birding information revolution. Premium rate phone lines broadcasting up-to-the-minute details of rare birds opened up twitching to the masses. No longer did you have to wait for someone to answer the telephone at Nancy's café or ingratiate yourself into the well-informed elite. One quick call to 0891 numbers and you could plan your next birding adventure. Lee joined Richard and Hazel Millington, Steve Gantlett and Roy Robinson to give the world 24/7 birding news at the touch of the telephone pad. There was not a serious birder in the country who did not know the hotline number and no excursion into the field could be chanced without having a pocketful of loose change to call from public telephone boxes.

'This is Birdline ...' Richard Millington would speak with the gravitas of a prime minister addressing the nation. Listening on the other end of the line the anticipation was electric. Had a new bird turned up? Was that long-stayer staying put? I must have pumped money into their coffers like an unlucky machine player in a Las Vegas casino. More often or not, I never had the time or inclination to see the birds being mentioned but there was something comforting to know that I knew they were there. No doubt Lee was watching them. At my expense!

The late 1980s also saw another major change in Lee's life. He met Carmel Pentecost. Hearing that Lee had found a 'new bird' had my news sense alarms blaring. The thought that Lee, a free spirit whose previous relationship had made the tabloids, had found love needed investigating. By now I was crime correspondent on the *News of the World*, but after hearing a summary of Lee's birding veritables and the suggestion that he had met someone who understood his birding passion was soul music for the news editor. He dispatched me to get the first interview. The final published article failed to do the story justice. A few paragraphs on a back of the book page of the paper affectionately known as 'The Screws' hardly touched the surface of the story Lee and Carmel had told me at their home in Buckinghamshire. But of all the articles I've written about Lee over the years, and for all its hackneyed puns, it is my favourite. It shows that deep within the genius there is an ordinary bloke. The article appeared in the *News of the World* in January 1989 under the headline 'Lee has a birdie to warm his nest'. It read:

Eagle-eyed Lee Evans is crowing over the new bird he has added to his record-breaking list. For Britain's undisputed bird-watching champ – his wife divorced him because of his obsession – has found a new partner for his lovenest. No longer does Lee, 28, have to worry about being hen-pecked when he flies off at the crack of dawn, because new love Carmel Pentecost is a birdwatcher, too.

Carmel said: 'We met in a nightclub. I thought he was a nice guy, but all his conversation was about birds. Our first date was birdwatching in Norfolk and Suffolk. While most couples go to restaurants, Lee takes me birdwatching – roughing it together in his car.'

Lee commented: 'My relationship with Carmel is good for me – and good for her. I can't survive without a woman. I need warmth and love.'

It all seems so terribly clichéd today but tabloid writing styles during the 1980s relied on puns and corn. Anyway, since that article, Lee's name has rarely been out of the news. Women's magazines, television documentaries, national and local newspapers and, of course, the birding press have profiled him, and reviled him, frequently. My own cuttings book is filled with stories about his adventures, his publications and his spats. His highly publicised contretemps with fellow twitchers Steve Webb and Adrian Riley have been a headline writer's dream. Who cannot resist lines like 'feathers are flying' when reporting on the rivalries between Lee and those who want to knock him off his perch. My review of Adrian Riley's now infamous 'Clash of the Titans' with Lee, as detailed in *Arrivals and Rivals: a Birding Oddity*, may give a hint at the lengths to which twitchers will go in order to claim records and the depths to which they will descend to when things go wrong:

If George Bernard Shaw had been a birdwatcher, you can imagine his views on twitching. In his Irish brogue, the great man would have mused about those lucky enough to have the time and money to chase rare birds – and wish them all the best. Twitchers are the SAS shock troops of the birding world. They are brash, single-minded and purpose-driven, sometimes to a fault. Non-twitchers love to criticise them, and recant tales of how they turn up at the location of a rare bird after a marathon drive and then spend a mere few minutes looking at their quarry before dashing off to the next sighting. Step forward Adrian Riley to put the case for the defence. Adrian would have won the admiration of old GBS in the way he put aside all the normal constraints of modern living to follow a dream that saw him entering the record books by spotting the most British birds in 2002.

With the support of his voluntary retirement package, an understanding wife, a healthy supply of caffeine and a Ford Escort that proved more reliable than Captain Kirk's Enterprise, Adrian crammed 380 species into a 12-month twitching marathon. It was a task of Herculean proportions that took him from the sublime Isles of Scilly to the storm-lashed outposts of the Shetlands. The expense and effort have now finally been revealed in a book titled *Arrivals and Rivals: a Birding Oddity*. The arrivals part is pretty straightforward. In short, these are the waifs, strays and mega-rarities that make Britain arguably the most exciting place to watch birds on Earth. Adrian's quest saw him spot more birds in 12 months than most keen birdwatchers see in a lifetime. His beloved car ended up with an extra 78,000 miles on the clock and his bank balance was £8,000 worse off, but his log reads like a birdwatcher's wish list. There was the strangely named Bobolink from across the Atlantic; a Sardinian Warbler from the Mediterranean; a Siberian Chiffchaff from Russia; a Two-barred Crossbill from the Finnish forests and an Ivory Gull from the polar ice floes.

While the romance of Adrian's quest is highly readable, it is the Rivals part that makes it so addictive. The way his friendship with Lee Evans – not the comedian, Britain's most fanatical rarity-chaser – degenerates into what amounts to contempt is the real driving force of a very entertaining book that will appeal to birdwatchers everywhere. Even non-birders who question what makes grown men sacrifice so much for often a fleeting glimpse of a bird as it flies away will find many of their questions answered.

Sunday Express, 12 June 2005.

The following month, this review appeared in *Bird Watching* magazine under my name.

Year-listing – seeing as many species of birds as possible in 12 calendar months – is arguably the most futile twitching activity. Building geographical lists – a local patch, national or international levels – is one thing, staking out the likes of Mandarin on duck ponds or Ring-necked Parakeet in west London during the first weeks of January is Sad with a capital S. This said, there is an ever-growing army of the un-dead ready to become willing zombies for this annual pursuit.

Since what seems like the dawn of time, Lee Evans has been the undisputed King of the Year-listers, performing Herculean feats to remain one step ahead of all-comers. But when challengers do throw down the gauntlet expect binocular cases at 30 paces. Adrian Riley's account of how he took on Lee Evans in the 2002 year-listing marathon reveals not only the insignificance and worthlessness of this achievement, but also questions the sanity of its exponents. It also makes fantastic reading.

Arrivals and Rivals: a Birding Oddity is the title of Riley's addictive and highly enjoyable book, which charts his 78,000 mile odyssey along the highways and byways of the British Isles to see an incredible 380 species… and costing him the princely sum of £8,000. Each bird has a story, some more than others. On occasions he risked life if not limb to get his tick. Whether it was suffering near hypothermia in the Shetlands or facing the wrath of Ireland's Garda, Riley's account of how he clocked up his 'arrivals' – the rarities that willingly succumbed to his checklist – makes great bedside reading.

It's the stories of his run-ins with rival Lee Evans, however, that make this book a must-buy. To read how a birding friendship degenerates to the point where libel lawyers are consulted is far more interesting than travelling to Bedfordshire to see Lady Amherst's Pheasant. The irony of ironies is that when Riley finally claims the crown which list does he use? – the one drawn up by Lee Evans' own UK 400 Club! Mmm...

Yes, controversy courts Lee. And he loves it. I love seeing him in full flow, too. No email newsgroup is complete without Lee pontificating his views. Woe betide anyone who challenges him – even if they are sure of their facts. I've learned my lesson. These days I prefer to light the blue touch paper of debate and retire before the fireworks explode. A wonderful opportunity to play agent provocateur arose at the 2009 Bird Fair when I was invited to attend a drinks reception to mark the early successes of the Great Bustard project by the RSPB's Director of Conservation, Mark Avery. It is fair to say that Lee does not like the idea of introducing one of the world's heaviest flying birds to Salisbury Plain. Another RSPB-supported operation – the culling of Ruddy Ducks in the UK – is also one of his biggest bugbears. The temptation was just too great.

'Hi Lee, I'd like to introduce you to Dr Avery of the RSPB.' I may as well have been announcing the contestants of *Celebrity Death Match*. There stood Mark, six-foot-plus and tipping the scales as a super-heavyweight, and Lee in his pinstripe jacket and hurling factoids about the waste of resources in preserving an extinct species or attempting to eradicate another as if they were left-hand jabs. Mark bobbed and weaved and landed blows for accepted scientific practice. The debate raged for an hour before the tent was cleared and the pugilists retired to their respective corners without conceding a point. It was pure theatre.

Looking back at my friendship with Lee, it has been more one of mutual respect and information exchange rather than as birding buddies. Besides meeting him at twitches or seeing him birding in

Bedfordshire and on Scilly, two of his favourite venues, most of our communications are by telephone or email. Before writing this chapter, I wanted to make one further attempt to try and understand what pushes him to see more than 350 species every year, clocking up thousands of miles and spending a small fortune in the process. I asked him to jump up on an imaginary psychotherapist's couch and answer a few questions. Here goes:

Me: You must have spent more time birding than anyone in history. How often do you go?

Lee: In an average week during the summer, I'll think nothing of actively birding 112 hours, that's a 16-hour a day. Even in winter I'll clock up 56 hours a week in the field.

Me: If that involves chasing rare birds, you must clock up a few miles driving?

Lee: Yes, I do. Pursuing rare vagrants and scarce migrants can see me driving anything between 48,000 and 63,000 miles in a year. When you add that to the additional 20,000 miles travelling across the wider Western Palearctic, it's fair to say that I am an obsessive individual.

Me: What do you mean by obsessive?

Lee: I think my passion and enthusiasm for birding is second to none. I literally live, breathe and sleep birds. I adore them, I love them. I suppose that when other really committed twitchers say I am mad about birds it means I have entered another dimension in terms of being obsessive. In addition to my commitment to all things listing, I have as perhaps the largest music collection in the UK. I have more than 90,000 recordings in a variety of formats including virtually every Top 75 single between 1958 and 2009. Besides that, I have a skin and stuffed bird collection that a museum would be proud of and I also own a massive collection of toy cars, particularly Dinky, Corgi and Matchbox

Me: I bet you have good bird list then?

Lee: Over the years I have earned an endless number of accolades. In 1986 I achieved the record-breaking number of birds seen in Britain and Ireland during a year – 386 species. In addition to having seen a record number of species in the wider Western Palearctic with 854, I have also recorded the highest number of species in that region in a calendar year with 637.

My British list is a phenomenal 566 species, placing me sixth in the UK400 Club table. Besides that, I am in the Top 10 of virtually every individual county list in Britain. Besides this, I have personally found more than 250 official rarities in Britain and several more across the Western Palearctic.

Me: Do you have time for anything else?

Lee: I run very successful national birding organisations in the British Birding Association and UK400 Club, and I write and produce the weekly magazine *Rare News Weekly*. I have written over 28 books, including the highly acclaimed *Rare Birds in Britain 1800–1990* and the best-selling *Ultimate Site Guide to Scarcer British Birds*.

Me: All this must put your head above the parapet?

Lee: I suppose I am the 'mover and shaker' of British birding. I am certainly the most prolific writer by far on the Internet and also the most contentious. People have labelled me 'Judge, Jury and Executioner' on the subject of rare birds. The birding press have even described me as a 'legend in his own lifetime.'

The thing is, I am not fearful of any of my critics and I'll push them to the limit, even getting underneath their skin if needed. I never shy away from confrontation and I'll attack any organisations if a subject touches my heart, say as in the case of Ruddy Duck culling or the reintroduction of species such as Great Bustard and White-tailed Eagle in England.

Me: So what worries you about the state of the nation's birds?

Lee: I have serious concerns about the future of our nation's wildlife and I am forever harping on about the drastic reduction in numbers of common farmland birds. My main passion is the plight of the European Turtle Dove, but I'm also constantly highlighting the ever-decreasing populations of Willow Tit, Tree Sparrow, Corn Bunting, Grey Partridge, Yellowhammer and Spotted Flycatcher. These relatively ordinary birds are very dear to my heart.

Me: Why are you so combative?

Lee: There's no doubting my commitment to birdwatching, and underlying this is my struggle to ensure that birding records are accurate. Yes, I am totally obsessed with the meticulous recording of rare vagrants and scarce migrant birds in Britain and Ireland.

Me: But you do appreciate other birders?

Lee: Of course I do. I have a full commitment to others. I enjoy nurturing and training new birding companions and I spend countless hours trying to inform and teach contemporaries on the Internet. I often answer more than 50 individual email enquiries each day. To be honest, I love to see the excitement and passion birding creates in other like-minded individuals. I am always making every effort to ensure that birding is as memorable an event as possible.

Me: So what has been your favourite birding experience?

Lee: The undoubted highlight was seeing my very first Wallcreeper in Cheddar Gorge in Somerset back in the 1970s. To this day, I continue to pay homage to the species by annually taking parties to Les Baux in southern France, where up to four of these exquisite, butterfly-like birds spend the winter.

Me: I am going to describe you as a birding genius. What's your reaction?

Lee: Me, a genius? I wouldn't say so myself. Like everyone, I am on a learning curve and I delight in all the new experiences and challenges of every day. That said, I do revel in my work.

Me: So are there any birding geniuses out there?

Lee: Chris Heard is without doubt the most knowledgeable and able field observer in Britain, if not the world. His abilities are second-to-none and he has proven time and time again just why he deserves that accolade. He is a joy to be with and much of my excellence is a tribute to someone who has been one of my closest associates for over 30 years. Hardly a day goes by when the two of us do not discuss birds on the phone.

Killian Mullarney is in a league of his own, too. He's a fabulous artist, a meticulous note-taker and a talent of the highest grade, with the ability to teach and educate in a particularly charming way. I love him.

Me: What disappoints you most about modern birding?

Lee: Sadly, the hobby is being hijacked by non-professionals and birders like me are being pushed out and replaced by technology. I know I was at the forefront of modern birding with my association with the Bird Information Service but now I feel like my grasp on the hobby is slipping through my fingers.

One particular bone of contention is the question of birding apprenticeships. At one stage, any birder worth his salt would serve a 10-15 year apprenticeship working a local patch and visiting frequently the great birding destinations. In doing so, they would learn off by heart the identification and jizz of the 360 most common British and European birds. Sadly, this premise has been replaced by the pager culture, subsequently resulting in a drastic reduction in birding ability and experience.

My biggest disappointment, however, is seeing the continuing demise of the Isles of Scilly as an October destination for birders. This was once the highlight of the birding year and an event not to be missed at any cost. From 1974 through to 2005, I was a permanent fixture of a Scilly October, but in recent years the soaring cost of visiting the islands has alienated birders like me and priced us out of the market. What a travesty. There really is nothing like it in the British birding calendar. This is where relationships were born, where world trips were planned and where birding apprenticeships were sealed and approved.

Me: So Lee, you have been described as a legend, what part have I played in making you birding's most talked about figure?

Lee: We have always been close friends, mainly because of our grass-root connections as Luton-based boys and our equal commitment and enthusiasm for birding. Over the years our paths have crossed and with your connections with the media and my passion for notoriety, this has kept us in close contact. You have contributed in your own way, bringing birdwatching to the masses through feature-writing and your weekly newspaper column. You've championed the hobby on countless occasions and this has brought to the fore many of those controversial subjects that affect conservation. I think you provide an excellent platform for ideas.

So there you have it, that is my small part in the legend of Lee Evans.

End of a Scilly Love Affair

The heart was made to be broken.
—Oscar Wilde (1854–1900) – Poet, Novelist, Dramatist and Critic.

The elbow caught me under the ribs with all the guile and power of a Floyd Mayweather body shot, lifting me off my feet and leaving me gasping for breath. I never saw the blow coming, although I would feel its effects for days. Neither did I see who threw such a well-timed, cunningly placed blow but I would hazard a guess it was someone who had played some form of contact sport in their life, say a cage-fighter, bare-knuckle boxer or Sumo wrestler. Anyway, the owner of the stiletto sharp elbow was not the kind of person you would expect to be carrying binoculars and standing next to you on one of the Scilly Isles' most tranquil of walks. Lower Moors is a nature lover's dream. In autumn, the tangled sallows still have enough foliage to shade the meandering footpath and provide refuge for tired migrants. Firecrests and Chiffchaffs long for its dark cloak of respite after their intrepid seasonal flights. Birders like it too, particularly as real treasures can be found among the commoner birds. When they are, something like a Klondike gold rush ensues.

Friday 10 October 1997 is date permanently engraved on my heart and ribs. It was the day I got the elbow and the day I decided to give Scilly the elbow, too. Anyone who enjoys seeing a rare bird will accept that playing the waiting game is an occupational hazard. Furtive species, say ground-hugging *Locustella* warblers or skulking pipits, need time to work their way into the open. For twitchers, especially those with a degree of masochism running through their veins, spending an hour or so at a stake-out waiting for a bird to raise its head only adds to the piquancy of the occasion. Even I accept that a cat-and-mouse game with a potential new sighting only increases the drama. But queuing to see a bird? Queues are for supermarkets, football turnstiles and motorway pull-offs. The moment I took that elbow in my right flank I vowed never to stand in file for a rarity again, especially for one regarded as a 'trash bird' on its home turf.

Only in America could a bird the colour of a mouth-watering fried egg sunny-side up be dismissed as trash. The very phrase trash bird is one of those awful State-side contributions to the English language that sticks in the craw like a soggy burger. Yank birders use it all the time. House Sparrow, officially Red Listed in the United Kingdom, is a trash bird. The Starling, another Red List species in the UK, is equally dismissed as a piece of trash whenever it decides to lay down roots in a downtown block. Trash birds do not necessarily have to be illegal aliens from the Old World. Grackles are trash birds, as are American Crows. Blue Jays are trash on the East Coast; Scrub Jays are castigated on the Pacific West Coast. Decidedly attractive birds such as cardinals, mockingbirds, juncos and Mourning Doves get the trash treatment if they dare to become too numerous in any single locale. Even the stunning American Robin, with its red breast and beautifully liquid song, gets canned on occasions. But the decidedly beautiful Common Yellowthroat a trash bird? Surely not!

Take a walk with an American birder on their home patch, especially if it has a fetid ditch or dank patch of sedge or reeds decorated with detritus, and you can bet your last dollar that even the most forthcoming of yellowthroats will be, at best, dismissed without comment, or enthusiastically passed off as trash, even adult males with their striking 'bandit masks.' I've heard it many a time. Yellowthroats are found in all of Lower 48 states of the Union. From California to

Connecticut, from Maine to New Mexico they scramble about, singing their *wichety-witchety-witchety* love songs, which may attract mates but will rarely be applauded by any passing birder. Place one this side of the Atlantic, though, and hell is unleashed.

Hell had been unleashed. One birder's elbow had creased me in two, another birder's size 12 boots had committed GBH on my metatarsals, yet I was determined to keep my place in the queue. The yellowthroat was in view, albeit only the posterior; and I was not going to let two hours of waiting go to waste. How many birders were shoehorned into Lower Moors that morning, I will never know: dozens, scores, hundreds? Whatever the head count, every single observer was desperate to see the American warbler, only the seventh of its kind to make the crossing. Trash it may have been on its home sod, but here on the Scilly Isles it was being hailed as the 'Bird of the Year'. The pager system had been sounding non-stop bulletins announcing its presence for 24 hours, but pinning the blighter down in such dense habitat, especially a species instinctively at home in sedge banks and reedbeds, was creating pandemonium.

I was already 24 hours behind the chase. The Wednesday Club's now annual tour to Scilly had seen us spending the night in Penzance the previous evening, which had become something of a nail-chewing experience when the pager service went into overdrive announcing the yellowthroat's arrival. As soon as we landed that morning, we had dumped the luggage at our B&B and ran to Lower Moors ... only to find us running into a thick, green-clad wall of birders spread along the Porthloo end of the Lower Moors nature trail, the last known place where the bird had been seen. It was then that the shout went up: 'It's in here.' And so the crowd squeezed and squirmed, wriggled and writhed, on the narrowest of paths into the wood. The motion, the buffeting, reminded me of standing and swaying on the terraces at a 1970s football match. Tempers were held; gallows humour prevailed, but when people started to fall into ditches and cries of 'don't push' echoed, tensions rose. Another suppressed shout of 'there it is' heralded another surge and then came that agonising blow to my ribs as fellow birders clambered for better views. Winded and stamped on, I managed only the briefest of glimpses of the yellowthroat's yellowish backside before it vanished once more. As soon as the first rank of bodies pulled themselves out of the ditches, casting a few unrepeatable admonishments at those who had pushed themselves to the front, another shout went up. The yellowthroat had reappeared on the other side of Telegraph Road! Another melee ensued. Once again, there was more pushing and shoving as everyone rushed out of the wood and began scrambling up the roadside stonewalls to look for the bird. I joined what had now become a rolling maul until.... There it was: perched in brambles and glistening nonchalantly in the sunshine of a new morning, oblivious to the commotion it had caused, the yellowthroat was radiating its beautiful plumage tones in open view. Who cared if disingenuous Yanks describe Common Yellowthroats trash birds? The pain in my ribs eased slightly, my metatarsals stopped aching and the warm sensation of adding another tick to my list momentarily transported me to twitching's equivalent of the Elysian Fields. But it wasn't to be for long.

Forty-eight hours later another American wood warbler, this time a Blackpoll on neighbouring Tresco, had been duly seen, identified and then added to my tally of sightings, along with a sprinkling of other rarities which have become Scilly's stock-in-trade over the years. For some, the return in terms of rarities per pound spent travelling to Scilly in autumn 1997 had not been good value for money (an all-in-week's stay cost about £500). As I penned my regular weekly dispatch for the *Daily Star*, I was still flushed with the golden memories of the yellowthroat's sparkling tones, but something was beginning to irk. I wrote:

> Looking up a bird's backside while being elbowed and trodden on may not be everyone's idea of paradise. But for a split-second the buffeting was worthwhile as I added a prized sighting to my checklist. It had taken two hours before the massed crowd caught sight of a flash of brilliant yellow radiating from deep inside a willow bog. The apparition was greeted with a chorus of 'wows' from scores of assembled twitchers.
>
> They had flocked to the Isles of Scilly to see Britain's seventh-ever Common Yellowthroat – a North American warbler that had somehow managed to cross the Atlantic. On a footpath just wide enough for one person, it seemed that the entire population of British birdwatchers had gathered to pay homage to this rare vagrant. Despite packing ourselves together more tightly than English defenders in Rome, tempers only frayed occasionally and frontline humour prevailed as the birders muscled and bustled their way into better vantage points.

As the call went up that the bird was on view, I focused my binoculars on the only yellow object in sight. It turned out to be the yellowthroat's bottom, which was enough to claim a tick but hardly the view you want of one of the rarest birds ever to touch down this side of the Pond. Only later, when the bird turned round, could you see why early ornithologists came up with its name. The bird's throat shone like a fluorescent marker pen!

Sadly many birders had to fly home from Scilly without seeing the bird. For those who stayed there was a bonus. Another American wood warbler – this time a rather drab Blackpoll – turned up on nearby Tresco. This bird also proved elusive and I needed a three-hour wait spread over two days before I was finally rewarded with good views. Waiting so long for a rare bird can be frustrating, especially when you are based on the Isles of Scilly where there are all sorts of rarities waiting to be discovered.

For some reason, many of the goodies which you can normally bank on seeing there were a bit thin on the ground this autumn. Although I caught up with an American Golden Plover, Tawny Pipit, Wryneck, several Firecrests and the long-staying American Black Duck, many list 'padders' – scarce birds rather than official rarities – were missing. This may have something to do with last month's Indian summer, which meant that many birds made it to their normal wintering grounds without getting blown off course. Or perhaps I simply planned my annual trip too early. Those heading for Scilly next week may be in for a bumper time.

Readers may have been left thinking that I was somewhat ungrateful that week. Of course, I was enjoying a wonderful stay in some of the most beautiful landscapes that England has to offer: windswept St Agnes with its sweeping gorse-clad Wingletang Down and the quaint, tree-lined Barnaby Lane, a favourite resting place for tired wanderers from across the Atlantic; Tresco and its Great Pool, a great place to see rare water birds; and St Mary's, not only the 'capital' of the Scilly Isles, but of British birding too. Yet behind the newspaper story, I could feel myself falling out of love with a place which over the previous couple of years had turned me into an infatuated devotee. To use newspaper slang it was the 'back story', the bits that I failed to mention in my dispatch, which was playing heavily on my mind.

The rough-and-tumble at the yellowthroat site would certainly have appeared ungainly, perhaps uncouth, to any casual passer by, but not only did the vast majority of birders present get cracking views of the bird, they came away energised and delighted by the occasion. Yes, I could accept the 'skirmish of Lower Moors'; the experience was almost fun at times. It was the events that I witnessed at the Blackpoll twitch and later while enjoying a quiet pint with my friends at the island's Scillionian Club that left the taste of the bitter living up to its name.

The Blackpoll has an incredible autumn migration. In summer, its thin, high-pitched song whispers through the cool, wet conifer forests of Canada and Alaska. But as the days shorten the birds prepare for their long 8,000km flight south to the warmer climes of South America, with many spending the winter in Brazil. It is a perilous journey that has to be completed in one flight, an adventurous sweep out into the Atlantic to take advantage of the Earth's curvature and shorten the flying hours. Long wings and a powerful heart assist the Blackpoll, but if prevailing weather systems interrupt the migration birds can be sent hurtling eastwards. Many die at sea, and a small handful make landfall in Western Europe. The Scilly Isles are in a strategic position to receive America's tired and straggling Blackpolls and, since the first record in 1968, more than 20 have turned up, although as warbler populations crash in North America the number that arrive on this side of the Atlantic is in decline.

The day after the yellowthroat adventure came the news that an 'odd' *Dendroica* (the Blackpoll Warbler's genus) had been seen near Tresco's Abbey Crossroads. It sparked similar frenetic scenes of excitement. Our little group was in (black)pole position to take advantage of the bulletin. We had been looking at ducks on Tresco's Great Pool when an excited birder holding a CB radio whizzed past, screaming 'Yankee warbler...' We followed in a state of optimistic expectation. Three hours later, we were still waiting. The crowds had gathered as news buzzed across the archipelago. Although only a lucky few had seen the bird, it was close enough to confirm its overall olive tones, striking double wing-bars and straw-coloured legs – the key features of an autumn Blackpoll. Woodland clearings were searched, tree-after-tree forensically examined and every flicker of leaf movement was optimistically greeted with careful scrutiny by scores of binoculars, but without success. My attention span began to diminish. I had already seen plenty of Blackpolls in the United States and also a vagrant bird in East Sussex. Out of loyalty to my friends I continued to search for a tiny, Great Tit size bird in a wood the size of several football pitches, but eventually my perseverance began to wane and I mooched off in the fading light. We had dipped.

The thought of spending another half-day on a hopeless quest filled me with dread the next morning when the Blackpoll's continued presence was heralded on the pagers. We filed back, retreading our weary footsteps and took the boat back over to Tresco. This time a crowd of several hundred had squeezed into a narrow gateway where the bird had been seen earlier, bringing back instant memories of the yellowthroat crush. I somehow found myself being propelled to the front, while my pals were scattered in all directions. The wait began. My mind fluttered off to a scene from the film *Groundhog Day*, which explores the frustrating world of a news reporter trapped in a *déjà vu* nightmare. I was in one, too.

A cry of 'there it is' brought me back to reality. Emerging from a cluster of decaying sycamore leaves, the warbler came into full view, flicking through a window of bare branches and picking at insects. Cries of 'where is it?' came from the back, calls of 'up there' were volleyed back. The 'them-and-us' attitude of the crowd persisted, not through selfishness or one-upmanship, but because altruism is impossible in a crush. Birders delight in putting colleagues on to birds, but only if they can point and provide a helping hand. I could barely raise my binoculars.

Since I'd had good views of the bird, I squeezed my way out from the gateway to let others in, only to be confronted by the sickening news that some 'low-life piece of scum', to quote one birder present, had stolen a woman's telescope. She had left it in good faith on the fringes of the mass gathering with the all other scopes and tripods. Mine was there, too. Hers was a latest model and the crafty sneak-thief had cunningly taken it off its mounting and thrown her tripod into the long grass while all eyes were on the Blackpoll. Scilly, a land still cocooned in an age of innocence, had arguably witnessed one of its most serious crimes. The joy of seeing the Blackpoll evaporated in an instant.

Sandwiched between the yellowthroat crush and the Blackpoll debacle was one other event that would sour my short-lived love affair with the islands. October 1997 saw Glenn Hoddle's England team travelling to Rome to play a vital World Cup qualifying match. The Three Lions needed just one point to ensure an automatic place in the following summer's competition in France, yet the odds looked long. Fifteen other countries had tried and failed to keep the rampant Italians at bay in the Eternal City in previous World Cup campaigns. Could Hoddle's men succeed in their Italian Job where so many others had failed? As match day dawned the excitement reached fever pitch.

England expects headlines were blazoned across the front pages. On the mainland, St George's Cross flags flew from bedrooms and car windows, while on Scilly birders put almost as much energy into finding somewhere to watch the match on satellite television as they did in tracking down rarities. There was only one place to be: the Scillonian Club. For once, Lower Moors, the Great Pool and Barnaby Lane had to play second fiddle to another mass gathering of twitchers. The game was classic theatre. Seaman, Campbell and Adams held the English line; Gazza jinked and Beckham's adroit right-foot sent terrorising crosses into the heart of the Italian defence; Sheringham was his imperious self. England fans cheered on their Gladiators from the terraces and in millions of homes and pubs. The atmosphere in the Scillonian was electric until one idiot approached me during half time. Drink had been had.

'You that Stuart Winter?' He asked with what sounded like a beery slur. 'You write a load of ****!'

I was nonplussed. The diatribe continued full on as my ability to report matters ornithological was questioned, each point being made with expletives for punctuation. Experience told me that things were about to get ugly. Luckily, two of the stouter members of the Wednesday Club could sense a scene developing. They sidled next to me *à la* Campbell and Adams to provide defensive cover. Fortunately the second half kicked off and England went immediately on the attack. The cheers in the Scillonian reached a new crescendo. My tormentor decided to return to venting his spleen at the television screen and its little figures playing in the azure blue of Italy.

The match ended in a draw. England got their passport to France '98. I felt as sick as the proverbial football manager's parrot. As a Fleet Street hack I do a job and with it comes criticism, sometimes threats. Writing a birdwatching column to the greater glory of something I loved was not meant to generate such anger, such venom. That was the moment I decided that I would not be returning to Scilly in the future. The next day's theft of the telescope was confirmation. As a footnote, I did return to Scilly one more time. The following year I had an opportunity to take an overnight trip to the islands. Luckily, the visit coincided with the arrival of an Eastern Olivaceous Warbler which had taken up short-term residence in the Parsonage on St Agnes. The crowds and the briefest of unsatisfactory glimpses of a rare bird only reinforced my vow: adieu Scilly.

Legends and Heroes

Heroism is the divine relation which, in all times,
unites a great man to other men.
—Thomas Carlyle (1795–1881) – British historian and essayist.

Twitchers are unmitigated name-droppers. They cannot stop themselves boasting about where they've been and what they've seen. They can roll off the tongue the contents of lists as obscure and inconsequential as the birds they have encountered while relieving themselves behind bushes. Check any bird-listing website and you will see lists of names listing their lists and then listing what's on those lists. The eagerness and clamour to say 'I've seen this and here's the list as proof I've seen it' is at the very heart of twitching. Its protagonists are not only measured by what's on the seemingly endless list of lists they keep in the UK, for instance – garden, county, day, monthly, year or all-time lists – but also what other types of list they keep. So an experienced birder living in the

UK and with a passport really needs to keep North American, African, Neotropical, Oriental and Western Palearctic lists if they want to be listed in the list of top listers!

Confused? Well, I am. I don't keep a list. I know roughly what birds I've seen in Britain, Europe, my home county of Bedfordshire and on my trips to North America. Adventures in Africa, India and South America have produced wonderful birds, wonderful memories, but I am far too long in the tooth to list what species I have seen and where I saw them. Anyway, when your life list – the sum of all the birds you have ever seen – does not contain Puffin, then name-dropping other bird names is rather a waste of time. That said, I am an unashamed dropper of names.

The importance of 'who-you-know-rather-than-what-you-know' was taught to me as a young cub reporter. Old Stan, our chief reporter, was a grizzled, irascible, veteran of local newspapers who had served in the war and loved to play raconteur. He would come to work in the mornings, his gravelly voice stoked by a thousand Woodbines, and talk about whom he knew and who knew him. My job as office junior was to go the local off licence each morning and pick up a bottle of Worthington White Shield, an award-winning Indian Pale Ale, to kick start his day and to keep the stories on tap. Names such as Telly Savalas and Audrey Hepburn would fly from his lips and around the office as if they were local parish councillors. I listened in awe.

'It's all about your contacts book, boy,' he would often nod sagely. 'A reporter's only as good as the people he knows. You mark my words.'

Wise words they proved. Looking back through my newspaper cuttings book – a file nowhere near as important as my contacts book, but a useful *aide-mémoire* when trying to recall tales from past – and there are names enshrined in newsprint that have rightly taken their places in the Pantheon of Birding Heroes and Legends.

Legends

Exactly what the difference is between a legend and a hero, I will leave lexiconologists and classics students to argue over, but for the purposes of this eulogy, I have divided them into two: the figures who have inspired, encouraged, motivated, enthralled and enchanted me over the years and who have now taken their place in birding's Valhalla, and those who still tread the path of mortals.

Sir Peter Markham Scott (1909–89)

Sir Peter Scott crash-landed into my life – literally. I must have been eight or nine and it was the school summer holidays. Calling in time had just been sounded by my parents and as I traipsed home in the gloom – in those halcyon days, children could play out late without social services or the police being called – the neighbourhood tom-toms began sounding. An aeroplane had crashed into our school playing field! There was no way I was going to bed. Soon the world and his wife descended on our primary school, scaling the perimeter walls to see the carnage. Instead of smoking debris and all sorts of ghoulish horrors, there in the middle of the grass football pitch stood a glider and a distinguished, bald-headed man in a flying suit talking nonchalantly to the village bobby.

'Don't you be touching that,' the constable warned the growing crowds as they circled the glider, which seemed totally unscathed despite its rude arrival in the middle of a densely populated council housing estate.

One of the adults recognised the pilot:

'That's Peter Scott, that is. You know, the bloke off the telly,'

'So it is,' said another.

'Go and get his autograph, son,' I was urged.

'He's real famous that bloke. His dad was Scott of the Antarctic.'

I had no pen, no paper and no real idea who they were talking about. He was not a footballer, nor a Saturday pictures star. They were the only famous people I cared about. It was not until the story of Peter Scott's crash landing appeared on the front page of the *Dunstable Gazette* the following week that I realised what excitement I had been wrapped up in. My mother explained that the pilot was the 'man on the television' who presented the 'serious' animal programmes. At the time there was Johnny Morris, the self-styled zoo-keeper and animal conversationalist who presented *Animal Magic*, and there was the 'posh man' who looked like my school headmaster and brought us *Look*, the prime-time black-and-white wildlife show which I was allowed to stay up and watch if I was a good boy. Locals still talk about the day Peter Scott ploughed into the school football pitch four decades on although, rather than a crash, it was a textbook emergency landing without risk to life or limb. Such derring-do was typical of the man. Like most of the things Sir Peter attempted in life, he became the supreme exponent.

At the time of the incident he was British gliding champion and was also teaching Prince Philip how to fly. How I wished I had asked for his autograph.

Seven or so years later, I had my chance to ask. To mark Sir Peter's centenary in 2009, I wrote the following article for the *Sunday Express* to celebrate the day I birdwatched, albeit briefly, with arguably the greatest British conservationist in history. Under the headline, 'Great Scott! Memories flood back', I wrote:

Childhood memories have a strange knack of throwing things out of proportion. Chocolate bars always seemed bigger, the summers were warmer and an hour's detention in those dim and distant days seemed like a life sentence. On the birdwatching front, the years have also played tricks on the mind's eye. The first Great Crested Grebes I ever saw are etched in my fuzzy memory banks as if they were the size of Mute Swans, and the sewage farm where I cut my birding teeth always appeared to be awash with more waders than The Wash.

One memory from a distant youth has never been distorted by the years. It was a sunny spring afternoon in the early 1970s and I was birdwatching with a group of school pals, including my birding buddy to this day, Johnny Lynch, at Tring Reservoirs, when we came across a group of middle-aged men and women looking across the water with a telescope. A real, proper telescope! In those days we were sharing a pair of £19 Dixons binoculars between us.

Out of the blue, one of the adults commented nonchalantly on the presence of a distant Gadwall. A Gadwall? We quickly looked it up in the field guide that we had in the duffle bag along with our sandwiches and squash. It was a duck none of us had ever seen before. For some reason, it may have been because I was the gobbiest, I was volunteered by my pals to ask if we could look at the Gadwall through the adults' telescope.

Over the next few minutes a crocodile of slightly unimpressed schoolboys got their first view of this rather scarce, albeit nondescript, duck. Back in the early 1970s Gadwall was very much a sporadic breeder in the UK, largely confined to East Anglia. We said our thanks and were about to walk away when a lady in tweeds asked in hushed tones: 'Do you know who just showed you the Gadwall?' Our combined look of ignorance encouraged her to speak again: 'That's Peter Scott! THE Peter Scott!' Even to a bunch of 13-year-olds hooked on *The Beano* and *Dandy*,

Peter Scott – he had yet to be knighted – was a household name, a figure sharing our same pantheon of schoolboy heroes as Doctor Who, Jimmy Greaves, Bobby Charlton and John Noakes. He'd even crash landed into our school's playing field.

For any youngster interested in wildlife and the countryside, Peter Scott's nature programmes, particularly his legendary *Look* series, were essential viewing and were one of the major factors that inspired me to pick up a pair of binoculars. Sharing a few moments in his company – and getting his autograph – on the banks of a Hertfordshire reservoir is a precious memory that has never been eroded by time.

John Eric Bartholomew OBE (1926–84)

In the opening section of *Bill Oddie's Little Black Bird Book*, the author, in his inimitable style, lists a number of eminent names with a 'supposed interest in birdwatching' who have NOT provided the foreword to his classic work. They include Prince Philip, Prince Charles, Billy Fury, Humphrey Lyttleton and Eric Morecambe (who was born John Eric Bartholomew). The fact that Eric Morecambe liked birds seems to have passed the greater birdwatching community by. There are no papers by him in *British Birds*. I guess there are no descriptions of rarities found by him gathering dust in the archives. I don't ever remember seeing him at a twitch or, indeed, at any RSPB reserve. But he loved his birds. I know. He told me once, in person, at perhaps the most incredible press conference I have ever attended.

Back in the early 1980s Eric, who, with his short, hairy-legged partner Ernie Wise, dominated television viewing figures, was already beginning to suffer from the heart problems that would tragically end his life all too prematurely in 1984. After one health scare, Eric was ordered to take a lengthy rest but when he felt recuperated enough he organised an 'open house' for Fleet Street's showbiz reporters to discuss his future plans.

I was working at a freelance local news agency that covered the Harpenden area where Eric and his wife Joan had a beautiful mansion, and was asked by the London *Evening Standard* to cover the 'presser' (press conference). My brief was simple: the conference starts at 9am, stay 25 minutes and file 750 words of Eric's 'quotes'. I duly arrived outside *chez* Morecambe and was ushered into a sumptuous lounge containing a grand piano decorated with silver-framed family photographs. Eric was dressed casually in a shirt, pullover and slacks. The Fleet Street 'luvvie' pack took their seats, Eric thanked us for coming and then, totally unexpectedly, he went into a routine that had the journalists literally rolling around on the floor in hysterics. Joke-after-joke-after-joke was interspersed with hilarious anecdotes and inside 'off-the-record' stories that left the assembled hacks agog. Time and again, Joan would enter the lounge to tell Eric to take things easy. He simply took off his trademark glasses, looked up to heaven in a 'yes dear' sort of way, and continued with an act that the BBC would have paid thousands to screen. If only I had taken a tape recorder, if only hand-held video cameras had been invented. The material would have been worth a fortune, a national treasure.

I remember at one point I tried to make my excuses and leave so that I could file my story from the nearest telephone box – it was long before the days of mobiles and laptops – but Eric ushered me back to my seat saying 'you don't want to leave yet.' I stayed. All three hours. By the time I sent over my story, I got one of the biggest b********** of my career. I had missed several deadlines, the only time in my career that I failed to file on time. But then again, I had been in the presence of a comedy legend. It was worth the catcalls.

Only when I was leaving, did I have a quick word with Eric about birds. He smiled and spoke of the beautiful colours of Kingfishers and the cheeky antics of Great and Blue Tits in his gardens. Perhaps he was not a 300-species-a-year twitcher, but one sensed how much he loved his birds. The presence of so many Chaffinches, Bullfinches, Great Spotted Woodpeckers and Robins thriving in the grounds of his home showed that they loved him, too.

Appropriately, Eric's association with birds and the RSPB has been honoured for posterity with the naming of a mere at the Leighton Moss reserve in his honour, while draped around the neck of his bronze statue on Morecambe Bay seafront is a pair of binoculars. It would bring a smile to the face of the man who had the nation in stitches.

Robert John Tulloch (1929–96)
The obituary that appeared in *British Birds* when Bobby Tulloch died in the spring of 1996 began with two poignant sentences that I consider to form one of the most beautiful tributes that I have ever

read. They came from the pen of the RSPB's veteran spokesman Mike Everett, who wrote in the great Scottish naturalist's honour:

> Like everyone who had the good fortune to do so, the Archangel would have found meeting Bobby on his home patch an unforgettable experience. Nearly 30 years have passed since it first happened to me, but the memories of our first full day in the field are still very fresh in my mind.

I never had the opportunity to birdwatch with Mr Tulloch, as I called him on the one and only occasion that we met. His natural lairdom was the wild, gale-swept islands of Shetland, a place as distant as the moon for a schoolboy listening to his wonderful stories of trying to photograph Snowy Owls while dressed in a pantomime horse costume. Bobby was the guest of honour at the first night of an RSPB film show at the National Theatre on London's South Bank. He was a long way from home, and so was I. Tickets for the film show had been a birthday present and, although we only lived 40 miles outside London, the event took on family holiday proportions. A new dress for Mum, collar and tie for Dad and I had a Friday night rather than a Sunday teatime bath. We came to town by train, 'took lunch,' to quote mum, in a Joe Lyons Corner House and then settled down in the plushest of theatre seats.

The tickets had been bought by a well-to-do family friend. Dr Muriel Radford, the wife of social reformer Maitland Radford, acquaintance of the likes of Virginia Woolf and Rupert Brooke, had worked among the poor of the East End as a paediatrician, striking up an unlikely friendship with my mother. Dr Radford was a keen supporter of the RSPB and each birthday and Christmas she would send a small parcel wrapped in string and sealed with crimson wax. Inside would always be something to nurture my interest in birds: my first *Observer's Book of Birds*; a nest box; membership to the Young Ornthithologists' Club and, of course, film tickets for RSPB premieres. On school holiday visits to her Hampstead home she would package up back copies of the RSPB's magazine, which would provide bedtime reading for months on end. The tickets for the film show were the best present of all; I can still remember the excitement of watching the Snowy Owls floating across the cinema screen in glorious Technicolor. It would be another 25 years before I saw them for real.

At the end of the film show, Bobby Tulloch stood up and gave a gripping account of his part in the story. I was spellbound. A 30-minute film had transformed my life. I dreamed of becoming an RSPB warden, of travelling to distant islands and seeing rare and exciting birds. At the interval I approached 'Mr Tulloch' and asked if he would sign my programme. I hope I asked some sensible questions, too. Time has fuzzed the moment. Ideally, it would be great to write that he had offered some sagacious words on how I could fulfil my destiny to work with birds. Anyway, just listening to him speaking and watching those delightful owls, blinking in the face of a Fetlar gale, inspired me for life.

Herbert Axell (1915–2001)

Whether it really was Bert Axell whose cheeriness and smiles brought the curtain down on my best ever day's birdwatching, I will never know. Bert's lack, for the want of a better phrase, of customer services skills dogged his career in turning Minsmere into probably the best nature reserve in the world. Bert's obituary in *British Birds* in 2001 dallied slightly on his somewhat brusque nature:

> Big, forceful, and fiercely independent, he could sometimes be opinionated and awkward, and, sadly, it has to be said that not all of his professional colleagues were endeared to him. The problem was, however, as often as not of their making as much as his, and perhaps not enough consideration and understanding were always given to his determined and single-minded approach to his job – which, for a significant part of his life, really boiled down to making the RSPB's reserve at Minsmere, in Suffolk, the best bird reserve on earth. He probably succeeded.

Would such an indomitable, single-minded figure really have had time to chat with and help two young birdwatchers wanting to engage with an adult in a way that only inquisitive teenagers can? Over the years, whenever I have told my story about engaging him in chit-chat, the most frequent response has been: 'Doesn't sound like Bert.'

I detailed the meeting in *Best Days with British Birds*. Johnny Lynch and I had been on an organised local natural history society field trip to Suffolk in the spring of 1970 (which was detailed on pages 20-23), and we had been simply overawed by the experience. We had seen scores of new birds; enjoyed encounters with iconic species such as

Avocet and Bittern; had seen a pre-invasion Little Egret and also been
given a lesson in how mankind can create natural wonders with time
and effort. It was as we trudged back to the car that we decided to buy
some mementoes from the reserve centre which, in truth, was nothing
more than a glorified hut in those days. I wrote:

> At last, feeling like a real birdwatcher, I nudged Johnny and said we
> should head back to the reserve centre in order to buy some souvenirs to
> help us remember – as if we would forget – such a memorable day. We
> said our farewells to the Scrape and walked out into the warm spring
> evening. Shadows were beginning to lengthen and the Nightingales,
> rehearsing their song along with the various other passerines that haunt
> the woods adjacent to the lagoons, made the walk back to the reserve
> HQ all the more pleasant.
>
> 'Had a good day, lads?' asked a rather friendly-looking man selling
> an assortment of Avocet-stamped memorabilia. Our faces gave an instant,
> self-explanatory reply; for good measure, I reeled off the unexpurgated
> day list. The salesman nodded approvingly, then added: 'Ah, didn't you
> see the shrikes?'
>
> 'What shrikes?' We asked.
>
> 'Those!'
>
> There, no more than 10 feet away from the sales hut, sat a pair of Red-
> backed Shrikes: a glorious blend of slate greys, warm pinks and chestnut
> browns of the male and the female's dowdier, dun plumage, all contrasting
> with the deep greens and brilliant yellows of their gorse bush perch.
>
> Sadly, a few years later, the shrikes disappeared as breeding birds
> at Minsmere, I fear never to return. Yet those last poignant moments,
> watching the shrikes' outlines slowly become silhouettes as the evening
> sun dropped, will remain with me forever. This was truly my most
> memorable day's birdwatching.

A quarter of a century later I was sitting in Bert's lounge and asked him
if he remembered me. I got a shake of a head.

'I'm sorry,' he said, apologetically. 'Rather a lot of youngsters visited
Minsmere over the years. The important thing is not whether I
remembered you, but that you remembered the shrikes. They are lost
forever.'

How true. *Bird Watching* magazine had asked me to interview Bert in the spring of 1997 to celebrate Minsmere's golden jubilee. With a smile and a firm handshake, he welcomed me into his pretty Suffolk cottage and over several hours we drank tea and talked about the masterpiece he had played such a considerable part in creating. I sensed that there was more he wanted to say about the politics of conservation and what he perceived as internecine rivalries that confronted his desire to do things his way. But he did not want to spoil my story with his own misgivings, and so he spoke long and eloquently about the prodigal Avocets and majestic Marsh Harriers. Bitterns brought smiles to his face and Bearded Tits made him laugh. My own recollections of the many visits I had subsequently paid since that first trip in May 1970 pleased him greatly. So did my avowal that of all the places in all the world, that's where I wanted my ashes to be scattered.

'Let's hope that's a very long way off,' said Bert. 'I am sure you have many, many more visits to pay in coming years.'

Before I left we swapped gifts. I gave Bert a copy of *Best Days* and he signed a volume of *Minsmere: Portrait of a Bird Reserve*. It has become a cherished possession, very much like my memories of the RSPB's flagship reserve and the man who made it happen.

Richard Richardson (1922–77)

A little like the fleeting glimpse I had of Holkham's Red-breasted Nuthatch or the Scilly Eastern Olivaceous Warbler that vanished the instant my binoculars brought it into focus, my memories of Richard Richardson, the so-called 'Guardian of the East Bank', are dim and sketchy, and the reason is not wholly due to the passage of time.

While Minsmere had enchanted, perhaps bewitched me, during the early 1970s the very name of Cley had remained tantalisingly out of my orbit. Not having a car and, for some inexplicable reasons, always failing to take advantage of organised natural history society field trips to the north Norfolk coast, the so-called 'Mecca of British Birdwatching' remained a distant Shangri-La to discover and enjoy on some auspicious occasion. The future Mrs Winter did not quite like the idea of having Cley as our honeymoon venue, and so it was in the autumn of 1976 that I finally passed the Cley-next-the-Sea village sign ... to host an impromptu stag party.

The stag do is a peculiarly British institution in a constant state of evolutionary flux, a bit like Yellow Wagtails (read John Gooders' *Birds of the World* part-work series, it will explain what I mean). You cannot go through an airport departure lounge these days without being confronted by groups of slightly inebriated young women dressed as fairies and nuns or beery guys in rugby shirts (nicknames stamped on the back) heading to places such as Prague, Krakow or Budapest to get bladdered. These international invasions are planned weeks in advance of the nuptials to allow time for the prospective brides and grooms to recover from alcohol poisoning. Back in the 1970s, things were simpler. Stag parties in Bedfordshire were invariably taken on the Thursday before the big day and involved going to the California Ballroom in Dunstable, arguably the finest soul venue in the south of the England, drinking copious amounts of beer and having your trousers pulled down by your mates. I fancied something different: a pilgrimage to Cley.

The itinerary went like a dream. Most of the Saturday was spent at one of the great British birding sites of the post-war period – Wisbech Sewage Farm, a five-star wader paradise which has subsequently vanished off the map. Our car-load finally arrived at Cley late in the afternoon of a blustery September day. We were full of optimism. The first course of Curlew Sandpipers and Little Stints had whetted our appetites, but there was only time for a cursory seawatch from the famous coastguards' car park before we retired to the George and Dragon for the evening, with the promise of more birding the next morning. I cannot remember much more of the evening other than sweet-tasting pints of mild, fish and chips, an awful feeling of nausea and spending the rest of the night trying to sleep in the back of the car. We parked back at the coastguards' car park and, at one stage, I attempted to sleep in the storm shelter. This was before today's sturdier, brick-built affair. Whether it was sleep deprivation, hunger, the mental cruelty of having to listen to our driver's single item of musical entertainment, an eight-track Beach Boys cassette, for hour-after-hour, or simply the horror hangover that only drinking pints of mild can create, I was well and truly wrecked when the sun finally rose over Cley's famous acres of wetland.

The fog of time, the fug of sleeping five in a car and the curse of beer has wiped most of the experience from my memory banks, except for one event. Somehow we managed to stagger the mile or so along the beach to the East Bank, where a dark figure dressed in leather and wearing a beret was holding court. He reminded me of a villain out of *Dr Who*.

'Who's he?' I asked one of the guys, most probably pointing in a way only a drunk can point.

'That's Richard Richardson. THE Richard Richardson,' I was told in no uncertain terms.

I think I smirked.

'Daft name? Sounds like a Scandinavian footballer.'

I was soon put right.

Richardson had already reached legendary status long before his premature death in 1977. His excellence in the field, an eye and deft hand for perfect field sketches and a slight speech impediment – 'warblers, waders and waptors' were his favourite birds – had turned him and his East Bank domain into a birding institution. Crowds would gather around him to listen to his gospels. I only wish my one and only audience with the great man had not been blurred by beer glasses.

Peter James Grant (1943–90)

A whole 1960s generation remembers what they were doing the moment JFK died. I suffered such a moment the day I read that Peter Grant was dying. I can still sense the shock and deep sadness that Saturday morning when I opened a newly arrived copy of *Birding World* and read that Peter Grant was suffering from terminal cancer. His death followed in days and robbed us of a figure whose vision and wisdom would have moulded the face of birdwatching well into the 21st century. And it would have done so very much for the better. I don't know if Peter had ever read Rudyard Kipling's *If*, but he certainly lived by its credo. He could talk to crowds and maintain his virtue, and also walk with the high and mighty of British ornithology and not lose the common touch.

Peter's personality was such that he never came across as bumptious or a know-all, and yet when it came to the technical, often esoteric, sometimes unfathomable, dimensions of advanced field identification, he had the brain of a Nobel prize-winner. To the 'tertial fringe' school of advanced birding he was the guru, and yet to those embarking on a primary course in basic gull identification there could not be a better teacher or guide. It was on the subject of gull identification that I first approached him and yet he treated my totally out of the blue telephone call as if a long lost friend was on the line. No doubt he had many unsolicited calls from birdwatchers wanting to seek his opinion on primary moult or scapular colouring. My question was very much reception class material – I wanted to talk about juvenile Mediterranean Gulls – but he listened and commented as if I was explaining some important new discovery. Not only did he put me right on a few points, but a few days later a back copy of *British Birds* with his seminal identification paper on gull ID arrived in the post.

In the spring of 1983 he asked me down to spend a few days birding at his beloved Dungeness, arranging for me to stay at the observatory where he was quite rightly fêted. Peter was as much a fixture at this obscure outpost, with its shingle desert and quaint beach houses, as the ominous nuclear power station that overshadows the entire area. The gurgling, warm waters pumped from the facility have created a unique area to observe seabirds known as 'The Patch.' I guess it was Peter's favourite place in the whole world. We sat in the small hide overlooking this bubbling, vortex of water, watching frenzied terns and gulls picking off prey fish stirred up in the eddies, and Peter reminisced about his favourite moments looking out to sea.

One day in particular came floating back to him. It was 8 April 1979, a day when only mad-dogs and birdwatchers would venture out into the dull, wet, breezy murk. Peter and seven other hardy souls crammed themselves into the hide, the same hide that we now had to ourselves, yet while our day's fare was largely Common and Sandwich Terns trying to pick off tiddlers, the dramatic account he gave was of one of the most incredible day's seawatching in history. In his own inimitable way, Peter combined the technical details of flock sizes and flight directions with a wonderful, eloquent account of what flew past the hide's observation slit with little nuggets of personal commentary. A count of 27,000 Common Scoter, including one flock of 1,360 birds which he said looked like a 'giant sea serpent' as it flew past, was just one of the many highlights. There were divers and grebes, wildfowl aplenty; a half-dozen wader species and even an unexpected fly-by in the shape of a male Hen Harrier. And, of course, his beloved gulls.

Throughout the time he spoke, Peter was gazing out to sea with Zeiss binoculars, punctuating his story with updates of what the terns were doing and what other species were out at sea.

'Early evening saw the numbers in the hide begin to dwindle as people bade their farewells,' explained Peter. 'Everyone said that it had been a day to remember. There had been no lifers, no rarities, in fact, there was not a single bird that would send the grapevine into overtime and set off a mini-invasion the following day. Yet, only those who have sat in this tiny seawatch hide can guess at the atmosphere that was generated on that day of days. It was non-stop birdwatching of the highest order, the kind only experienced once in a lifetime.'

Chris Mead (1940–2003)

The world of birdwatching was robbed of another of its great personalities when Chris Mead died in his sleep in January 2003. Chris's premature death was a great loss for popular ornithology. His ability to communicate the most esoteric subjects in juicy, easily digestible sound bites was a journalist's dream. His name and telephone number was one of the first that any environment correspondent wrote into their contacts book, for they knew that if they wanted a good story, a difficult subject made easy or wonderful, snappy quotes, Chris was the expert to ring.

Chris's knowledge was not only imparted in media briefings. His easy to use, fact-filled *The State of the Nations' Birds* would be a strong candidate for my Desert Island Book. My copy is kept in a strategic place on the bookshelf; the dog-eared, tea cup stained pages a testament to its indispensability. When it was published at the Millennium, I raved about its usefulness. Here is the review I wrote in My Strictly for the Birds column. Little did I realise when I was writing it that I would be writing a similar tribute three years later:

> Few people deserve the title 'Bird Man' as much as genial giant Chris Mead. He hasn't got a TV birding series and you won't see his large bearded frame at the front of a big twitch. But if you want any facts or figures – or just need wise counsel on any birdwatching issue – Chris is your man. Over the years he has been a vital reference source for anyone writing about birds. Few, if any, have the wealth of knowledge about Britain's birdlife to match Chris's. A lifetime's work at the British Trust of Ornithology has given him an insight into an incredible range of subjects. Take a peep in the *Who's Who of Ornithology* to see how he has become an expert on ringing, migration studies, population dynamics and longevity.

I'm sure many birders have even thought about getting rid of mountains of weighty volumes and simply plopping Chris on their bookshelves. At 6ft 5ins, this might be difficult, so he's come to the rescue by writing what will become one of the most studied bird books of the decade, if not the new century.

The State of the Nations' Birds is the book we've all been waiting for. It's a 300-page investigation into the status and prospects of the 250 species that most regularly grace our islands. Chris charts the history of all our breeding birds, including Ireland's, analyses their status and predicts their future. From the Wren, the commonest bird with an estimated 9.9 million pairs, to rarities like the Black-winged Stilt, Chris studies each species and calculates the chances of seeing them during the summer months. Some pages make gloomy reading, though much is optimistic. I will not be a spoilsport and reveal too much, because anyone mildly interested in birds will want their own copy. But as a tease, Chris has revealed the 'winners and losers' of the past century. Top of the pile is the Red Kite, which appears on the cover and is hailed for surviving from one breeding female in the mid-1930s to today's 300-plus pairs. The worst loser is the Red-backed Shrike. Described as common at the start of the last century, it became extinct in the early 1990s.

The tragedy for all us is that Chris is no longer here to write the sequel. Over the last 10 years, the impact of climate change, the pressures on our summer breeding birds, both in Europe and Africa, the long term decline of farmland and woodland birds and other, as yet unknown factors, continue to whittle away the numbers of many species. Without Chris's expertise to analyse, interpret and then sing from the rafters about what is happening to our natural heritage, the fight to conserve and protect is seriously compromised. Like the loss of Peter Grant, I felt terribly empty that Friday morning when I learned that Chris had passed away. I remember talking to his colleagues, both at the BTO and also at the RSPB, and besides the personal feeling of grief among his many friends, there was one recurring question: 'Who shall we ask now?' Sadly, there was no answer – Chris was truly irreplaceable. That fact became only too apparent when I wrote the following obituary:

Birdwatching lost one of its most important figures and the birds one of their best allies when renowned ornithologist Chris Mead died. The phrase 'bird expert' is a term used far too often, but Chris filled the role like no other person. He was the experts' expert.

A lifetime dedicated to birds had given him an encyclopaedic knowledge that ranged wider than any library. Every time I called on his advice while writing Strictly for the Birds, he was only too willing to help, explaining the most complicated of subjects in an easy, 'tabloid-friendly' way.

Unlike many scientists, Chris had no problem dealing with the sharp end of the media. He excelled in coming up with stories for papers, a task he loved due to his wickedly sharp sense of humour. One of the first stories he gave me was during the early days of the Internet when his studies of Great Tits had become a worldwide cyber hit for sleazy surfers looking for other kinds of tits. Indeed, when anyone asked him about Bearded Tits he often replied: 'I'm always getting called that.' And Chris's legendary Santa Claus-style whiskers were a trademark that he always put to good use. He once shaved off his shaggy beard for charity, not forgetting to recycle the copious amounts of white, fluffy leftovers for nest-linings for his beloved garden birds. They were simply his life.

He joined the British Trust of Ornithology in 1961, and even when he retired a few years ago after a stroke, never lost his links with the trust, acting as its friendly face. During his 'retirement' he even wrote one of the most significant and useful bird books ever, *The State of the Nation's Birds*.

Tragically, Chris was only 62 when he died in his sleep at home in Thetford. His untimely death has robbed ornithology of one of its gurus – and birds of one of their greatest champions.

There are many other people I have been privileged to know who I am sure are keeping Peter Grant and Chris Mead company in some fantastic place. The talented Laurel Tucker, a wonderful bird artist who died tragically young, and David Hunt, the Scilly Birdman; Guy Mountfort, who kindly wrote a chapter for *Best Days* while well into his 80s, and Stanley Cramp whose foresight, drive and commitment brought us the landmark *Birds of the Western Palearctic*. Death is always a tragedy but it immortalises those who deserve to be immortalised.

Heroes
The wonderful thing about birdwatching is that it brings together rather than separates. Friendships are forged that last lifetimes.

Partnerships create works that advance our knowledge. Experiencing the natural wonder of birds is something always better shared. As Mark Cocker explains in his modern classic *Birders: Tales of the Tribe*, we are a brotherhood, a class, a breed, ruled by time-honoured traditions: together we bird, divided we wither.

Mark is one of my heroes, a writer as deft with the pen as the Peregrine is with wings, beak and talons. To read his prose inspires; to birdwatch with him is to see someone tutored in the old skills of observation and note-taking. Another of my favourite writers is Dominic Couzens, who vast knowledge of the secret lives of so many common birds would remain so if it were not for his prolific writing.

Then there are frontline birders such as Martin Garner, whose hunger to push back the frontiers of bird identification fill me with admiration. His drive to discover the diagnostic features of Yellow-legged and Caspian Gulls also filled my nostrils with the rancid, decaying stench of landfill sites but, then again, I did ask him to give me a crash course in Larid ID. Russell Slack and Dave Gosney are two birders who have become good friends by virtue of their knowledge and my need to ask questions.

I must admit that one birding hero not only has my admiration but does generate feelings of jealousy. Chris Packham will become the public face of birding in coming years. His film-star good looks, ease in front of the television camera and outstanding skills as a naturalist make him the natural successor of the doyen of wildlife broadcasting, Sir David Attenborough. Chris has the charm and presence to take on the great man's mantle. We can only hope that in decades to come there are still the natural spectacles and broadcasting budgets available to bring the wonders of the world into our homes. If so, another friend who I met through birdwatching will surely be involved. Stephen Moss is the man behind the scenes of so much of the great BBC Natural History Unit's television. Over the years he has produced many of Bill Oddie's television series as well as being a prolific writer of books, including the ground-breaking *A Bird in the Bush: A Social History of Birdwatching*.

Mention has already been made of Sir David Attenborough, whose persona and charm have given all aspects of wildlife viewing great credibility. Many of my republican friends say that if Britain was not a monarchy, then Sir David, with his charisma and gravitas, would be their choice as head of state. Millions, no for that read billions, across the planet have been entertained, inspired and, most importantly, educated by watching Sir David in full flow, bringing images and stories of the planet in action and often with the message that so much of this rich biodiversity is under imminent threat. I have been lucky enough to see Sir David in action many times, too. Sadly, not in some remote stretch of tropical cloud forest or on a lonely coral atoll, but at press conferences, book launches and public engagements, where audiences are left enraptured.

On one occasion I was invited to interview him at his home in south-west London. One whole hour, one-to-one, Sir David relaxed and talking about his favourite wildlife encounters and me sitting like a child invited into Santa's grotto. It is a top contender for my favourite day in 30 years of journalism. Under the headline 'Something's stirring in the Undergrowth', here is the article I wrote in full in autumn 2005:

David Attenborough's soft whisper, so often copied by other naturalists but never fully emulated, has been bringing the marvels of the natural world into countless homes across a threatened planet for 50 years. Perhaps his crowning moment was the poignant encounter, almost 30 years ago, with a family of gorillas high in Rwanda's mountain country. As they welcomed him out of the mists and into their very midst, the future of wildlife film-making was defined. These magnificent creatures, endangered to the very brink of extinction by Man's activities, were so welcoming to the fair-haired stranger and his film crew.

For those watching at home, an estimated 500 million of us shared the experience worldwide, it was the day that Man's closest relative, the savage beast demonised in folklore and fiction, was shown in its gentle, intelligent majesty. The moment the gorillas began to gently groom Sir David in the ultimate act of primate friendship has been hailed as one of the greatest events in television history.

Making landmark television is Sir David's stock in trade. It's widely accepted that he has brought more colour and excitement into the homes of British viewers than any other broadcaster. As controller of BBC2 he gave us our first colour TV pictures, *Match of the Day*, *Monty Python* and a raft of award-winning, landmark documentaries. In later years, nature, in all its forms, has been his focus. His style is light years from the modern genre of wildlife programmes, the 'grab-'em-and-show-'em' brand perfected by all-action crocodile-wrestlers and death-defying snake-catchers.

Now the latest in Sir David's study of the planet's amazing kaleidoscope of creatures and plants is being screened. *Life in the Undergrowth* promises to amaze, entertain and educate in equal measure, peeling away the mystery of the world under our feet where invertebrates have ruled for 400 million years.

At home, relaxing among his books, bird paintings and artefacts from his innumerable foreign adventures, Sir David reminisces about his encounters with nature in the same style as his films, with hushed tones, fond smiles and passionate hand movements. A grin spreads across his face as he expresses his feelings of luck and gratitude for having witnessed things that most naturalists have experienced only through the pages of dusty zoology tomes.

'I suppose I have been very fortunate to have travelled to so many countries and seen so many wonderful things, the things that I feel really passionate about,' he says. 'Filming the gorillas is one of the most famous and certainly one of my most memorable encounters, but there are many others, too. Watching birds of paradise displaying in the wild was mind-blowing, as was seeing a Blue Whale, the largest creature on the planet, in Pacific waters off the coast of California. Witnessing the emergence of Horseshoe Crabs was equally incredible. We show this in the first programme of our new series. We filmed the crabs in Delaware Bay and it was a truly amazing experience.

'Then there was my first dive on a coral reef,' he says, his slow, deliberate hand movements imitating a scuba diver in the weightless world under the sea where brilliant, multi-coloured fish sparkle in the azure waters. 'The first time you put on scuba gear and find yourself in a world where you can move in three dimensions and then suddenly see these colours and forms is fantastic.

'When talking of colours, then butterfly migration is an extraordinary thing. I was once in Paraguay, camped by the side of a river, and suddenly these butterflies began to appear in their millions. There were probably 15 different species and they came through in a solid blizzard that continued for three days.'

Some of his encounters with nature have been life-fulfilling, others heart-rending and upsetting. Australia's Superb Lyrebird is a remarkable mimic that turns the sounds it hears into its own mating calls. On one filming expedition, Sir David came across a lyrebird imitating the chainsaws that were robbing it of its forest haunts.

There are also creatures he still dreams of seeing in the quiet moments between filming. 'There are lots of things I would love to see. I have never been to the south-west corner of China, there are lots of wonderful creatures there,' says Sir David. 'The Golden Snub-nosed Monkey, for instance, is a fascinating creature. It has a brilliant blue face, golden fur and a little snub nose and I would dearly love to see it.'

But journeying to the remotest corners of the planet is not always necessary; there is much we do not see right under our noses, as this latest journey into the world of the creepy-crawly, the myriad tiny creatures that make life on Earth possible, proves. There are estimated to be 1.6 billion invertebrates for every human. The series has been three years in the making and uses the latest technology to film a world as alien to us as anything in the farthest reaches of the galaxy. *Life in the Undergrowth* promises to add another award-winning title to the impressive Sir David filmography. With its array of poisonous bat-eating centipedes, cicadas that emerge once every 17 years and belligerent ants that wage wars on termite colonies, the series is also expected to achieve high viewing figures.

'There are some things you ought to be squeamish about,' he says of the many people who have phobias about insects. 'For example, there are very big centipedes which are 18 inches long and extremely poisonous. They can kill a human baby with a bite,' he adds. 'But I don't think I'm particularly squeamish about anything else. I suppose spiders as big as your hands can make you jump but that's quite irrational, really, as they seldom bite.'

And this is one of the reasons he was so keen to give people a window on this extraordinary world. 'I've wanted to make the series for a long time because of the importance of the subject.'

With an incredible array of equipment, including a remote-controlled camera dubbed the 'Frankencam' and the latest in fibre optic, cold lighting and infrared technology, Sir David's team are bringing natural events to the screen that have never been witnessed before. But then, pointing out of the window of his delightful cottage to its neatly tended garden, he explains that the fascinating world of the mini-beast can be explored in our own backyards.

'Making this series was not about making important discoveries,' he says. 'For instance, ask the public how earthworms copulate and they have no idea; most people have never seen worms mating in their own gardens. But when we show them worms doing it on a warm summer evening after it's been raining, just yards from where they are sitting, it will blow their minds.'

Of course, there are many others whom I both admire and respect. One only has to look at a bookshelf to see the collective knowledge of a legion of birders whose drive, commitment and know-how has made ornithology arguably the most understood of all scientific disciplines. Remarkably, it is not only academics that make important discoveries and interpret vast volumes of data. Birdwatchers make brilliant citizen scientists. Field skills honed over decades and theory learned as much on the frontline as from books has produced an army of experts who can stand shoulder-to-shoulder with Oxbridge zoologists in the field before returning to their jobs as factory workers, builders and tradesmen. Science salutes you.

Sex, Sins and Scandals

You cannot hope to bribe or twist (thank God!) the British journalist.
But, seeing what the man will do unbribed, there's no occasion to.
—Humbert Wolfe (1885–1940), poet and civil servant.

Ask any successful tabloid editor the secret of a good 'red-top' – those newspapers that have red mastheads on the front page and often feature 'scantily-clad lovelies' inside – and they are bound to have their own secret formula. Lots of 'gossip, girls and games' (Fleet Street slang for sport) is certainly one way to appeal to a mass market. Or 'sex, soccer and showbiz' are another popular blend of downmarket tabloid ingredients. One particular editor's favourite alliterated recipe for the perfect newspaper was a blend of subjects that all began with the letter C that included crime and cricket and a few others that cannot be printed here. No matter how much an editor professes to want serious news from his journalists, the desire to titillate and entertain has always dominated the popular end of the industry. It is a largely British phenomenon but, then again, we are the nation that gave the planet Carry On films and saucy seaside postcards. Laughing at sexual innuendo and being embarrassed about body parts and awkward situations is part of the Anglo-Saxon psyche. Birdwatchers are not exempt. And it makes news!

Most birders have stories about catching couples *il flagrante delicto* while out in the field. Fresh air, open spaces and remote car parks are not just the preserve of people dressed in khaki and carrying binoculars. Indeed, the best time of year to find an overshooting Mediterranean rarity or to get up early to enjoy a dawn chorus also coincides with the prime season for alfresco sex. The old adage of 'hooray, hooray, it's the First of May, spring migrants are on their way' has been commandeered by a new generation who sing: 'Hooray, hooray, it's the First of May, outdoor sex begins today...'

One of my most embarrassing birding situations came during a particularly warm May when I was looking for early butterflies and orchids rather than late spring migrants. The location was a beautiful patch of open downland high in the Chilterns where ancient tribes had worked the chalky ground into a series of undulating knolls, which is perfect habitat for plants and butterflies – and also for discrete couples. Picture the scene: there I was, binoculars on close-focus, trying to track an early Common Blue and blissfully oblivious to what was happening around me. As the butterfly alighted on some trefoil on the precipitous edge of a chalk cut-away, I got down on my hands and knees, fumbled for my camera and began focussing slowly on the butterfly's beautiful underwing pattern. It flinched and then fluttered gently over the edge of the chalk cliff. I scrambled forward. The butterfly, I presumed, was resting inches away down the slope. I kept my camera to my eye and gently peered over the top, slowly twirling the focus wheel. Suddenly, a banshee wail smashed through the tranquillity. I took the camera away from my eye and there, 15ft below, was a young woman on her back, her arms and legs spread-eagled and what looked like a pair of black, lacy knickers strategically coiled around one ankle. Her modesty was covered by the back view of a male, moving rhythmically. She screamed again as our eyes meet, her partner unaware of my presence and mistakenly believing that her ecstatic cries were due to his love-making skills rather to than my innocent, voyeuristic activities. I vanished in an instant and never did get a photograph of the butterfly.

Most birders have similar stories. The heaths, woodlands and cereal fields that give sanctuary to Dartford Warblers, Common Redstarts and Corn Buntings also provide safe havens for illicit liaisons. While birders should always be on guard and try to avoid upsetting the sensibilities of others, sometimes they cannot avoid the careless abandon of free love. One particular bird hide I know – I will keep its location a secret – became a perfect location to not only study the courtship behaviour of Water Rails, but also that of *Homo sapiens*. Saturday mornings, it seemed, were not only a time for a small gathering of half a dozen birders to cram into the hide and look out for passing waders and wildfowl, but also for a young couple to stage secret assignations. It was so obvious that there was something suspicious about their trysts. They would meet at the same synchronised moment every weekend, arriving in separate cars, which were then parked off the road away from passing traffic. While she was climbing into the back seat of his car, he went through the same rigmarole of making sure they were not being watched ... totally oblivious to the rank of telescopes 100 metres away peeking out the perfectly camouflaged bird hide. Discretion and respect meant that the birders would always avert their eyes as the car windows slowly became steamed, but the irony of watching a couple go to such lengths to keep their secrets away from prying eyes always ended in the hide erupting in laughter.

Apart from the weekly outburst of hilarity, at least that particular hide was used for its intended purpose. The suggestion that birdwatching hides are being used for nefarious activities made banner headlines across the national newspapers in the summer of 2009. Lincolnshire Wildlife Trust was forced to remind visitors that hides were there for the 'quiet enjoyment' of nature after a complaint that one had been put to other uses. A trust official warned:

> There are certain things that happen at nature reserves that really shouldn't. People need to remember that when they visit there are regulations in place to protect the habitat and environment. Nature reserves are for quiet enjoyment only and anything else could possibly disturb or cause harm to the animals that live there.

The story not only appeared in hard print but also found its way on to newspaper internet sites, with one particular broadsheet deciding to use a photograph of a silhouetted birdwatcher supposedly looking in one direction while a flock of Pink-footed Geese flew suspiciously in the other. Of all of the photographs that could be used from the newspaper's vast archive, the one chosen just happened to be of the RSPB's Grahame Madge, the hard-working stalwart of the society's media office. Although the backlighting obscured his facial features, any sharp-eyed observer could easily make out his trademark bushy moustache, leading to much merriment at his expense at The Lodge – and a quick visit to the barbers.

Grahame is one of my key contacts and has to put up with a barrage of inquiries every week, ranging from obscure questions on European conservation law to the up-to-date status of our common birds. His excellent knowledge and cheeriness is respected by the small legion of environment correspondents, but it took all of his quick-thinking and experience when he was once approached by a lads' magazine who wanted the RSPB's reaction to the news that one of its heathland reserves had been voted as one of the top four places in the country to enjoy outdoor sex.

'I had to think on my feet,' Grahame later told me. 'I supposed they wanted some Middle England outrage but I proceeded to tell the magazine about the importance of heathlands to biodiversity and the rarity of some of the birds and other fauna that this type of habitat supports. I explained how seeing Dartford Warblers would be one of the major draws for the particular reserve in question, but then warned that such places were not particularly good for other so-called types of outdoor recreation, especially when it was our aim to recreate a habitat that would actively encourage more prickly gorse and snakes!'

Disturbing a Schedule One species such as Woodlark while having a lark in the woods could actually result in an appearance before the beak under the Wildlife and Countryside Act, but as an environment crimes go it would pale when compared to some of the appalling depths certain individuals and, more seriously, organised gangs will stoop in order toto get their kicks or make money. The appalling impact that rogue gamekeepers, bird collectors, eggers and habitat destroyers have on the countryside has dominated my columns over the years and has been one of the most gut-wrenching and upsetting parts of my job. Saying that, getting opportunities to name and shame the kind of scum who can kill a beautiful Peregrine Falcon or plunder the nest of a Red-throated Diver is arguably the most important contribution a journalist can make towards conservation.

In recent years, the courts have begun handing out stiffer sentences to those convicted of wildlife crimes, and the RSPB and RSPCA are to be congratulated for the skill and determination they exercise in bringing the crooks to justice. Crook is the right word – others I'd like to use would be censored – for those who can brazenly put out poison bait or set a trap, knowing full well that they are condemning a living creature to a horrible death. The following *Sunday Express* article was written by me in July 2008, but it summarises two decades of frustration and spleen aimed at those who continue to ride roughshod over our wildlife and the laws to protect it:

> A society should be measured on the way that it protects the most vulnerable, and the levels of persecution targeted against some of our rarest and most spectacular birds is an outrage. One set of statistics you will not find by poring over the Home Office's recently released British Crime Survey is the record number of crimes against birds of prey. Poisoning, shooting, trapping and nest destruction continues unabated. Last year (2007) witnessed a massive 40 per cent rise on 2006 figures, with a serious incident reported every 33 hours.
>
> Among the worst areas for raptor persecution are North Yorkshire, Northumberland, Shropshire and Cumbria, which together accounted for 132 incidents, almost half of all the offences. The fact that these counties are traditional game-shooting areas, where rogue gamekeepers and birds of prey have long been at odds, is worthy of note. The only way to bring errant elements within the game industry to book is through committed law enforcement.
>
> Not that wildlife crime is the reserve of cowboy keepers. Egg collectors, misguided pigeon fanciers and criminals exploiting the value of wild falcons are also responsible for serious offences. Without doubt, the most insidious crime is laying poisoned bait to kill defenceless birds. Last year there were 49 reports of birds of prey being poisoned, including 17 Red Kites – the highest number recorded in a single year – and one half of the only breeding pair of Golden Eagles in the Scottish Borders.
>
> The Wildlife and Countryside Act is a powerful tool in combating these offences, but making prosecution and conviction a certainty also

requires commitment from senior police officers and politicians. Ian West, the RSPB's head of investigations, told me: 'We are still seeing only the tip of the iceberg. It's hard to say whether the problem is increasing or we are just getting to hear about more of the offences that are taking place. What is clear is that very large numbers of birds are being illegally killed every year, which is totally unacceptable in a civilised society. There has to be a greater effort to enforce the law.'

Mr West is calling on the Home Office to make it clear to police forces that wildlife crime needs to be given a higher priority. He added: 'The public's help will continue to be vital if we are to identify where the problems are and try to do something about it.'

While the forces of law and order rely upon public help, workable legislation, supportive courts and increasingly sophisticated crime-fighting techniques, the criminals are ever more cunning in their attempts to evade capture. One of the most worrying trends to have developed in recent years has been the determination of egg collectors to continue adding to their secret stashes by exploiting EU freedom of movement.

A combination of budget flights and wave-through passport controls saw eggers turn to the lakes and woods of Scandinavia and the Spanish steppes when nest-raiding in the UK became too dangerous. It was an issue that needed raising urgently in the spring of 2003 when the RSPB began gathering intelligence about the movements of key egg collectors who had discovered a glaring loophole in the law. With the help the RSPB's investigations department, I wrote the following article under the headline: 'Egg thieves plunder Europe'.

A new breed of British criminal has joined the ranks of football thugs and drug traffickers wreaking havoc across the Continent – the international egg collector. Wildlife crime investigators have discovered that nest raiders are now taking their cruel obsession into Europe to escape Britain's tough conservation laws.

The eggers are even exploiting a loophole in British law with their foreign sorties. Possession of wild bird eggs is not illegal if it can be shown they were taken abroad. It means the thieves can bring back their booty without the threat of being jailed.

Graham Elliott, head of the Royal Society for the Protection of Birds'

Investigations Unit, told me: 'We are campaigning for a change of law to close a loophole which will enable prosecution for the possession of eggs taken abroad and also help protect all birds in the European Union. To date, our laws only protect birds here.

'The most worrying thing for egg collectors is the fact that we know where they are and where they are going. This unit is not only building up an increasingly detailed picture of the egg thieves but we are also using increasingly sophisticated techniques to bring them to court. The message is simple: try to steal an egg, attempt to rob society of a piece of its natural heritage, and we will catch you and there's every-likelihood that you'll go to prison.'

Defra, the Government department responsible for conservation legislation, says it is aware of the problem and that it will be looked at when the Countryside and Wildlife Act is reviewed later in the year. Conservationists are hoping that any new penalties imposed under the review would include the confiscation of convicted egg thieves' passports.

Over the coming weeks of the nesting season, up to 300 British egg collectors will be pitting their wits against some of the finest wildlife investigators in Britain. The investigators with the RSPB have had a successful run in catching and locking up eggers who threaten some of our best-loved and rarest birds such as the Osprey, Avocet, Golden Eagle, Peregrine Falcon and Dotterel. A combination of high-tech security devices, covert operations that have even included a Gurkha surveillance team, and the near certainty of immediate jail sentences have driven the eggers overseas.

Countries such as Poland, Estonia, France, Spain, Portugal, Norway and Finland have become the key destinations for egg thieves keen to plunder the nests of some of the most elusive and beautiful birds in the world. In Norway the key target is the White-tailed Eagle, a magnificent fish-eating bird of prey that breeds in the UK only on a few remote Scottish islands. Arctic taiga bogs, with their rare wading birds such as Spotted Redshanks and Broad-billed Sandpipers, are also hot-spots for the jet-setting egger.

Another target is Poland with its ancient woodlands and water meadows. Law-abiding birdwatchers are drawn to Eastern Europe each spring to see Ural Owls, Black Woodpeckers and Red-breasted Flycatchers. Sadly, these birds have also caught the eye of egg collectors who boast their own intimate network of contacts in order to discover nest sites.

Portugal and Spain, with their small breeding populations of bustards and sandgrouse, are also popular destinations. Eggers can begin plundering the nests of some of Europe's most exotic birds within a couple of hours' drive of Faro airport. Egg collecting is virtually unknown in other European countries. Although most have conservation legislation, few have enforcement agencies such as the RSPB's unit.

'The chances of an egg collector being caught on the European mainland are far less likely than at home and so we have seen a huge increase in the numbers travelling abroad,' said a senior RSPB investigator. 'As more legitimate British birdwatchers travel to foreign destinations to watch exotic birds, so the amount of information on bird populations and the location of nest sites also increases.

'Egg collectors are almost as obsessive about building up intelligence files on rare birds as they are about stealing the actual eggs and they'll go to great lengths to get the latest news. We know that many of them visit bird fairs, glean legitimate birders' trip reports, read holiday brochures and also scan the Internet to find out what bird is breeding where in Europe. Once abroad, they'll go to incredible lengths to steal an egg. They'll wade across freezing Arctic bogs or scale precipitous Mediterranean rock faces, risking their lives to get a prized egg.'

Egg collecting is a throwback to Victorian times when gentlemen in top hats plundered the nation's wildlife to decorate drawing rooms. Stuffed birds and egg collections in display cases were as much a part of the 19th century parlour as gas lamps and pianos. Sadly, their excesses were responsible for the dramatic decline of several species. The Red-backed Shrike is today extinct in Britain, largely because its beautifully marked egg was such a prize for the gentleman collector.

The profile of today's egger could not be further from the gentleman of 100 years ago. He is invariably male – there are no known female egg collectors – in his mid-30s with an unskilled job and often has previous convictions for petty crime. Some are suspected of having links with extreme right-wing groups.

Hopefully, my article played some small part in Defra's review of wildlife legislation later that year, which resulted in the loopholes relating to non-native but European birds being closed. Today, anyone found in possession of a wild bird's egg from an EU member state species faces the full weight of the law.

One successful *Sunday Express* conservation campaign mounted in association with the RSPB also resulted in a high-profile victory. In the winter of 2004, English Nature, the Government conservation organisation charged with protecting wildlife and wild places, had decided to explore the idea of controlling the number of Hen Harriers as an obtuse way of preventing the illegal persecution of this beautiful moorland raptor. The thinking was that agreeing to 'limit' the Hen Harrier population with grouse moor managers would prevent more birds being killed unlawfully. After a tip-off that the subject was to be discussed by English Nature, I went to town, describing the idea to limit harrier numbers as 'outrageous' and warning that it could set a 'damaging precedent' in nature conservation. Dr Mark Avery, the RSPB's Director of Conservation, was particularly concerned about the idea of culling a species that had declined to just a few nesting pairs.

'The harrier is very rare in England so no grouse moor can seriously claim to have suffered economic damage,' he told me. Within a week, the idea was dead. Outraged *Sunday Express* readers, angry birders, RSPB members and a sensible approach by English Nature board members saw the idea blasted out of existence. The following weekend I reported the following story under the headline '*Sunday Express* saves the Harrier':

Controversial plans to cut down numbers of a rare, spectacular bird of prey have been shot down, after the scheme was exposed by the *Sunday Express*. English Nature had been looking at the idea of 'limiting' the birds, Hen Harriers, because of the damage they do on grouse moors. Scientists had suggested the scheme to stop illegal killings of the harrier. But the Royal Society for the Protection of Birds called the suggestion 'outrageous'. And English Nature's ruling council blocked it.

The Hen Harrier is one of Britain's most beautiful birds – and one of the rarest, with as few as 10 pairs nesting on English uplands. Earlier this year, police launched a nationwide campaign, Operation Artemis, to save it from persecution. When the ruling council of English Nature met last week, they were given copies of the *Sunday Express's* article on the bird's plight – and ruled out the idea of a cull. Instead, they launched a five-year recovery project.

A spokesman said: 'The council decided that culling would not be in the new project's brief, but said it must pursue other conservation actions and try to resolve the conflicts between Hen Harriers and the management of commercial grouse moors.'

Chairman Sir Martin Doughty said: 'We know there is evidence to show that Hen Harriers will eat Red Grouse, but to suggest that we should consider the legality of culling a near-extinct bird, decades away from recovery, is out of the question.'

A spokesman for the RSPB said: 'We're delighted. The combined strength of the RSPB's members and the large *Sunday Express* readership has proved a powerful union.'

Sadly, wildlife persecution continues. As I write this, a copy of the RSPB's *Birdcrime 2008* report sits open on my desk. It makes depressing reading. That year, there were 1,206 reports of potential offences against wild birds, in other words, one every eight hours. These included: 210 reports of shooting and destruction of birds of prey; 133 poisoning incidents; 36 egg collecting reports; 27 illegal disturbances of Schedule 1 rare species; 42 reports of illegally taking, possessing or selling raptors; 64 cases of finch trapping and 682 reports of shooting or the destruction of wild birds other than raptors. Together, they amount to an awful indictment of cruelty and vandalism against our national heritage. What is needed is a thematic review of wildlife crime by the Government, which would hopefully update laws, increase penalties and force police chiefs to put more resources towards enforcing the law and tackling this much-neglected area of criminality.

While criminal acts blight the conservation of birds and wildlife in Britain, more nefarious activities have stained and besmirched the good name of ornithology over the decades. The infamous case of the Hastings Rarities is writ large in the murky annals of bird collecting and created a tale of intrigue and foul deeds worthy of a Conan-Doyle novel. If ornithology wanted to look for an arch villain in the role of the malevolent Professor Moriarty, then Colonel Richard Henry Meinertzhagen CBE DSO stands accused of being a bounder and a cad. They are two of the more diluted comments that could be aimed at a historical figure that lived a dozen mens' lives, or so we thought. Stories of his boys' own adventures and acts of derring-do have largely been discredited, and certainly his claims that he met Adolf Hitler on several occasions and, another time, helped bring about a vital victory for the British Army with a classic intelligence ruse, have been dismissed as whimsy.

T.E. Lawrence – Lawrence of Arabia – said of him in his biography *Seven Pillars of Wisdom*:

> Meinertzhagen knew no half measures. He was logical, an idealist of the deepest, and so possessed by his convictions that he was willing to harness evil to the chariot of good. He was a strategist, a geographer, and a silent laughing masterful man; who took as blithe a pleasure in deceiving his enemy (or his friend) by some unscrupulous jest, as in spattering the brains of a cornered mob of Germans one by one with his African knobkerrie. His instincts were abetted by an immensely powerful body and a savage brain....
>
> For all his intellect, Meinertzhagen was not averse to using brute strength. In India, he once killed one of his assistants in a fit of rage and then persuaded the local police to cover his tracks. His place in history, or should it be infamy, however, was reserved for the way he unscrupulously tried to win acclaim as an ornithologist of standing. Forty years after his death he has been exposed as the perpetrator of an incredible fraud. A review of his bird collection at Tring Museum in the 1990s revealed that the Colonel had stolen the best specimens of other people's collections and then fabricated data to support his records. His *Birds of Arabia*, published in 1954, is also believed to have been based upon the unpublished work of another naturalist.

The aroma of corruption and malevolence has fortunately wafted well away from modern ornithology. Our scientific community is under the focus of the all-seeing eyes of peer review, Internet access and global chatter. On an amateur scale, bird reports and records have never been more transparent. Local scientific and rarity committees attached to bird clubs and societies do sterling work collating the massive mountain of data and information that comes their way. There is something comforting about the unwritten rules of integrity and honesty that underpin modern birding. Just like golfers who cheat, birders who try to win self-aggrandisement through deception are quickly found out. The attempts still make great stories.

One recent attempt to deceive the birding community came in early 2009 when an email with an attached photo of a mystery bird found its way through to a recorder in North Wales. The picture showed a female Steller's Eider, a rarity of mega magnitude and one of the most eagerly sought-after birds among today's generation of twitchers. The hunt was on. Many began the pilgrimage to Anglesey to see the bird that had been purportedly swimming close inshore. However, another photograph already existed of the eider, one that had been taken three years earlier – in Finland. The culprit had simply taken the photograph, reversed the image and attempted to start a twitch of mass proportions. Fortunately, the acute eyes of the more sceptical elements of birding were able to expose the fraud before too much damage was done.

The summer of 2009 also witnessed one of the most profound confessions I have ever seen from a birder. *Birdwatch* magazine reported how a man from Essex finally owned up about how he fabricated the record of a North American Hermit Thrush in his home county in 1994. For 15 years the account of how the transatlantic vagrant had been discovered exhausted in Chipping Ongar, along with supporting photographs, had been archived by the birding authorities as authentic. Although doubts had been initially raised about the supporting evidence – the so-called exhausted bird was photographed in the hand of someone using a classic ringer's grip – the record remained inviolable ... until the culprit, to use his words, 'came clean.' His *raison d'être* for such an elaborate hoax was his mounting frustration over the number of records appearing in the Essex county bird report which had been suppressed.

Suppression is arguably birding's dirtiest word. Long before Tony Blair's government introduced the Freedom of Information Act, birdwatching had its own unwritten 'legislation' that basically amounts to this: 'if you want to see the birds I have found, you MUST tell me about the ones you find'. It largely works. BirdGuides and Rare Bird Alert provide a five-star service to thousands by publishing sightings within a blink of a nictitating membrane. The way the birding brotherhood acts in altruistic unison on these occasions is a sight to behold. When rarities settle in residential or private areas, with all manner of parking and disturbance issues, friendly negotiations often open the doors. Of course, birds can turn up in places which cannot physically host a mass twitch. Military bases, airports, secure industrial areas and royal estates remain strictly out of bounds. Health and safety fascism will undoubtedly increase the number of no-go zones, but we are a prosaic bunch. What really gnarls birders is when a rarity turns up at a site which is regularly watched by an individual or a group and the information is kept secret. It has been written that birders can still remember where they were and what they were doing when they heard the news that a Tengmalm's Owl had spent the winter at Spurn Point in 1983. For quite understandable reasons, there was a news blackout. The peninsular could not have coped with a mass influx of cars and could have made access to the lifeboat station impossible. Lives could have been lost at sea. Yet mention Tengmalm's Owl and Spurn in the same sentence to 99.9 per cent of most twitchers of a certain age and then listen for the gnashing of teeth.

Fortunately, not all birding hoaxes, ruses or, as in the case of the Tengmalm's Owl, justified suppression, have caused ill-feeling or resentment. Some attempts to pull the 'Wallcreeper over the eyes' of twitcherdom have been masterful. Okay, there have been no attempts as far as I know to create a hoax Wallcreeper sighting, but over the years some of the most esteemed figures in ornithology have not been averse to have a laugh at others expense.

The great Richard Richardson used his artistic skills to cause something of a kerfuffle during the days he was the esteemed 'Guardian of the East Bank.' On one occasion, he painted a small *Calidris* sandpiper on metal sheeting and strategically placed it on the open marshes of Cley. Being particularly mischievous, one side displayed the features of a Least Sandpiper, the other a Semipalmated. Having been involved in the finding of Britain's first Semipalmated Sandpiper in July 1953, he was patently aware of the identification issues involved in nailing both species and one can imagine the heated exchanges as various birdwatchers reported one or other species, detailing – accurately – the fieldmarks of both birds, depending on what side of the bird they were watching. Richardson must have been creasing up. Richardson's biographer Moss Taylor, a stalwart of the Norfolk birding scene, also admits to executing a similar ruse himself as a trainee doctor. Moss, who wrote the excellent *Guardian Spirit of the East Bank* tribute to Richardson, put his combined birding and medical skills to use by creating a model of a Black-winged Stilt. Plaster of Paris that would normally fix broken limbs provided the body, bits of black plastic were used for other features and, as a finishing touch, Moss bought some pink nail polish to give the stilt authentic bubblegum-coloured legs. Picture the excitement of anyone picking out this incongruous bird seemingly holding territory on the north Norfolk coast back in the 1960s – remember this was long before the days of Sammy the Stilt. The sight of the 'birdwatchers trying to guess why the stilt was motionless' hoax left medical student Moss in stitches but it did not go down well with Cley's legendary warden Billy Bishop. You can still hear the fear in Moss's voice 40 years later as he recalls the moment Billy marched up and stormed: 'Whoever did this has 10 minutes to bring it back or there'll be big trouble...' The stilt vanished as quickly as it had arrived!

Exposing scandals is part of a newspaperman's job but sometimes I have felt duty-bound to defend unfortunate souls who have fallen foul of unfair whispering campaigns. Back in 1995, one young birder told me how he had been pilloried for doing no more than picking up an injured bird in a car park, a kind-hearted act that got the twitching tom-toms drumming venomous tones. The following article was published in the *Daily Star*, under the headline 'Top twitcher in flap':

> Soccer has had its bung scandals, politics its sleaze and now there are murmurings of dark doings in the world of birding. The unfortunate victim of a sinister whispering campaign is Rob Stinger, who is the target of claims that he passed off a caged bird as a mega-rarity.
>
> At the centre of the furore is the beautiful Meadow Bunting, a species never before seen in the wild in Britain — and which was spotted by Rob as it careered into a parked car last week. After making an overnight recovery, the bird was released the next day, much to the delight of 400 hastily assembled twitchers. But as the bunting, a native of the wastes of Siberia and China, vanished into the wild blue yonder, so began the Chinese whispers and accusations that all was not what it seemed.
>
> Rob, 20, stormed back: 'Someone's putting around stories that I bought the bunting from the Cage and Aviary Bird Show in Birmingham and then released it. It's completely peed me off. Why would I waste good money to buy a cagebird just to let it go? It doesn't make sense, especially as the Meadow Bunting is a species that would never be accepted in this country as a genuinely wild bird.'
>
> The bunting, a reasonably popular strain among British and continental aviculturalists, had no coloured leg ring, the normal sign of a

captive bird. Rob came across it last Friday after a lunchtime drink at a pub near the Marton Mere local nature reserve in Lancashire. The bird, feeding with a flock of Reed Buntings in a car park, was spooked by a passing car and crashed into another parked vehicle.

At first, Rob thought it was dead, but after noticing it was still breathing he set about trying to put a name to the mystery bird. After travelling up to see some friends in Preston, they were finally able to identify the bird as a first-winter male Meadow Bunting. The news was circulated and the next day birders from all over the country gathered to watch the bird's release.

Rob added: 'There has been talk that I had bought the bird at the Cage and Aviary Show but that that didn't open until 2.30pm on Friday afternoon, and I found the bird a short while later that afternoon. There is absolutely no way I could have got back from Birmingham to Lancashire in such a short space of time. Anyway, if someone was trying it on, they would not pick a species like the Meadow Bunting because they know it would never be regarded as truly wild.'

Glad to set the record straight, Rob.

Television and the
Corridors of Power

Television! Teacher, mother, secret lover.
—Homer J. Simpson, *The Simpsons.*

Ask my family about the pinnacle of my journalistic career and they will, without hesitation, allude to one event. As a hack of 30 years, you would think it might be some scintillating front-page world exclusive, or an exposé that brought down a Government minister, or a hard-hitting article that highlighted some grave miscarriage of justice. Over four decades, I have worked on some of the big stories of the late 20th century and early 21st century – the death of Princess Diana, the 9/11 attacks and the Hillsborough disaster – as well as covering several of the most infamous crimes and murders of the generation. For my daughters, however, one event stands out: introducing the 2002 final of *Pop Idol*, which pitched a youthful Will Young against an even more youthful Gareth Gates. How a humble hack managed to enter the world of Simon Cowell and all that showbiz razzamatazz is a convoluted story that led to a speaking part in front of an estimated 20 million viewers on peak-time Saturday night television. My girls still eat out on it.

The spotlight came down on me at a time when I was working on the *Daily Star* news desk, where reality television and all its spin-offs were an incredible readership draw. *Big Brother* and its ilk pulled in thousands of young readers and so when *Pop Idol* hit the screen, we gave the programme front-page billing. I was part of a team thinking up 'blue-sky angles' for the newspaper's coverage and, as the contestants were whittled away to the two finalists, our team dreamed up the perfect metaphor for the show's climax – reality television's equivalent of the General Election. The Blair versus Hague contest had taken place the previous spring and so there were plenty of comparisons to be made when Mssrs Young and Gates mounted the musical hustings. Pop Idol's producers loved our take and soon got into the act themselves, providing both singers with 'battle buses', colourful rosettes and their own presidential-style campaign trail. The *Daily Star* offices were one of their first ports of call.

Over the years the Star's newsroom, in its palatial splendour on Blackfriars Bridge, had hosted many VIP visits. Mrs Thatcher was there when the newspaper first moved from Fleet Street, and throughout the 1990s, as it became acknowledged for insightful popular television and contemporary music coverage, the stars seemed only willing to come in and say hello. Take That, Boyzone, East 17 and the Spice Girls were just a few of the acts to put in guest appearances on the news desk, while hundreds of teenyboppers screamed and fainted outside. Nothing was to prepare us for the scenes when the Young and Gates roadshow arrived. There were thousands besieging the building while inside every secretary, cleaner and advertising rep in the office wanted to get a peek of the two performers made as they made their guest entrances. And what entrances. The guys were ushered into the building with hysterical scenes reminiscent of Beatlemania. Once inside, they headed straight to the news desk for handshakes, interviews and to chat to fans over a special *Pop Idol* hotline. It was during all this commotion that I made a passing remark to a producer that the final had caught the national psyche in a way the last General Election never had. Within a flash, a camera was in my face and I was being pressed to repeat what I had said. Over the following days the Young versus Gates contest continued to dominate the pages of the red-top tabloids, and on the Saturday evening most of the nation settled down in front the television to watch the final sing off.

I was one of the exceptions. A long-planned dinner date with friends meant I would be oblivious to proceedings. Well, for all of five minutes. Unbeknown to me, the producers had decided to use my off-the-cuff remarks as the introduction to the show. Within seconds of sitting down to eat, my mobile phone was burning. Dozens of friends, workmates, and relatives were calling to say they had seen me on television. Long forgotten acquaintances I had not seen for years made contact. Even my daughters were mightily impressed. For once, in their eyes, I was more than a middle-aged, real life Homer Simpson impersonator.

What the *Pop Idol* experience taught me was the power of television. One only has to visit the Bird Fair to sense the celebrity aura of that small band of wildlife presenters who appear regularly on the Box. Chris Packham, Simon King, Mike Dilger and David Lindo work extremely hard in a very competitive medium and deserve the adoration they get. Fame is nice, and can bring riches, but you have to be cut out to be a TV birder. And, if the truth be told, I am simply not an in-front-of-the-camera person. Besides being told by one television executive that I have a 'face for radio,' my one and only attempt at a screen test ended in crushing embarrassment. The idea of presenting regional news bulletins seemed like a good idea and, after making an application to be a newsreader, I sailed through the early stages which involved putting items in order of current affairs priority. Then came the 'Good evening, this is the six-o'clock news' bit. Seventeen takes later and I had still not delivered a full news summary. The production team had picked up on my inability to pronounce aspirates correctly and had me reciting a particular pay-off line, which I delivered as 'This is Stuart Winter reporting from the 'Oliday H'inn 'Otel h'at 'Eathrow H'airport.' I sounded like Manuel from *Fawlty Towers*. My parents' Cockney roots had turned me into a laughing stock. I was told, in no uncertain terms, not to give up my day job and to stick to newspapers.

Having taken the advice about concentrating on a written journalism career, I have still found myself flirting with notions of television grandeur on occasions. While working as a crime reporter I was shadowed by a BBC crew for a documentary on Scotland Yard and also had a speaking part in Channel 4's *Encounters* programme that focussed on Scilly's twitching season. One *Daily Star* column was to put me in full glare of a live television discussion with a hostile audience baying for blood. Mine. The article was about one of my pet aversions, Peregrine Falcon persecution, and saw me aiming two barrels at those rogue elements who are more than happy to attack one of our most beautiful birds of prey to pursue their pastime. It created one of the paper's biggest mailbags. Under the headline 'Pie in the Sky', it read:

> If there's one bird that's better on a plate than flying through the air, it's the feral pigeon. They are boring, scruffy, disease-ridden and prone to leaving nasty little messages. The only form of life lower down the pecking order are pigeon breeders who want to obliterate some of our rarest birds of prey in a misguided bid to save their precious pigeons. There has been a growing lobby of pigeon-fanciers demanding the destruction of Peregrine Falcons and Sparrowhawks because they prey on racing birds. Top racing pigeons are worth their weight in platinum. The sport is big business across Europe and the fastest racers change hands for thousands of pounds. That's why fanciers get peeved when their birds' internal compasses go haywire and they get lost.
>
> Unfortunately, it's the Peregrine Falcon that has taken the blame. There have been calls for the Government to grant licences to cull birds of prey, but new evidence is emerging that will acquit the Peregrine. The latest issue of influential magazine *New Scientist* says that the stress of being transported to the start line for racing is killing some pigeons. Lack of water and high temperatures generated by birds in cooped up conditions also weakens them.
>
> Chris Harbard, of the Royal Society for the Protection of Birds, told me: 'Peregrines do feed on pigeons but they form a small part of their diet. There are many more factors that can result in pigeons going missing. They face bad weather or may fly into pylons or find a mate in Trafalgar Square.'
>
> The next time your council spends a small fortune trying to eradicate the local feral pigeon population, you may wish there were more Peregrines around to do the job naturally.

Within hours of the newspaper hitting the streets the complaints were coming in thicker than a flock of Rock Doves. Angry telephone callers baying for an apology were followed by even angrier mailbag demanding that someone wring my neck. I stood steadfast but the Editor decided to publish some of the more printable letters under the headline 'Coo! What a flap' and followed by a short introductory sentence which read: 'Readers' feathers were really ruffled when the *Daily Star's* birdman said pigeons were only fit for pies ...' Here are a few of the examples the spleen vented in my direction:

> The Queen is a top breeder of racing pigeons and would no doubt be outraged to discover that you regard her as 'lower in the pecking order than a dirty, disease-ridden Trafalgar Square feral pigeon'. J.O., Bolton.

> I've been a *Daily Star* reader since the day it was born and, until now, I have enjoyed the Strictly for the Birds column. Writer Stuart Winter should realise that the pigeon fanciers he despises raise thousands for charity. We just don't squawk about it! B.H., Northumberland.

> Problems have arisen because the RSPB has bred hawks and falcons and then released them into the wild. These birds have no fear of man and often attack pigeons in their own lofts – yet fanciers don't want to see them wiped out. A.L., Merseyside

> During the war, Peregrine Falcons were destroyed on Government orders – to protect racing pigeons carrying vital messages. That alone is proof that these birds frequently attack pigeons. J.V., Ulster.

> Pigeon breeders do not want to obliterate the Peregrine Falcon or the Sparrowhawk, they merely ask that numbers be controlled. These birds kill large numbers of pigeons and are decimating the songbird population. J.H., Shropshire.

> Stuart acknowledges that pigeon racing is big business across Europe. So why not cover some of the races instead of printing a load of negative rubbish? M.H., Cheshire.

The row simmered for days and sparked a much wider debate. Before I had time to write a follow-up article, a television producer made contact and asked if I would like to discuss the issue on a late-night current affairs show. For the *Daily Star*, it was all good publicity and I was as good as told to fight my corner on screen. Fight was the operative word. What the producer had not told me was that I would be appearing on the nearest thing to mortal combat since the Colosseum closed down.

Central Weekend Live was a far too innocuous name for a show that was real bear-pit television. Some of the country's best television talent presented the show – Nicky Campbell, James Whale, Paul Ross and Victoria Derbyshire – and its guests and subject matter were served up like raw meat for the baying mob handpicked to create the show's unique atmosphere. The week before I was appearing, a group of self-confessed drugs dealers had to be given a police escort to protect them from the audience. Our particular show would see Peter Stringfellow defending lap dancing to a crowd of feminists and yours truly attacking those who wanted to see the poor Peregrine culled. Our host was Adrian Mills, formerly of the Esther Rantzen vehicle *That's Life*, and a skilled exponent of this live debate genre. He simply asked me to repeat the opening lines of my pigeon column as if he was lighting the blue touch paper at a firework display. I did. And the audience went wild.

Over the next 15 minutes the Pigeon men and the Bird men slugged it out. Peregrines were painted as ravenous beasts. I defended their honour. On stage with me was a leading light in the pigeon fancying world, accompanied by one of his racing birds in a cage. Quick wit and ready repartee has never been my forte but, if I say so myself, I took one look of the pigeon and noticed its caged was lined with a copy of *The Sun* – the deadly rival of my own newspaper.

'The only good thing about that bird is that it's ******* on a copy of *The Sun*,' I said with a growl.

The comment brought the house down. There were cheers among the mass contingent of bird lovers shipped into the studio to give their voice to the 'live debate', for want of another word for this shock TV pugilism. Angry looking pigeon people on the other side of the studio hissed as if they were at a pantomime. Arguments and insults were traded until the show's compère requested a show of hands on the motion that Peregrines should be controlled to protect pigeons. The result was overwhelming victory for the falcon. There were cheers and standing applause. Back in the Green Room – the hospitality suite where guests can chill out with chilled beers – there was still an air of tension. While some of the pigeon fanciers were gallant losers, a couple eyed me with contempt and refused to shake hands. Tough.

For all the adrenalin rush appearing on a live television debate produced, it was the after show socialising that was to have a profound impact on my bird journalism. Among the invited guests that night were Chris Whittles of CJ WildBird Foods, one of the most influential figures in the bird world, and David Cromack, Editor of *Bird Watching* magazine. Over a beer or two, I was not only invited to become a writer for David's magazine but forged strong links with Chris, whom I am delighted to say, today sponsors my weekly column in the *Sunday Express*.

Although the combination of a somewhat portly physique (they say that you look a stone fatter than you are on screen) and an inability to pronounce aitches means that I'll never have a career in front of the camera, television has always featured heavily in all aspects of my birding. At one time, ticking off birds on screen became a pastime in itself, with my television list becoming almost as precious as my proper outdoor list. During the late 1980s and into the 1990s every wildlife documentary was watched assiduously in the hope of seeing birds on screen that appeared on the official British list. It meant watching some pretty naff programmes to get much needed rarities such as Spotted Sandpiper and Song Sparrow. I even counted American Robin from the 'Spoonful of sugar' sequence from *Mary Poppins*, although I had misgivings because the bird looked stuffed! The whole thing became very addictive. To make sure I never missed potential new sightings I began to build up a video library of natural history documentaries as I recorded hour after hour of programmes with the hope of getting a new tick. Then, one day came the satellite age and Sky Plus. Hundreds of programmes and a limited hard drive meant recording birds on video had not only become obsolete but the excitement of picking out Snow Buntings on a Scandinavian news report or Ring-billed Gulls in a New York gangster film seemed suddenly futile. Today, my loft still heaves under the weight of cardboard boxes filled with hundreds of unwatched video tapes. I am waiting for an opportunity to sell them on eBay.

The one thing about watching out for birds on television is that it gave me an opportunity to ogle shows such as *Baywatch*. When I told the *Daily Star* news desk that I always watched the show because of the number shorebirds in the background rather than Pamela Anderson's shapely contours encased in a red swimming costume, I was persuaded to write a whole feature on how to spot the Californian, Western and Heerman's Gulls, Willets and Brown Pelicans that haunt Malibu Beach. The piece also made reference to watching out for boobies.

Mainstream American shows were to provide a good revision tool ahead of my first venture at the World Series of Birding in New Jersey in the spring of 1995. Competitors in this event have to rely heavily upon song and call notes, and although there are several bird-sound CDs on the market, listening out for background warblers and thrushes in cowboy films or cop series is also great way to revise. One particular event that produces a cacophony of American bird song is the annual US Masters golf tournament at the Augusta National. Northern Cardinals and Carolina Wrens serenade the likes of Tiger Woods and Ernie Els as they tee off at the famous Amen Corner. Listen really carefully and you can pick out the wonderful spiralling notes of Wood Thrush. Not being a golf fan, it certainly turns the game once described by Mark Twain as 'a good walk spoilt' into a watchable event.

Birding by ear on television is not an exact science. Television's obsession with canned laughter and music also sees some very strange background soundtracks. Everyone must have heard the eerie Arctic song of the Great Northern Diver and Australian Kookaburras bringing African jungle adventure films to life. One thing which always amuses me about Westerns is that the skies are never darkened by the clouds of Passenger Pigeons which were so numerous until the 1860s that nesting colonies could number 100 million birds. Costume dramas suffer the opposite effect on this side of the Atlantic. For all the attempts by film-makers to get the settings right in terms of dress, language and historical fact, there is always one thing that lets these big-budget dramatisations down – bird noise. Jane Austen, the Brontë sisters and the odd piece of Shakespeare have all suffered from the strident sounds of one particular species, a fact that lent itself to a column headlined 'Coo, what a Bloomer' in November 1997:

BBC Chiefs have been left red-faced by their latest Sunday night ration of bodice-popping cleavages and bouncing buttocks. It's nothing to do with the vast expanses of naked flesh on show, or the scenes of bawdy 18th century sex. For despite spending an astonishing £10 million to make Henry Fielding's classic *Tom Jones* – and claiming to have made every effort to keep faithful to the plot – TV drama-makers have made a bigger boob than any poking out from those low-cut Georgian dresses.

An astute reader took time to point out this week that all the puffing and panting on screen had not softened his birding skills. As viewers watch randy Tom bed his way through a bevy of buxom wenches, the radar-eared twitcher picked up the dulcet tones of Collared Doves doing a bit of billing, and cooing themselves. As any keen birder knows, the chances of hearing a Collared Dove anywhere in England during the 1700s would have been just a little bit more improbable than seeing it perched on top of a red London bus at the same time. This is because the first Collared Dove to set foot on British soil did not arrive until the 1950s, in one of the bird success stories of the age.

Until 1930, the Collared Dove's nearest breeding area was 2,000 miles away in the Balkans, but because of its own rampant sex drive the dove dramatically spread westwards. In the space of just 30 years, it managed to colonise most of Europe. The reason for this astonishing success is its extended breeding season. Collared Doves can mate and raise young in almost any month of the year. They also have the very useful ability to eke out a living around urban areas, which allows them to survive even the harshest of our European winters.

We felt obliged, on behalf of all birders, to point out the error of their ways to the BBC. A surprised drama department spokesman insisted that they had gone to great lengths to keep faithful to the original book – and had also warned viewers before every episode about the full frontal nudity on show. But he did admit: 'Despite all the lengths we have gone to, to make the drama authentic, it seems that our soundman was not much of an ornithologist.'

The BBC's ability to see Auntie drop a few bloomers has provided me with a few scoops over the years. My favourite relates to the presenter I regard as the finest writer in the English language today. Love him or loathe him, Jeremy Clarkson's curare-tipped pen can fascinate, infuriate, inspire, provoke, anger, amuse and generate belly-laughs – sometimes all in one sentence. His observations are perceptive and his ability to tap into the national consciousness makes him unique. His outspoken views and his love of the heavy throb of V8 engines have hardly endeared him to the green lobby. One particular diatribe on aviation in Britain and the rise of nimbyism was aimed at an organisation very close to my heart. To use the Clarksonmeister's words about 'the most fearsome organisation in the world' he says of it: 'In a straight battle between this lot and Al-Qaeda, Osama bin Laden would end up killing himself to escape from the hounding. It can nit-pick a man to death from 400 paces. Its members are terminators. Ladies and gentlemen, I give you ... the Royal Society for the Protection of Birds.'

In an essay on the debate that surrounded the building of a new London airport on the north Kent marshes, he suggested that the only way through the 'eco-twaddle' is to expand Heathrow because, and here is the punchline: '...best of all, the RSPB can't object because any birds native to the reservoirs of Staines were long since sucked into the Trent engine of a passing 777 and shredded.'

As someone who regularly birded on Staines' famous causeway during the 1980s, I could easily find such remarks offensive. I guess all those who have watched such birds as Baird's Sandpiper and Wilson's Phalarope through the reservoir railings would love to take sheep-shearing scissors to Clarkson's trademark curly locks. But the man is at the front of the queue to join my genius list. He writes what so many people would love to think and also writes in a way that no single popular wordsmith can emulate. I know, I've tried, and with almost disastrous consequences. On one occasion I tried to review a certain product for a magazine in the style of Clarkson – I borrowed one of his terms, saying it felt like it had been made from a melted down Action Man – and sparked demands by the manufacturers that the publication pulp its entire print run! Fortunately, everything was resolved amicably.

For all my admiration for Clarkson, it has not stopped me from letting rip when I have felt he has overstepped the mark. I wrote a piece about *Top Gear* angering conservationists when the all-action car show decided to go on location to the Makgadikgadi salt-pans in Botswana, the setting for Africa's biggest zebra migration. The idea of leaving tyre tracks across the flat, unspoilt 'thirstlands' had angered conservation organisations and gave me a full-page article, headlined: '*Top Gear* stars speed through zebra crossing'. The BBC argued that the *Top Gear* team had used 'ordinary cars' and not 4x4 vehicles for filming in Botswana and that the tracks would be washed away when the rainy season started. But for environmentalists, driving in such a pristine wilderness was anathema because it threatened to open up the idea of driving on the salt-flats to others.

There was no room for manoeuvre when Clarkson really put his accelerator foot in it during the making of a television series about our Continental neighbours and visited France to savour one of their more appalling Gallic traditions – eating Ortolan Buntings. Within hours of the show being broadcast my sources at the RSPB were incandescent. Complaints were coming in like Starlings to roost. Under the headline

'Bird-brained', I told the story in the following weekend's *Sunday Express*. By his own admission, Clarkson was expecting a backlash.

TV motormouth Jeremy Clarkson bit off more than he expected when he savoured one of France's finest delicacies. The curly-haired presenter, famed for his fast cars, tight jeans and outspoken views, enraged conservationists by dining on one Europe's most threatened birds.

Millions watched Clarkson lick his lips and extol the virtues of feasting on the tiny Ortolan Bunting, a migratory bird related to the Yellowhammer, on his new BBC2 show.

Worse was to come as Clarkson dismissed the way the tiny Ortolans are trapped, fattened up and then killed by being drowned in brandy.

As he popped the bird into his famously voluminous mouth, Clarkson could be heard salivating about the taste and admitting: 'Mmm...Mmm... How many letters of complaint? This could be my absolute record in terms of complaints.'

Britain's leading conservation organisation set the ball rolling by condemning Clarkson for his exploitation of a bird which is rapidly declining across the Continent. A spokesman for the Royal Society for the Protection of Birds said: 'We have received several complaints. This programme was highly unpopular with our million members.

'It's a shame that Mr Clarkson thinks he has to entertain us by eating such a rare bird. We know that the French think the Ortolan Bunting is a delicacy, yet given the Ortolan's rare status not only in France but also the rest of Europe we believe the French Government should be looking to outlaw the hunting of this beautiful bird. Programmes like this do not do the conservation cause any good.'

Clarkson sampled Ortolan as part of a tour of Europe for his series *Jeremy Clarkson Meets The Neighbours*. Ortolan numbers are declining rapidly in Europe. Each spring they migrate from Africa to Europe but have to run the gauntlet of French hunters. Up to 50,000 are captured. The birds are kept in blacked-out boxes for two weeks and encouraged to feed continuously before being taken out and drowned in Armagnac.

The appalling treatment of wild birds by our European partners has been one of the saddest continuing themes of my columns over three decades. France, Spain, Italy, Malta and Cyprus have all stood accused of failing to crack down on cruel, bucolic practices that have no place in the 21st century. Trapping and netting migratory songbirds for the pot or simply blasting them for fun is something that northern Europeans eschew, and the forces of law and order in the United Kingdom thankfully take a dim view of these illegal practices. The Wildlife and Countryside Act has been a powerful tool in the war against the countryside's eco-vandals. Egg collectors and those who kill birds of prey no longer walk from court with derisory financial penalties. Courts are handing out short, sharp custodial sentences. In both Whitehall and Westminster there is a general feeling that biodiversity must be preserved and that birds, in particular, are part of the nation's heritage. Indeed, the barometer value of birds is seen by the Government as an important gauge of not just the health of the countryside but of our overall feeling of well-being in modern Britain. Wild bird populations are one of 15 headline 'Quality of Life Indicators', which also include education, crime, cultural diversity, employment and economic prosperity. For any Government department, it is easy to understand how any positive increase in these vital indices is something to proclaim. When Environment Minister Michael Meacher did so, it ended in the two of us squaring up to each other in an amazing display of verbal fisticuffs, with me accusing him of falling victim to New Labour spin tactics.

The kerfuffle began in the late autumn of 2001 when the Department for the Environment, Food and Rural Affairs (Defra) released bird population figures in an all too triumphant press bulletin. My sources in the bird conservation world were spitting feathers and urged me to get writing. Under the headline, 'Tale of Decline They're Trying to Hush Up', I wrote in the *Daily Star*:

> The curse of the Government spin-doctors has jinxed the world of birds. Whitehall smooth-talkers suggest it has achieved a true conservation success.
>
> 'An increase in rare and common wild birds,' the Department for the Environment, Food and Rural Affairs boasted this week. 'New figures show that the populations of UK common wild birds have reached their highest level since 1990. Populations rose by three per cent in 2000,' the bulletin added.
>
> Indeed, Environment Minister Michael Meacher's statistics show the Great Spotted Woodpecker and Goldcrest are flourishing and some of our rarest species – Corncrake, Bittern and Black Grouse – also benefit from

conservation. But like most Government spin, there's another side to the story.

Mr Meacher did NOT tell a conference that farmland birds in Britain have declined by 40 per cent in the last 30 years – the worst record of 30 European countries. This is catastrophic.

More than 75 per cent of Britain's land is farmed and birds are key to it. Species such as the Skylark, Grey Partridge and Lapwing must not be allowed to die out. Corn Buntings, Turtle Doves, Mistle Thrushes, Cuckoos and Bullfinches are all far less common since Britain joined the EU and its agricultural policy.

Millions have been spent on appeasing farmers for the foot and mouth crisis, but it's time some money was spent on saving our birds by:

- Using less pesticide;
- Encouraging organic farming;
- Leaving more stubble over winter.

Only then can New Labour talk about improvements.

As far as weekly rants went, it was one of my favourites, mainly because it went down well with the birding community. My attitudes to farming and farmers have changed much over the past decade and today I find many people in agriculture much more in tune with good environmental practices. The day after publication, I was one of the first in the office when the Editor's secretary phoned down to the news desk to say she had Michael Meacher on the line, demanding to speak to the Editor himself. The Minister of State wasn't very happy, she warned. She put the call through and I got it – both barrels.

'I do not want to talk to you,' the Minister stormed. 'I want to speak to your Editor. I am bloody furious.' Dealing with angry readers was very much part of my news desk brief, and I like to think that I can take the anger out of most situations. This was proving far more difficult. A Government minister certainly does not like to be placated when he's in full swing...

'Yes, minister,' I found myself answering like the BBC comedy's bumbling Sir Humphrey, the irony lost on me as Mr Meacher threatened all sorts of recriminations from the Press Complaints Commission. But I was not going to recant. I knew in my heart of hearts that birds were still having a hard time for all his ministry's triumphalism. After we agreed to disagree, a compromise was reached. My column would carry a letter from Mr Meacher. In my last *Daily Star* column of 2001, the

Environment Minister and I both put our cases in the following article.

Government high-flyer Michael Meacher was spitting feathers this week after I said his party was too triumphant about the latest wild bird breeding figures. The Environment Minister got in a flap after my report claimed the Government had missed out the most damning statistic of all – that Britain was bottom of the league of 30 European nations for its decline in farmland birds. These have crashed by more than 40 per cent in the past 30 years and the future still looks bleak. Mr Meacher has asked us to print his letter putting forward the Government's case. We're only too happy to do that. At the same time, I've written an open letter to the Environment Minister.

Dear Sir,
Stuart Winter has a nerve to claim the Government tried to hide figures showing a decline in farmland birds ('Tale Of A Decline They're Trying To Hush Up', 21 December), when he was not even at the press briefing when I announced this. Had he been there he would know, as journalists attending have reported, that I clearly stated that the recent stability in farmland birds and a small increase in woodland birds contrasted with the rapid declines of the 1970s and 1980s. However, we are not complacent. That is why we have adopted farmland birds as one of our key targets and we are aiming to reverse the long-term decline by 2020. We are also doing much to help these birds by increasing spending on agri-environment measures and introducing new arable options in the Countryside Stewardship Scheme. I am disappointed that Mr Winter failed to spot this information in the Defra press notice issued on Wednesday morning.
Yours faithfully,
Michael Meacher, Environment Minister.

I responded:

Dear Mr Meacher,
As I could not get a word in edgeways when you called last week (you were 'bloody furious,' I seem to remember), please take time to read the following. The Department for Environment, Food and Rural Affairs did make what is still a worrying, if not dire, situation seem far too cosy.

'Increase in rare and common wild birds,' bugled the news release.

'New figures show that populations of UK common wild birds have reached their highest level since 1990. Populations increased by three per cent in 2000 and are now six per cent up on three years ago,' it said. It all sounds very good. That is, until you look at one key fact highlighted by the compilers of your statistics, the British Trust for Ornithology.

The current boom in 'common' bird populations has more to do with nature than conservation initiatives – it's largely down to the run of mild winters we have all enjoyed in recent years. Birdwatchers everywhere will be praying that January 2002 does not witness a major freeze. Even New Labour, for all its success in office, has not yet found a way of controlling the weather.

The aim of my article was to highlight the fact that 11 farmland species are still suffering declines. These are birds that hold a special place in the hearts of the British public, and birds that depend on good agricultural practices to survive. According to the Defra report, the Skylark, Grey Partridge and Cuckoo all enjoyed mini booms in 2000 — up 42 per cent for the partridge alone.

But it's the underlying trend that should worry bird lovers everywhere. Between 1994 and 2000 the Grey Partridge was down 22 per cent, the Skylark 7.9 per cent and the Cuckoo 19.4 per cent. How long can they survive if this trend continues?

I used my column to put forward practical suggestions to ensure the survival of our farm birds. The Government must be prepared for the biggest agricultural revolution since we joined the EU. It must ensure we have more organic farming; more spring cereals are sown; more fields are left as stubble, and fewer pesticides used.

From the level of the anger voiced to me, I can tell that you are concerned about the future of our wildlife. If you can harness this passion into forcing our farmers into adopting these simple but effective techniques, we may have found the politician who will give us back our farm birds.
Happy New Year,
Stuart Winter.

The brouhaha abated. The minister and I went back to our day jobs of trying save the planet. Some weeks later, I met Mr Meacher at a ministerial reception and we shook hands. The impression he gave was that there were no hard feelings. We were both people passionate about preserving the countryside. Talking to many high-ranking conservationists, Michael Meacher is still regarded as the best Environment Minister the country has ever had. His grasp of conservation science was second to none, according to my sources at the RSPB. Sadly, he does not hold high office in a Gordon Brown administration in desperate need of strong environmentalists, particularly when the last *State of the Nation's Birds* report showed that farmland birds are still suffering heavy declines.

When Michael Meacher's ministerial tenure in the Blair administration came to an end in 2003 with his unceremonious sacking, he was replaced with arguably the best birdwatcher ever to hold high office, Elliot Morley.

I first met Elliot Morley at the Bird Fair and it was obvious from the outset that he held both a deep passion for and knowledge of birds. The fact that he could bring his own field experience into the inner sanctums of Government was a positive boon for conservation. On one occasion I had a briefing from him in his ministerial office on the Ruddy Duck issue and it was patently obvious that he had far more understanding on the subject than his aides. Besides birds and the countryside, he was also a strong anti-whaling voice. One of his duties was Fisheries Minister and, after he had championed cetacean rights during tough talks at an international conference in Japan, I dubbed him the 'Prince of the Whales'. It seemed to go down very well. Whenever we met at press conferences or at official functions, he would always chat and loved giving updates on his garden birds, particularly his beloved Tree Sparrows. The way he had turned his constituency home into a miniature bird sanctuary seemed a great feature – the Environment Minister with his own nature reserve – and so with arrangements made through his office, Mr Morley happily posed up for photographs of him putting out Tree Sparrow feeders at his family home.

The following piece appeared in the *Daily Star* in April 2002:

> The Tree Sparrow is fighting its way back from the brink of extinction, thanks to a one-man Government initiative. But the conservation battle for the sparrow's survival isn't costing taxpayers a penny.
>
> Deep among the ivy-clad ash trees of Animal Health and Fisheries Minister Elliott Morley's country home, this delightful chocolate-and-cream songbird is proving it can still have a future in Britain – after 30 catastrophic years.
>
> In that time numbers have fallen by 87 per cent, and it has entirely disappeared from many of its former haunts. But now its plaintive chirp is

once again ringing out in Mr Morley's rambling garden in the north Lincolnshire village of Winterton, courtesy of an environment operation that has become a labour of love for the Labour minister.

When Mr Morley is not in his Westminster office at the Department for Environment, Food and Rural Affairs looking at such issues as fishing quotas, whaling and animal welfare, he's poring his efforts into his one-man conservation campaign. He has turned his garden into a miniature nature reserve bedecked with feeders and nest boxes that help to support thriving populations of tits, finches and thrushes. Yet it's the arrival of the Tree Sparrow that has so delighted Mr Morley, a life-long birdwatcher.

'This has been the family home for 16 years and in that time we have put up feeders and nest boxes, hoping to attract birds like tits and House Martins,' he said. 'It costs a small fortune in seed, but is very rewarding. Watching birds come into the garden is a joy. But this winter I noticed two Tree Sparrows had suddenly arrived from nowhere. They have become a very rare bird in these parts, mainly due to changes in the way we farm.

'Lack of winter stubble and weed seeds means that there is no longer enough food when the weather's harsh and, as an added problem, farms today are just too tidy with less spilt grain about. Tree Sparrows like to nest in holes in tumbledown buildings and the like, and these sites are no longer available. It has seen a marked decline in the species in Britain. That's why I was just so pleased when the first two turned up. Over the winter the flock grew steadily and we now have 14 feeding here regularly.'

The next stage is to encourage the Tree Sparrows to remain in his garden to breed and raise young. Mr Morley added: 'Tree Sparrows are colonial nesters and I have put up a special nest box system that could encourage several pairs to breed. The box has a number of entrances; it's a bit like a little terraced housing estate. Sadly, I am not always here to see them but I do try to get out into the field when I am at home with the family on Sundays and the family are taking a keen interest.'

In May 2009, Mr Morley announced that he would be standing down as an MP at the next General Election after the well-publicised story of his expenses claims for mortgage repayments on his home, which led to him making the following statement:

'This is my choice after discussing this with my family and my constituency party officers. The last two weeks have been traumatic for me and I have to think of my family and my health, both of which have suffered. Nor do I want in any way to undermine the strong position the Labour Party has in this constituency in what will be a crucial election.

In saying this I want to stress that I made a genuine mistake over my expenses. There are reasons for this and I am confident that my name will be cleared and I am ready to make my case to the Parliamentary Commissioner for Standards as soon as that can be arranged, and to co-operate fully.

I have never tried to duck responsibility for my mistake and I have repaid the amount in full. I do understand peoples' anger over the whole issue of MPs' expenses and their frustration.

For those who condemn me I would simply ask to be allowed the opportunity to present my case. For those who have supported me, particularly those who have urged me not to stand down, I'd like to thank them for their support and would ask them to give that backing to my successor.'

I could make play of the irony in the second sentence of my Tree Sparrow article after recent events, but would not stoop so low. Sadly, Elliot Morley's decision to stand down as an MP in 2010 saw ornithology lose a powerful voice in the corridors of power.

While politicians come and go, one institution remains not only at the heart of Government, but also at the heart of conservation in the United Kingdom. Much is made of the Royal Family's love of field sports. Fox-hunting, before it was made illegal, and pheasant shooting run through their blue-blooded veins, and this no doubt contributes to the strong feelings of republicanism among the animal welfare and conservation movements. I take a more pragmatic view. Royal patronage of organisations such as the RSPB and the Royal Society of Wildlife Trusts is a force for good. The Duke of Edinburgh and the Prince of Wales have both been outspoken over many aspects of conservation. Prince Charles, in particular, is a campaigning voice in the climate change debate and a fervent champion of rainforest preservation. Charles has also been a leading light in the global efforts to save the albatross. His service in the Royal Navy helped to instil in him a passion for these most iconic of birds, having watched them from the bridge of his warship as they flew effortlessly across the waves.

In March 2005, the appalling losses of albatrosses because of fishing practices in the South Atlantic began making headline news. Horrific photographs of these stately birds drowned by the long-lines became graphic conservation symbols. It moved Prince Charles to make an impassioned plea for their conservation in my weekly *Sunday Express* column.

Only those who have ever gazed upon an albatross as it careens across the swirling seas can fully comprehend the majesty of nature's finest flying machine. To be honoured with such an audience can be life-changing, a communion with a creature so perfect that it inspires feelings that transcend into a higher plane.

One man who has obviously been touched by the grace and mystique of the albatross is Prince Charles. At a time when his every action is scrutinised, when questions are raised about his forthcoming marriage and, treacherously, even his right to ascend to the throne, the Prince's adoration for these most regal of birds shines like a distant beacon in a maelstrom. He has become the albatross's champion. Conservationists are devoting their lives studying, monitoring and attempting to prevent the seabird's freefall into oblivion, but it is the Prince's personal crusade that may yet save the day for this king of birds.

Early sailors believed that albatrosses were the lost souls of shipmates swept to their doom. To kill one was to be cursed for all time. Coleridge immortalised the albatross's supernatural mystique in his *Rime of the Ancient Mariner*. His portentous lyric has gone unheeded. Albatrosses are dying out. And they're dying out fast. Every hour of every day, a dozen of these magnificent creatures suffer unimaginably cruel deaths at the hands of long-line fishermen, so callous is the slaughter that it risks dooming the bird to wholesale extinction.

Some 100,000 albatrosses are killed annually by these ships with their deadly fishing filaments armed with up to 10,000 hooks. Albatrosses and petrels lured by baited barbs swallow what first appears an easy meal, but are then dragged to their deaths as the lines sink below the waves. Both BirdLife International and its UK partner, the RSPB, have been lobbying on the issue at an international conference in Rome. But on the other side of the world, the Prince's personal struggle to help the albatross became a key moment in his royal tour of Australia and New Zealand.

One of the most powerful speeches he has ever given, he revealed his passion and despair for a creature that may not be long for this world. One only has to listen to his words to sense his fears for the albatross almost surpass any of the travails that have surrounded his own troubled life in recent years.

He said: 'Like many other one-time mariners, I have a very special affection for the albatross. I remember so well, while serving in the Royal Navy, standing on the deck of a fast-moving ship in one of the southern oceans, watching an albatross maintaining perfect position alongside for hour after hour, and apparently day after day. It is a sight I will never forget. I find it hard – no, impossible – to accept that these birds might one day be lost forever.

'Yet that does now seem to be a real possibility unless we can make a sufficient fuss to prevent it. In 1996, three of the 21 species of albatross were listed as threatened. Four years later, when I sat down to write an article expressing my concerns about the decline of these magnificent birds, the total threatened species had risen to 16. Another five years on, and 19 of the 21 species of albatross are now under threat of extinction with the populations of some species now numbering under 100 individuals. The albatross family is now the biggest single bird family with every one of its members under threat.

'I have always felt that if birds' wanderings should cease through Man's insensitive hand, and that magical moment of a swallow's first arrival or an albatross's return disrupted forever, then it would be as if one's heart had been torn out. If this was to happen – and we are rapidly approaching the very real possibility with all 21 species of albatross – then we would sacrifice any claim whatsoever to call ourselves civilized beings. We will have violated something sacred in the inner workings of nature, and our descendants will pay dearly for the consequences of this and other acts of short-term folly.'

Such folly is avoidable. Conservation organisations know it. The Prince has highlighted it. Yet world governments continue to turn a blind eye.

A few weeks later I was invited to attend an RSPB gala dinner where Prince Charles would be making a keynote speech to underline his message about saving the albatross. As I struggled to get my expanding girth into what seemed like a shrinking dinner jacket, I had little idea that I would get an opportunity to speak to Charles about his love for these sublime flying machines. Moments after his arrival at Trinity House, a Clarence House aide approached me and said that the Prince would like to personally thank me for what I had written about his campaigning. Minutes later, I was in a line of RSPB officials, awaiting my audience and pondering the protocols of using 'Your Royal Highness' and 'Sir' at the appropriate moments and remembering only to answer questions and not ask them. Suddenly, Charles was smiling in front of me, not as tall as I imagined, but with the firmest and friendliest of handshakes, delivered with a reassuring grip that he was genuinely pleased to be talking about a subject dear to his heart. My mouth turned to rubber. Charles asked if I had ever seen an albatross and urged me to get my editor to send me to New Zealand and visit Taiaroa Head, the only mainland breeding ground for the awesome Northern Royal Albatross. The heartfelt emotion he held for these birds was evident in his every word. I could have listened for hours but royal duties meant there were other hands that needed to be shaken.

Later that spring I was invited to visit Prince Charles's country estate at Highgrove, and also his working Duchy farm. The Soil Association hosted the visit and we were met by both his farm manager and head gardener who provided insight into Charles's commitment to organic farming. Highgrove would make a beautiful nature reserve. Delicate snake's head fritillaries coat the lawns with a glorious purple sheen, Common Buzzards mew overhead and the trees and hedgerows – many of them personally laid by the Prince – are awash with farm and woodland birds in numbers that hark back to a time before industrial agriculture. Listening to the Duchy of Cornwall staff enthuse about the Prince's commitment to conservation and their joy of managing an estate in tune with nature sowed the seeds of an idea that brought about a project that would finally see my name flashed up on the credits of a television programme.

Watching Song Thrushes go about their slug- and snail-clearing duties in the inner sanctum of Highgrove House – an important part of Prince's credo to clear pests without resorting to chemicals – left me thinking about the ways in which the Royal Family engages with birds. Everyone knows the story about the Tower of London's Ravens, who are cared for by the Monarch's most trusted and loyal guards – the Yeomen Warders of Her Majesty's Royal Palace, the so-called Beefeaters – but there are many areas of court life that bring birds and official duties together. Researching the roles of the Queen's Swan Warden and Swan Marker, looking into the activities of the Royal Pigeon Loft and also the way that the Crown estates are managed to give sanctuary to wildlife provided a fascinating insight into another world.

In 2008, I approached Discovery Channel with the idea and *The Royal Birdmen* was given its ascent. Getting a budget from a television company was the easy part. I needed to get permission from the Royal Household to germinate a concept into film footage. It was a long, protracted process but by the summer I had teamed up with an independent television company and we were on location in the grounds of Highgrove, with its reedbed sewage system, dense woodland and open meadows. Although much of the filming took place during the August lull when bird song was muted and passerine activity was at its quietest, Charles' vision of a natural garden rich in birds and bugs was there to capture in glorious High Definition. My main task that day was to find birds for cameraman Adam Kennedy, a fine birder himself, to get up close and personal with, as they say in TV circles. Few birders, if any, have had almost free-run of Highgrove's verdant pastures and woodlands, which are heavily protected by a security machine in place to protect the heir to the throne and his heirs. It was idyllic. Linnets, Greenfinches, Yellowhammers and Skylarks abounded in the farmed areas, while Robins, Common Whitethroats, Great Spotted Woodpeckers and Song Thrushes were in numbers you would be pushed to find on a nature reserve, let alone a country garden.

One of the 'birdiest' scenes of the entire documentary came when the crew was on location at the Queen's private estate in Sandringham. Filming centred on a pigeon race when Her Majesty's birds were pitched against those of her humble subjects. The film followed the pigeons on their 150-mile flight from Yorkshire, only to see them flounder at the last hurdle. Before the birds could enter the loft, a lone Common Buzzard circled overhead, making the pigeons take cover for vital minutes in which the race was lost. The manager of the Royal Pigeon Loft, Carlo Napolitano, a charming man with a strong Norfolk accent that belies in his Italian ancestry, looked on philosophically as the raptor quartered over the lofts while Her Majesty's birds skulked. Only after filming was completed and my role of 'associate producer' flashed up for a nanosecond in the rolling credits, did I learn that the Queen herself had signed the memo allowing us to film at Sandringham, and that somewhere my name appears on a piece of paper which carries the regal signature, Elizabeth R. Not bad for a council estate lad who became a tabloid twitcher.

Other Birding Titles by New Holland

Atlas of Rare Birds
Dominic Couzens. Amazing tales
of 50 of the world's rarest birds,
illustrated with a series of stunning
photographs and colour maps.
Endorsed by BirdLife International.
£24.99 ISBN 978 1 84773 535 5

Birds of Africa South of the Sahara
Ian Sinclair and Peter Ryan. More
than 2,000 species covered in full
colour. The most comprehensive field
guide to the continent's birds.
£29.99 ISBN 978 1 86872 857 2

Birds of Indian Ocean Islands
Ian Sinclair and Olivier Langrand.
The first comprehensive field guide to
the birds of Madagascar, Seychelles,
Mauritius, Reunion and Rodrigues.
Covers 359 species in full colour.
£17.99 ISBN 978 1 86872 956 2

Chris Packham's Back Garden
Nature Reserve
Chris Packham. A complete guide
explaining the best ways to attract
wildlife into your garden, and to
encourage it to stay there.
£12.99 ISBN 978 1 84773 698 7

Colouring Birds
Sally MacLarty. Ideal gift to help a
child's developing interest in birds.
Features 40 species outlines, including
such favourites as Robin, Chaffinch,
Green Woodpecker and Blue Tit, and
a colour section depicting the birds as
they appear in life.
£2.99 ISBN 978 184773 526 3

Common Garden Bird Calls
Hannu Jännes and Owen Roberts.
Invaluable book and CD featuring the
songs and calls of 60 species likely to
be encountered in gardens and parks.
Each is illustrated with at least one
photo and a distribution map.
£6.99 ISBN 978 1 84773 517 1

Creative Bird Photography
Bill Coster. Illustrated with the
author's inspirational images. An
indispensable guide to all aspects
of the subject, covering bird portraits,
activities such as flight and courtship,
and taking 'mood' shots at dawn
and dusk.
£19.99 ISBN 978 1 84773 509 6

A Field Guide to the Birds of Borneo
Susan Myers. Features more than
630 species. The only comprehensive
and accurate field guide to the varied
avifauna of this island biodiversity
hot-spot, which comprises Brunei,
the Malaysian states of Sabah and
Sarawak, and the Indonesian states
of Kalimantan.
£24.99 ISBN 978 184773 381 8

A Field Guide to the Birds of
South-East Asia
Craig Robson. The only
comprehensive field guide to the
region, fully illustrated in colour and
covering all 1,300 species recorded
in Thailand, Vietnam, Singapore,
Peninsular Malaysia, Myanmar, Laos
and Cambodia.
£35.00 ISBN 978 184773 341 2

The Garden Bird Year
Roy Beddard. Gives both birdwatchers and gardeners insights into how to attract resident and migrant birds to the garden, and how to manage this precious space as a vital resource for wildlife.
£9.99 ISBN 978 184773 503 4

The History of Ornithology
Valerie Chansigaud. The story of the development of a science that endlessly inspires us. Richly illustrated with numerous artworks, photographs and diagrams, including a detailed timeline of ornithological events.
£17.99 ISBN 978 1 84773 433 4

The Naturalized Animals of Britain and Ireland
Christopher Lever. Authoritative and eminently readable account of how alien species were introduced and naturalized, their status and distribution, and their impact. Includes everything from the Ruddy Duck to the Red-necked Wallaby.
£35.00 ISBN 978 1 84773 454 9

New Holland Concise Bird Guide
An ideal first field guide to British birds for children or adults. Covers more than 250 species in full colour. Comes in a protective plastic wallet and includes a fold-out chart comparing similar species in flight. Endorsed by The Wildlife Trusts.
£4.99 ISBN 978 1 84773 601 7

New Holland European Bird Guide
Peter H Barthel. The only truly pocket-sized comprehensive field guide to all the birds of Britain and Europe. Features more than 1,700 beautiful and accurate artworks of more than 500 species.
£10.99 ISBN 978 1 84773 110 4

SASOL Birds of Southern Africa
Ian Sinclair, Phil Hockey and Warwick Tarboton. The world's leading guide to southern Africa's 950 bird species. Each is illustrated in full colour and has its own distribution map.
£19.99 ISBN 978 1 86872 721 6

The Slater Field Guide to Australian Birds
Peter Slater, Pat Slater and Raoul Slater. Fully updated edition of the comprehensive field guide. Features more than 750 species, each with a distribution map, and 150 plates.
£15.99 ISBN 978 1 87706 963 5

Top 100 Birding Sites of the World
Dominic Couzens. An inspiration for the traveling birder. Brings together a selection of the best places to go birdwatching on Earth, covering every continent. Includes 350 photos and more than 100 maps.
£35.00 ISBN 978 1 84773 109 8

See ww.newhollandpublishers.com for further details and special offers